Mass Hysteria in Schools

Mass Hysteria in Schools

A Worldwide History Since 1566

ROBERT E. BARTHOLOMEW
with BOB RICKARD

Foreword by Glenn Dawes

McFarland & Company, Inc., Publishers
Jefferson, North Carolina

ALSO OF INTEREST AND FROM MCFARLAND

*The Martians Have Landed!
A History of Media-Driven Panics and Hoaxes*
(by Robert E. Bartholomew and Benjamin Radford, 2012)

*Little Green Men, Meowing Nuns and Head-Hunting Panics:
A Study of Mass Psychogenic Illness and Social Delusion*
(by Robert E. Bartholomew, 2001)

LIBRARY OF CONGRESS CATALOGUING-IN-PUBLICATION DATA

Bartholomew, Robert E.
   Mass hysteria in schools : a worldwide history since 1566 /
Robert E. Bartholomew with Bob Rickard ; foreword by Glenn
Dawes.
      p.   cm.
   Includes bibliographical references and index.

   ISBN 978-0-7864-7888-0 (softcover : acid free paper) ∞
   ISBN 978-1-4766-1426-7 (ebook)

   1. Educational sociology. 2. Social psychology.
3. Hysteria (Social psychology) 4. Witchcraft.
5. Psychoanalysis and education. 6. Education—
Psychological aspects. 7. Education—History. I. Rickard,
Robert J. M. II. Title.
LC192.3.B37 2014
302'.17—dc23   2013045108

BRITISH LIBRARY CATALOGUING DATA ARE AVAILABLE

© 2014 Robert E. Bartholomew and Bob Rickard. All rights reserved

No part of this book may be reproduced or transmitted in any form or by any means, electronic or mechanical, including photocopying or recording, or by any information storage and retrieval system, without permission in writing from the publisher.

Front cover: vintage schoolbell © iStockphoto/Thinkstock

Manufactured in the United States of America

*McFarland & Company, Inc., Publishers
  Box 611, Jefferson, North Carolina 28640
    www.mcfarlandpub.com*

Table of Contents

Foreword by Glenn Dawes   1

Introduction   3

1. Witch Hunts and Schoolchildren   11
2. Twitching Epidemics and Pregnancy Panics: Historic Tales from Europe and America   26
3. Fear 101—Fates Worse Than Homework: Modern Tales from East and West   44
4. The Demon-Haunted Classroom: Tales from Asia   71
5. The Students Who Laughed for a Week: Accounts from Africa   94
6. The Meowing Schoolgirls of Fiji: Accounts from the Islands   121
7. Strange Tales from Latin America   134
8. Strange Schoolyards and Unusual Field Trips: Cases from Beyond the Classroom   146
9. Global Lessons   173

Chapter Notes   187

Bibliography   211

Index   223

Foreword
by Glenn Dawes

This book examines one of the strangest chapters in the study of the social sciences: the history of contagious conversion disorder (aka "mass hysteria") in schools. Robert Bartholomew and Bob Rickard analyze these outbreaks, which span different cultures and time periods, seeking to identify their underlying patterns of origin and spread.

This book helps bridge the gap in our knowledge about seemingly unrelated cases of extreme behavioral changes among young people in schools through reference to a number of case studies. These studies cover outbreaks going back to one in 1566 in Holland that mystified observers and fostered a variety of folk theories meant to explain bouts of twitching, shaking and supposed demonic possession still common in parts of Asia and Africa today. Other case studies document changes to student behavior, such as mass faintings or unexplainable bouts of laughter, to illustrate the pervasiveness of conversion disorder across global boundaries and cultures.

Bartholomew and Rickard provide a convincing analysis through reference to cross-disciplinary theories to provide plausible explanations as to why these events occur. They demonstrate that schools, in addition to educating students, often are hotbeds of gossip-mongering and misinformation that gives rise to rumors and folk theories with real consequences. As sociologists Peter Berger and Thomas Luckmann famously concluded: reality is socially constructed, and if a group of people believe something, no matter how strange and bizarre it may seem to outside observers, they act as if it were real. This book is a valuable resource for educators, parents and students who seek a rational explanation for outbreaks of bizarre behaviors and illness symptoms in school settings and an understanding of their impact on the rest of society.

Glenn Dawes is the former chair of the Department of Anthropology, Archeology and Sociology, James Cook University, Townsville, Australia

Introduction

In a Malaysian classroom, a young girl gets a wild look in her eyes and begins flailing about and screaming. She soon falls to the floor and curses her principal in a gruff, eerie voice, as if a mysterious force has seized her. A student in Tanzania starts to laugh, followed by another, and another. Some students laugh intermittently for days. Before long, thousands are stricken and schools are forced to close for weeks. On the Pacific island of Papua New Guinea, a nursing student is stricken with a headache, is struck deaf and attacks bystanders. Over the next two weeks a dozen classmates are seized with similar symptoms.

These strange outbreaks of mass hysteria also affect students in Western countries. During a British jazz gala, 130 band members tumble over like dominoes. Near London, a young English girl feels nauseated; her stomach bloats. Girls around her experience similar symptoms and begin to suspect that they are pregnant. Tests reveal that no one is pregnant; all are victims of a rare psychiatric condition. An itching frenzy that lasts for months sweeps through dozens of American and Canadian schools. In the Middle East, odor from a school latrine almost leads to war when students fall ill, believing it is poison gas. In Soviet Georgia, reports tell of government forces unleashing a powerful chemical to break up a protest. The incident makes such a deep impression on 400 schoolgirls that they develop symptoms of gas poisoning, despite being nowhere near the rally.

Mysterious tremors have been occurring among students in Western schools for over a century. In 1906 a student at a girls' school in Germany was attending penmanship class when her writing turned to scribbles, her hand shaking violently. In the coming days and weeks, more classmates were stricken. Like falling ten pins, one girl after another fell victim to "the trembling disease." There were other oddities: the same girls went to other classes without the slightest trouble. These outbreaks took place when writing instruction in many European schools was agonizingly dull and repetitive. To "cure" the students, Dr. Johannes Schoedel hooked each girl to wires and gave them electric shocks, thinking it would render them open to his suggestions. At their next writing session, an announcement was made: "Since you are not able to write, you must unfortunately have mental arithmetic again."[1] The trembling soon stopped.[2] Writing tremors in Europe were common during the late nineteenth and early twentieth centuries.[3]

In most episodes, popular myths and preoccupations shape stress or fear, leading to the spread of rumors, panics, scares, and hysterias. Stress can affect the body in many different ways. An anxiety attack can transform ordinarily confident students into ones who are certain they are dying of a heart attack as their heart begins to pound rapidly. In the aftermath of a frightening event, post-traumatic stress disorder can emotionally cripple the most confident of witnesses, who are left to wrestle with baseless fears and unrelenting nightmares. One of the most fascinating medical conditions is conversion disorder. In devising the term, Sigmund Freud described it as the conversion of psychological conflict and trauma into aches and pains that have no physical basis. An examination of the patient reveals normal reflexes and electrical activity. A classic example is the pacifist whose arm freezes when trying to fire a gun in combat. In other cases, a person may think that he or she is sick and unknowingly mimic the imaginary condition. The symptoms commonly mimic their illness scenarios. For instance, stomachache, nausea and diarrhea are common after food poisoning rumors,[4] while false alarms involving gas leaks typically induce headache, dizziness and over-breathing.[5]

Any place where students gather, be it a classroom, schoolyard, sports field or class trips can be fertile soil for the growth of rumors and social delusions, because the everyday adolescent world swirls with turmoil and passions: insecurities, jealousies, rivalries, fears, and suspicions. Under certain conditions, episodes may develop into full-blown mass hysteria, which has been known to occur in every country. The result is a strange mosaic of responses depending on the culture, context and era. While *conversion* aptly describes the process of converting conflict into symptoms,[6] *hysteria* and *mass hysteria* continue to be used by many doctors, psychiatrists and historians.[7] When we use these terms, it is to describe conversion disorder and nothing more. We must tread carefully here, as the word *hysteria* has been used for centuries to inappropriately describe an array of different behaviors under one label: mass suicide, communist "Red" scares, Nazism, the fear of AIDS, the Martian invasion panic, rock concert stampedes, land booms and stock sell-offs. These events have been described as mass hysteria, but they have little to do with the subject. Other fallacies include assertions that women cannot handle stress and are prone to the condition.[8] Such claims come from a bedrock of long-standing prejudice and stereotypes that view women as the psychologically weaker sex. They are without scientific merit. The term *social delusion* is not used as a psychiatrist would, to indicate mental disorder, but as sociologists use it, to describe the rapid spread of false beliefs.

In chapter 1 we analyze witch scares in European schools dating from the sixteenth century.[9] In a Dutch classroom in 1566, boys and girls went into frightful seizures and trance states, kicking and shaking on the floor, at times behaving like cats and crawling across the school roof. The episode coincided with witchcraft fears and the then-widespread European belief that cats were familiars of the devil.[10] During a French witch scare in 1639, villagers were preparing to burn the students alive after overzealous interrogators convinced the impressionable youngsters to confess to everything from eating babies to flying on broomsticks. Suddenly, the specter of guilt fell upon the female headmistress, who fled for her life, sparing the children a fiery fate.[11] Equally remarkable is a series of modern-day witch hunts occurring in American and European preschools during the 1980s and '90s. These imaginary nursery crimes ruined the lives of hundreds of innocent adults with allegations of satanic ritual abuse. The real culprits were poorly trained investigators who asked leading questions, and overzealous therapists using dubious techniques to retrieve so-called hidden memories.

Chapter 2 documents tremors and other bizarre maladies that became common in Europe and North America between the mid-nineteenth and mid-twentieth centuries, including twitching, convulsions, blackout spells, and phantom pregnancies. Appearing in the strictest schools, episodes reflected pent-up stress. Most cases corresponded to the adoption of a new educational approach, "mental discipline," at a time when the brain was thought to work like a muscle, requiring repetitions in math and penmanship. Even high-interest subjects such as English, reading, and social studies were reduced to drudgery, as little thinking took place. Most lessons consisted of "memory work."

Chapter 3 is a survey of outbreaks of psychological illness in European and North American schools since the mid-twentieth century. Episodes featured terrorism and contamination fears that developed after exposure to a real or imaginary threat — most often an odor or rumors of food poisoning. Common reactions included over-breathing, fainting, nausea, stomach pain, and headache. The cases reflect concerns over the quality of food, air, and water, and safety in the wake of foreign threats. Since September 11, 2001, there have been many terror scares in American schools resulting in the evacuation of students who felt ill after smelling an odor. Shortly after the anthrax mail attacks of 2001, the "Bin Laden Itch" struck dozens of U.S. schools. Amid rumors that the outbreak of rashes was a bio-terror attack aimed at schoolchildren, the Centers for Disease Control launched a major investigation. They soon found the culprit to be a variety of common ailments. Some ambitious pupils were even caught sandpapering their arms in order to be excused from school.[12] Also documented are terrorism false alarms in schools *before* September 11, in the United States, Asia, and the Middle East.[13]

In chapter 4, we examine conversion disorder reactions in Asian schools, which vary with local superstitions and beliefs. In Thailand, anxiety from ghost scares often leads to breathing problems and a belief that spirits are choking the children.[14] In Malaysia, group spirit possession is common among Malay girls in Islamic boarding schools that are notorious for their strict rules and lack of privacy, where students must account for their whereabouts at all times.[15] Interaction with boys is forbidden, as is dating. Even visits by family and friends take place in rooms that resemble fishbowls—under the watchful eye of adult monitors. The formula for mass hysteria here is simple: all work and no play fosters abnormal states of mind that reflect local beliefs in the existence of an array of supernatural creatures. Within this atmosphere of fear, students may collapse on the floor and enter trances, leading to a widespread belief that they have been the victims of demonic attacks. A few girls act as a mouthpiece for the class, publicly voicing complaints and frustrations with the way the school is being operated. The spirits are thought to be speaking through the girls, who negotiate better conditions with administrators, such as more recreation time and less homework.[16] In reality, their subconscious is expressing what they cannot voice aloud. The girls avoid punishment for speaking out because the spirits are seen as wresting temporary control of their minds and bodies.

In chapter 5 we describe unusual behaviors in African schools. For several days in 1976, students at a school in rural Zambia twitched, laughed, and wandered aimlessly about the campus grounds. Weary teachers could only look on in disbelief. After several days many of the 120 students were still meandering about as if in a hypnotic trance.[17] Similar incidents, known by locals as "laughing mania," have been plaguing African schools for decades.[18] Some students claim to be in contact with ancestors, from whom they seek advice. Outbreaks usually affect Western-run missionary boarding schools. Elders seeking the best education for their children send them to these schools in spite of the risk of exposing them to new ideas that often conflict with traditional beliefs. Trapped between worlds and unable to serve two masters, pupils are caught in a cultural and psychological tug-of-war. The result is a kind of mental gridlock as they enter trances and "communicate" with their ancestors for a solution to their dilemma.[19] "Talking" with ancestors in times of crisis has been part of the African religious landscape for centuries. These and other strange outbreaks in Africa show no signs of abating.

Chapter 6 is an exploration of bizarre behaviors in exotic island schools in Papua New Guinea, Fiji, and the Philippines. Island culture can be isolating and restrictive, helping to create ideal conditions for hysteria outbreaks. Episodes here occur when the teachings of Western schools conflict with native beliefs, especially over the changing role of women. In 1973, in the highlands of Papua New Guinea, students at an Australian-run school complained of drowsiness and headaches, entered trances, and attacked relatives. They returned to normal within hours, only to suffer more attacks. It is no coincidence that in this culture, local tribesmen dominate their wives, restricting them to cooking, gardening, and tending children and animals. Elders arrange marriages, and their decision is final. The students' contact with the school left them wanting more from life. Caught between the liberal Western values that they were exposed to at school and their traditions, some chose a bold step: to stop taking their elders' advice and pick their own partners. The cost was high: their families shunned them, and the crippling stress that developed triggered fits during which students lashed out at relatives.[20] Ordinarily, they would be severely punished for these behaviors, but in this case, they were seen as victims who had been possessed by demonic forces.

In chapter 7 we look at cases in Latin America, in particular, an outbreak of walking difficulties that affected over 500 students at a Catholic girls' school near Mexico City in 2006 and 2007. The episode was triggered by the use of a Ouija board to try to alter the outcome of a basketball game. When the girl using the board was expelled for trying to communicate with the devil, she was rumored to have cursed the school. The outbreak occurred shortly after. A number of factors contributed to the episode, including strict study and prayer regimes, an absence of leisure activities and the fear of expulsion, but the most influential was a belief in ghosts, witches and demons. Also examined is an outbreak of *grisi siknis* ("crazy sickness") among northern Nicaraguan schoolgirls.

Chapter 8 documents outbreaks of mass hysteria and kindred behaviors occurring outside of the classroom in such diverse settings as track meets, football games, chorus recitals and band competitions. In 1972, 130 members of several school bands began collapsing like unstrung marionettes along a parade route in England. Shortly after marching into a foul odor, the first student fell down, followed by dozens more. The students made a quick recovery upon learning that the stench was from a pigsty.[21] Not a single local student or onlooker fell ill—presumably they were used to the smell and knew what it was. There are many other incidents of collapsing school bands.[22] Over-breathing is a common culprit. Occasionally, outbreaks occur on buses. In May 2000 near Peoria, Illinois, a bus of fourth graders was returning from a field trip when a student began gasping for air, followed by a second student. Within minutes, eight of the twelve students on board were panic-stricken, gasping for air. The driver pulled off the road and stopped the bus, allowing the passengers to scramble out for fresh air. Rescue personnel quickly pieced together the circumstances: The first two students had asthma and began to worry about their breathing after realizing they had left their inhalers behind. The others then began to panic, thinking the bus was giving off toxic fumes. The children recovered quickly in the hospital.[23]

In chapter 9 we examine different explanations for the events in this book. Many cases fall under the category of mass hysteria, of which two key types are common.[24] The first type, anxiety hysteria, typically lasts only a day and involves sudden fear in the wake of a false or exaggerated threat. It is common in modern Western schools in response to terrorism and fears about the contamination of air, food, and water. A second type, motor hysteria, builds slowly. Weeks or months of relentless pressure soon disrupt the motor neurons that send messages to the muscles and control coordination. As a result, students' bodies go haywire, twitching, shaking, and convulsing. Interference with brain function results in trance states and emotional instability; students scream, cry, and laugh uncontrollably. Such outbreaks are common in Africa, Asia, and the Pacific, but a similar pattern also arose in Europe during the late nineteenth and early twentieth centuries.

Outbreaks of these seemingly strange school behaviors mirror preoccupations that define each era and unique beliefs about the world. In Africa, Asia, and the Pacific, the belief in spirits and demons continues to trigger reports of possession and ghost attacks. In the early twenty-first century, Western school episodes reflect terrorism fears and environmental concerns. In the case of modern-day sex abuse scares in preschools, episodes are a response to deep-seated anxieties. Scientists classify these incidents as "moral panics" that coincide with the breakdown of the traditional family and a search for scapegoats to explain why society seems to be falling into moral decay. They are cautionary tales that convey concern and guilt over the weakened family and its diminished capacity to protect children in a world where they are being raised by strangers in preschools.[25]

These accounts from around the world highlight the creative ways in which the human mind adapts to fear, uncertainty and distress. From afar, outbreaks may seem to have no rhyme or reason, yet on closer inspection, clear patterns emerge. Episodes are the outcomes of unique cultural contexts and fears. They are group problem-solving exercises that need to be recorded and understood. But beyond their fascinating storylines, they often have serious repercussions, for outbreaks are far more common than most realize and are impossible to eradicate. Each year the financial costs run in the tens of millions of dollars as schools in Western countries are forced to temporarily close while costly tests are conducted in a vain attempt to identify the cause of a mysterious odor or illness. When the results come back negative, the community is often thrown into social upheaval, as parents may keep their students away from school or even transfer them, under the belief that the mysterious triggering agent remains on the school grounds. Suspicion of a cover-up by public health authorities, who are seen as hiding the "real" cause, is common and may foster longstanding ill-will between the community and government. Then there is the cost of wasted resources such as emergency responders, consulting physicians, and stress-related disorders among students who are anxious because they believe that they are continuing to be exposed to harmful agents. In African and Asian schools, the belief in evil spirits commonly results in schools being closed indefinitely until witchdoctors can be called in to rid the premises of the demons. The sanctioning of native healers who try to cast out the offending spirits often backfires if the symptoms do not immediately subside, prolonging episodes for weeks or months. In some instances they can endure for years. Occasionally, teachers, principals, and even students have been forced to flee after accusations that they had caused the outbreak by practicing witchcraft or black magic. As always, the best way to combat episodes is to educate people about the history of outbreaks.

CHAPTER 1

Witch Hunts and Schoolchildren

Speak of the devil, and he is bound to appear.— Proverb

Witchcraft. The very word, whether spoken in a whisper or shouted as an accusation, was once enough to make grown men tremble. For those accused, it was often a death sentence. For others, it meant languishing in a dank prison for months or years, or enduring unspeakable tortures: flesh seared with hot irons, teeth and fingernails ripped out, bones crushed with thumb screws. The number of ways to inflict pain on the human body was seemingly endless. Across Europe during the Middle Ages and early Renaissance, for many people the night sky was filled with soaring evil and even the outwardly innocent could harbor the spirit of the devil, to say nothing of those who were considered eccentric or odd. Those poor souls who failed to conform to community standards were often meat for the maw of the brutal campaign against witches.

It is not surprising, then, that the earliest known outbreaks of bizarre behavior in schoolchildren took place in Europe during the sixteenth and seventeenth centuries, sparked by the widespread fear of witches and accusations of witchcraft. To the average European of the time, fear of the "dark arts" was every bit as real as the threat of terrorism today. A witch could take any shape or form, and potential witches were lurking everywhere. The threat is reminiscent of the global anthrax mail scare of 2001, when people were afraid of something they could not see with the naked eye and did not know when or how it would manifest. So it was with the fear of witches, that various misfortunes were taken to confirm the existence of Satan or his cohorts: sudden death, miscarriages, barrenness and impotence, crop failures, illness, droughts and floods, even unrequited love.

The *Malleus Maleficarum*, or *Hammer of Witches*, written in 1486 by

German demon hunters Heinrich Kramer and Jakob Sprenger, encouraged the identification and punishment of witches.[1] Historians credit this notorious book with triggering the great witch inquisition of the late Middle Ages.[2] As a result, many historians estimate that between two hundred thousand[3] and half a million souls[4] were ruthlessly butchered or burned at the stake: men, women, children, unborn and newborn babies; even family pets. Countless others endured years of suffering in prison; many died there. The lucky ones lost property or were banished from their communities. More recently, some historians have taken issue with these older estimates of the carnage, but all agree that the death toll was significant and the sufferings were immense.[5]

It is difficult to convey the depth of the fear of witchcraft that was prevalent at that time, and the number of learned people who accepted the reality of witches. Even eminent scientists such as the father of chemistry, Robert Boyle (1627–1691), and the father of deductive reasoning, Francis Bacon (1561–1626), were deeply influenced by the *zeitgeist* or "spirit of the times." Boyle suggested interviewing English miners to determine whether they had met "subterraneous demons." Bacon seriously pondered the likelihood that malicious spirits were responsible for witchcraft.[6] English philosopher John Locke (1632–1704), in his supposedly enlightened *Essay Concerning Human Understanding*, wrote, "Spirits can assume bodies of different bulk, figure or configuration."[7]

Witch Scares and Schoolchildren

It was within this simmering cauldron of cruelty, suspicion and fear that in 1566, about thirty boys and girls at a Catholic orphanage school in Amsterdam, Holland, were stricken with strange fits and compulsions. The attacks would suddenly strike one or more children, their arms and legs seizing up in violent spasms lasting from thirty minutes to an hour or more. Later, the children would compose themselves, struggle to their feet and act as if everything were normal, astonishing onlookers with their assertions that they could not recall any of their previous seizures, and instead claiming to have just awoken from a deep sleep.[8]

Some of the students' actions were bizarre by any standard. Sometimes they would fall into trance-like states and behave like cats, and even walk across rooftops on all fours. On several occasions they ran toward rivers or ponds as if about to drown themselves, only to stop abruptly at the edge and cry out: "The big man [God] does not permit it."[9] It may be that such behaviors expressed their unhappiness by threatening suicide by drowning; yet they failed to commit the act, as it would be considered sinful. When angry, the children demonstrated a feline ferocity dramatic enough to scare onlookers. After appearing to enter a trance, they sometimes spoke a strange, unintelligible language.[10]

Why did these children behave like cats? There may be a simple explanation. In much of Europe during the late Middle Ages, it was widely thought that cats were familiars of the devil and could temporarily possess the human soul. Cats were despised for their sinister profile: sleek killing machines silently prowling the countryside with sinewy grace, piercing eyes, and razor-sharp claws built for the kill in the dead of night. As a result of their satanic association, medieval historian Robert Darnton writes, the killing and torturing of cats was a popular pastime during the period, especially at public events and carnivals[11]: "In the Metz region [of France] they burned a dozen cats at a time in a basket on top of a bonfire. The ceremony took place with great pomp ... until it was abolished in 1765."[12] This fear of and disdain for cats undoubtedly shaped the children's actions.

During the later Middle Ages, Europeans who were thought to be possessed by the devil often acted like cats.[13] Wolves were also feared at this time, and there were thousands of lycanthropy cases recorded during the fifteenth and sixteenth centuries. Some of these people were no doubt mentally disturbed; others may have been entering stress-induced trance states, with their werewolf behavior reflecting the popular culture.[14]

Back in Amsterdam, orphanage authorities sought doctors to treat the "cat children," believing their strange, feline behaviors to be a natural ailment. Medicine, though, was still in its infancy, and the physicians were ill-equipped to solve the mystery. Soon many residents were convinced that the children were possessed by demons, so authorities brought in exorcists. From today's perspective, it is clear from descriptions that the children were having hysterical fits. It is nearly impossible to fake powerful muscle spasms and body contortions that continue for hours. It is equally clear that these savvy street kids were not averse to using melodrama to gain the attention and sympathy of spectators. Some children made it appear that they were vomiting hair, cloth, thimbles, needles, pins, bits of broken pottery, even shards of glass. The exorcists failed, and the episode endured for two more months.[15]

Physician Johann Weyer (circa 1515–1588) was certain of Satan's reality but skeptical that witchcraft was the culprit in this case. As a recognized expert on witches, his views held considerable sway. Weyer surmised that the devil was making the children vomit objects in order to spread the idea that sorcery was to blame. His diagnosis was seemingly confirmed when the children began showing up on the doorsteps of certain women and going into fits, as if to accuse them of witchcraft. Weyer thought the children were acting at the devil's behest to ruin the lives of innocent women. If not for Weyer, the women could have easily been thrown in prison, tortured, or even burned alive.

A lady street peddler named Bametie was despised by the children and accused by them of casting spells. Upset that she wasn't arrested for bewitchment, the children threw tantrums and began scaling the bell tower of the Holy Spirit Chapel. Inside, they were seen tapping out melodies with their fingers and singing, "We shall not leave until we have seen Bametie burnt at the stake." Surmising that the children held a grudge, Amsterdam authorities took no action. While little more is known about this case, it is recorded that the children's symptoms eventually stopped after they were temporarily boarded with foster families.

The convulsions and amnesia; the urge to run, climb, and imitate animals; the blaming of innocent women; and the purported vomiting of various objects are themes occurring time and time again during mass hysteria outbreaks of the period, as though the children were conforming to some stereotypical image of possession.[16] During the fourteenth and fifteenth centuries, there were dozens of similar outbreaks among repressed nuns in European convents who exhibited convulsions and would bark or meow, apparently vomit improbable objects such as living reptiles, and accuse others of witchcraft.[17] Many of the accused were tortured into confessing to witchcraft; some were burned at the stake.

The Black Angels of Lille

In 1639, a witchcraft scare erupted at a girls' school in Lille, France, where Antoinette Bourignon (1616–1680), a pious headmistress, founded a convent. One day she shocked her students by telling them that she could see tiny "black angels" flying about their heads, warning them that the devil's imps were hovering around them. Each day Miss Bourignon repeated the story, and before long Satan was the sole topic of conversation, even among the teachers. Despite her claims she continued to perform her duties and no one sought her dismissal.[18]

Whether she had an overactive imagination or suffered from mental illness may never be known. In any event, her claims terrified the children. One of the frightened girls ran away. She was caught, but during her interrogation she denied having run off, insisting that the devil had carried her away. Under pressure, she broke down, admitting that she was a witch and had been since the age of seven. After this news was announced to her classmates, fits of hysterics broke out. When they came to their senses and under further questioning, they too confessed to being witches. Eventually, all fifty students confessed to witchcraft. Before long, the children were in such a state of bewilderment that they confessed to flying on broomsticks, dining on the flesh of infants, and creeping through keyholes while doing Satan's work.

Many clergy were sympathetic, suggesting that the affair was a figment of the imaginations of suggestible youngsters; but the children were in grave danger as the Lille residents were in an uproar, calling for them to be burned at the stake. Appearing before a council of Catholic friars, the parents begged that their kids' lives be spared, arguing that the children were not witches but the innocent victims of bewitchment. This idea soon took root among the townsfolk, who blamed the headmistress. Miss Bourignon was interviewed by the council and charged with being a witch. Just hours before she was to be sentenced for witchcraft and burned by judicial decree, she put on a disguise and slipped out of town dressed as a man.[19] She eventually found her way to a convent in Friedland, Prussia, where she attracted many followers and became a famous visionary and religious writer until her death in 1680.[20]

Witch Panics in Northern Europe

In other schools during this period, rumors and false accusations made by students about the evil deeds of witches illustrate just how easily children can be led astray and generate imaginary stories. One of the most notorious episodes of this social hysteria began in the village of Älvdalen,[21] in central Sweden.[22] On July 5, 1668, fifteen-year-old Eric Ericsen accused Gertrude Svensen of stealing children for Satan. Soon more and more children were questioned about the accusation. Overzealous investigators soon had confessions from three hundred children who told wild accounts of flying on farm animals to meet the devil at the witches' sabbat. King Charles XI appointed a royal commission to investigate the claims.[23] When it met in August 1669, interest was so great that three thousand people came. As a result, seventy adults and fifteen children were burned at the stake. Dozens of other children were ordered to "run the gauntlet," that is, run through lines of men who struck them with whips. Those under nine were struck on their hands once a week for a year.[24]

The next year, 1670, five hundred children in Rättvik (20 miles southeast of Mora) testified to priests that female Satanists had abducted them from their beds in the dead of night and, as at Älvdalen, flown them on animals or humans to feast with the devil and his cohorts at Blåkulla, a legendary meadow in which the sabbats were held that could only be reached by flying.[25] At these gatherings sinister acts supposedly took place—drinking alcohol, swearing, sexual misdeeds and eating babies—all with the Evil One looking on with delight. The allegations spread, with children implicating others during interrogations. These children, in turn, implicated still more innocent victims. In the confusion and under the pressure of questioning, many children came to believe that they really had attended the witches' sabbat, weaving tales that were likely based on a combination of hearsay, stereotypes, and suggestions put forth by interviewers who were already convinced of their guilt. These episodes are far from being a relic of the past. A similar outbreak of false accusations has occurred in more recent times among schoolchildren in Western countries. Poorly trained, overly enthusiastic investigators asking leading questions were largely to blame in the modern-day cases.[26] The Rättvik scare spread to Finland, and later to Stockholm, where physician Urban Hjarne ended the slaughter by convincing authorities that the persecution resulted from children's fantasies, aggressive inquisitors, confusion, fear and malice.[27]

Psychologist Richard Sjöberg found a similar pattern in stories of visiting the witches' sabbat during the Great Swedish Witch Panic of 1664 to 1676. In these accounts, as a child lay sleeping, the witch, usually a neighbor, was said to enter the room after shrinking and crawling through a keyhole or walking through a wall. After being escorted to the roof, the child was placed on the belly of a farm animal such as a cow, which was hovering upside down. As they flew to Blåkulla, they picked up more children on the way to a big house for a feast at a huge table. Flames from hell shot through a hole in the floor as people sat around eating, cursing, and paying homage to Satan. A flock of white birds from heaven tried to stop the meeting but failed. The devil asked each child if he or she would serve him, and they could only say yes. The child's finger was cut, and the devil took some blood. The children were given gifts, such as knives to use in killing their parents, and books of curses. A witch brought the children home before morning, by which time their gifts had become shavings and twigs. The children said they were sworn to secrecy at the risk of being beaten.[28] That so many children could believe that they had met the devil—and accuse others of the same—is a testament to the power of social conditioning.

The Barking Children of Hoorn, Holland

At about the same time as the Swedish witch scare, there were strange happenings at an orphanage school in Hoorn, Holland. It was 1673. The orphanage was a haven for a gang of troubled street kids who were stricken with fits of shouting and barking. There are many cases during this period of Europeans thought to be possessed by demons, barking like dogs. Canines, too, were often thought to be in cahoots with the devil.[29] The screams and yelps would start with one child and quickly spread to others.

Amsterdam theologian Balthasar Bekker (1634–1698) was an eyewitness to these events, observing that the children would suddenly collapse and get a strange look in their eyes: "They tugged and tore at themselves, striking at the ground with their legs and arms and even with their heads, crying, yelling and barking like dogs so that it was a terrifying thing to see," he wrote.[30] Even more bizarre, Bekker went on to report that some of their bellies

> pounded so fearfully, that one would have said there was a living creature moving about inside them or even that a barrel was being rolled within their bodies. So strong were these movements that it took three, four, five or even six persons to hold them: one would take the head, two others the hands, one sat on the legs and sometimes another to sit on the belly to prevent them moving.

Eventually they would lie motionless, their bodies as "stiff as a bar of iron, so that with one person holding the head and another the feet, they could be carried anywhere, without making any movement. Sometimes this happened for several hours on end, and even at night, until 11 P.M., midnight, one, two or three o'clock."[31]

Bekker saw a girl named Catherine suffer an attack as the 8:00 A.M. breakfast bell rang, remaining in this state until 4:00 P.M. "when the bell called the children to their evening collation.... [Upon regaining her senses] she believed she had been in that state only for a moment, because she could hear the bell still ringing, and when she heard grace being said for the evening meal she thought it was for breakfast."[32]

Like the other children, Catherine had been forced to undergo monotonous religious instruction and prayer. Within this emotionally stifling setting, the children's fits grew common. As they were made to endure lengthier prayer sessions in hopes of curing their strange malady, the fits intensified. Prayer gatherings were held at churches across the city to save the children from the devil's clutches. Soon after, the orphans were lodged with local families and recovered.

The Great Preschool Scare: Modern-day Witch Hunts

In reading accounts of witches and witchcraft during the Middle Ages, one could be forgiven for thinking they could never recur in modern times, especially not in the seemingly more developed, civilized West. However, their ancient roots, overwhelmed perhaps by the topsoil of modern society, have never been eradicated by advances in education or knowledge. The reason for this persistence lies in the personal and social psychology that we share with our ancestors, and hence, the underlying causes of such panics or fears are the same now as they were in times past. In the 1980s and '90s, a modern witch hunt broke out in some of the most educated societies on earth. Preschoolers across the United States and Europe — and as far away as Australia and New Zealand — began making bizarre accusations about their instructors, who, they said, had not only sexually molested them but forced them to join in ghastly Satanic rituals. Like the early witch scares and witch hunts in European schools centuries earlier, these modern outbreaks were also incubated in an atmosphere of ignorance and fear.[33] The first director of the National Center on Child Abuse and Neglect, Douglas Besharov, once described the biggest challenge facing the agency: identifying the many unfounded claims of abuse — with 65 percent of all allegations being dismissed after an investigation by child protective services.[34]

One major example of reported abuse centered on seven teachers at the Virginia McMartin Preschool in Manhattan Beach, California, who were charged with the heinous crime of molesting children and flying them by helicopter to a remote farm where a series of incredible events were said to have taken place.[35] As the media reported the allegations, it appeared all but certain that the teachers were guilty, for how could the testimonies of 360 children be wrong? The prosecution even had the preschoolers' testimonies on videotape. It seemed that it would be only a matter of time before the teachers were sent to prison for a long time. Many news reports insinuated that some or all of the "McMartin Seven" were guilty. An article in *People* magazine was typical, referring to the preschool as "California's Nightmare Nursery," while *Time* described the charges under the heading "Brutalized."[36] Television coverage was equally biased in favor of the prosecution.[37] But during the trial, the children's accounts of what happened were revealed to be outlandish, and serious doubts were raised about how the interviews had been conducted.

Many of the children's stories included details and situations that were clearly impossible, such as descriptions of teachers and students frolicking naked in the playground near a heavily traveled road. One child claimed that the school janitor had sex with him while going through a public car wash, though vehicles with passengers were not allowed in the tunnel and the time factor made it impossible. Then after seven years and $15 million in legal costs, in a stunning reversal each of the accused was acquitted of all charges. During the trials, which were the lengthiest and costliest of their type in United States history, suspicion was focused on scores of other preschools scattered across the U.S. and Europe, and assertions were made that children there were also victims of abuse. Hundreds of innocent people were falsely imprisoned. But by the early 1990s, with the aid of experts on child development, memory and suggestibility, the Great Preschool Scare waned as it became evident that the spate of Satanic ritual abuse claims had been a witch hunt.

Context of the McMartin Nightmare

In the early 1980s, the Los Angeles area experienced an explosion of media coverage about a variety of sexually related social ills: juvenile prostitution, rape, child abuse, and advertisements with sexual overtones. It was against this backdrop of suspicion and fear about declining sexual morals that, in the late summer of 1983, there was growing anxiety about the safety of preschools. The epicenter of the scare was the elite McMartin Preschool, owned by Peggy McMartin Buckey and her mother, Virginia McMartin. The school had a good reputation for minding Manhattan Beach children for thirty years. Six years earlier, school founder Virginia McMartin had even been named local citizen of the year, and at the time of the first allegations, there was a six-month waiting list to get in the facility.[38]

On August 12, Judy Johnson, a 39-year-old mother of a two-and-a-half-year-old boy, told police she was convinced that a school aid named Ray Buckey — Peggy Buckey's son — had molested her son. She noticed the boy's bottom was red and itchy after he returned from the school. Police placed the facility under surveillance. Meanwhile, Mrs. Johnson continued to press her case by making a series of unsubstantiated claims, including charges that Ray's mother was a Satanist and that Ray had taken her son to a church where a baby was beheaded and the boy was forced to drink its blood. It was later determined that the Mrs. Johnson was mentally ill.[39]

On September 8, Manhattan Beach police chief Harry Kuhlmeyer, Jr., made a fateful decision. He sent a letter to two hundred parents, alerting them that Ray was a suspect in a child molestation investigation. "This Department is conducting a criminal investigation involving child molestation.... Ray Buckey of ... Virginia McMartin's Pre-School, was arrested September 7, 1983 by this Department." It continues: "Please question your child to see if he or she has been a victim. Our investigation indicates that possible criminal acts include: oral sex, fondling of genitals, buttock or chest area, and sodomy, possibly committed under the pretense of 'taking the child's temperature.'" The letter went on to state that nude photos might have been taken of the children and asked if any parents had observed Ray "leave a classroom alone with a child during any nap period, or if they had ever observed Ray Buckey tie up a child."[40]

Buckey was arrested but was quickly released for lack of evidence. Ordinarily when police conduct criminal investigations, they interview suspects separately and leave specific details out, to see if they are corroborated. By mentioning so many details in the letter chief Kuhlmeyer had unwittingly corrupted the investigation, as the children and their parents had a rough blueprint of what might have happened — but however flawed the chief's letter, it paled in comparison to the scripted way in which the interviews with the children were handled.

The Scare Escalates

The McMartin episode and similar scares across the Western world during this period share common elements. At the time of the allegations, the child witnesses were preschoolers who disclosed their abuse claims *only after* coaxing by relatives, law enforcement and health professionals. Typically, the children said they could not recall *any* of the abuse until their memories were jogged by people mentioning specific details or asking leading questions. A leading question is one that suggests a specific answer, such as, "Have you stopped beating your mother yet?" Whether you answer yes or no, it implies that at some point you have beaten your mother. While an adult would easily see such questioning as biased, these molestation scares occurred to children who were preschoolers at the time of the allegations — a period in life when children are highly suggestible.

Another common theme in these cases was the lack of corroborating physical evidence. Further, even after co-defendants were convicted, and despite the possibility of plea bargaining for reduced sentences in exchange for confessions, the accused continued to maintain their innocence. In each case, jurors were faced with a similar dilemma: should they believe the children, whose testimony grew more and more unbelievable?[41] Each episode was an emotional community event that drew intense media coverage, which often suggested that those accused were guilty. Few reports put the McMartin Seven in a favorable light or suggested their innocence. Ironically, even when the accused were found not guilty, there was a widespread assumption that they had gotten away with it and the justice system had failed. The McMartin debacle was typical, for after acquitting Ray and Virginia Buckey on all charges, the jurors were asked if they felt that some of the kids had been molested. Eight raised their hands but said they didn't have enough evidence to convict the Buckeys under the law.[42] How weak was the evidence against the defendants? During the saga, district attorney Glenn Stevens switched sides to join the defense, remarking that the evidence on which the original charges were based, was "very weak, if not false."[43]

Creating False Memories

Transcripts of the interviews show that the children's memories of abuse were inadvertently planted or modified during the repeated interviews by the parents, police officials, therapists and social workers, and were reinforced by the media. Their memories were vague at best. Consider the following courtroom testimony. Under questioning by prosecutor Lael Rubin, one boy said that Ray Buckey had placed his penis in his mouth. It was at this point that defense attorney Daniel Davis cross-examined the boy, who told a bizarre story of watching Ray beat a horse with a baseball bat. It quickly became obvious that the boy did not have a clue as to what had happened, had pieced his story together based on hearsay, and had been coached on what to say, as the following excerpt from the transcript shows:

> Did you see a horse get killed?
> Yeah...
> Do you know what color it was?
> I don't know.
> How did the horse get killed?
> Ray hit it with a bat.
> Where?
> I don't remember.
> Did they ride the horse before it got killed?
> I don't know.
> Were other kids there when the horse got killed?
> I don't know.
> Who was your teacher when Ray killed the horse with the bat?
> I don't know.[44]

At this point it became obvious that the boy had been coached, and he admitted that he had gone over his responses with Lael Rubin.

> Lael Rubin asked you questions and you'd practice answers?
> Yes....
> Did you practice the names of the teachers?
> Yes.
> Was your mom there practicing with you?
> Yes....
> You remember how far from the horse you were when it got killed?
> No.
> Did the horse make a sound?
> I don't know....
> How many times did he hit the horse?
> I don't know.
> Did the horse jump around?
> I don't know.
> Was there any grownup there when it happened?
> I don't know....
> Did Lael Rubin practice your testimony with you?
> No.
> Did anybody practice your testimony with you before the trial?
> No.
> Last Friday, Lael was at your house showing you pictures?
> Yes.
> Did you practice questions and answers?
> Yes.[45]

Then came a series of damning responses as it soon became evident that the boy had no conscious memory of the detailed events he had previously testified to.

> Was there a time you forgot about the molestation?
> I forgot everything.
> Did grownups help you remember?
> Lael?
> Were there other grownups that helped you remember?
> Yes.
> How about the puppet lady? Did she help you remember?
> Yes.
> Would it be fair to say you didn't remember anything about molestation?
> Yes.
> Did your mother tell you you were molested at the preschool?
> Yes.
> Did she tell you [other children] were molested at the school?
> Yes.
> Did you believe her?
> Yes.[46]

Another striking aspect of the interviews was the dominance by the interviewers who did much of the talking, and the leading questions they asked. How bad were the interview techniques? One videotaped interview with a six-year-old girl was typical. Dr. Astrid Heger asked, "Maybe you could show me ... how the kids danced for the Naked Movie Star [game]." When the girl replied that they did not dance, it was a song, Heger tried pressure to get the girl to agree that the game was real:

> Well, what did they do when they sang the song? ... I heard ... from several different kids that they took their clothes off. I think that [— —] told me that, I know that [— —] told me that, I know that [— —] told me. [— —] and [— —] all told me that. That's kind of a hard secret, it's kind of a yucky secret to talk of but, maybe, we could see if we could find...

Despite this pressure, the girl continued to insist that it never happened. Later, when she denied having been touched sexually, Heger said: "I don't wanna hear any more no's."[47]

We should remember that the interviewers in the McMartin case were high status adults: parents, legal officials, and health professionals, who were often asking leading questions. We also see here an example of the children's natural resistance to being guided—covertly or overtly—to give the answers that the inquirers were expecting or for which they were fishing. But how did memories of playing something as specific as the Naked Movie Star game, and tales of fellow kids playing this game while naked in the school, come to be accepted as reality in the first place? Based on the testimony of different children, it became evident that the "game" was actually a rhyme that was used to tease children. As one boy explained on the witness stand, "There was no naked movie star game. If someone made fun of you, you'd say, 'What you see is what you are. You're a naked movie star.'"[48] It was through the use of leading questions and scripted interviews that these fictitious events took on their own reality.

The case against the McMartin preschool workers eventually collapsed once the shoddy interviewing techniques became apparent. Many of the recorded interviews were textbook cases of how *not* to conduct an interview. Leading questions were the order of the day. One research team who watched some of the interviews wrote: "There was not one spontaneous 'disclosure' on any of these tapes.... On all of the videotapes shown, the children repeatedly denied witnessing any act of sexual abuse of children. The interviewer ignored these exonerating statements and continued to coax and pressure the child for accusations."[49] The consequences for those accused of these terrible crimes were devastating. While all of them were eventually freed, they have had to live with the stigma of having been accused of being a child molester. The school, its reputation in tatters, had to shut down.[50]

Ironically, many of the children came to believe that they had been molested by Ray Buckey—like the Lille novices in 1639—and convinced themselves of the reality of their fantastic adventures; yet, these memories of abuse were as shallow as the interview techniques used to extract their stories. The case against the McMartin Seven did not fail due to a lack of money; at the time it was the most expensive criminal trial in United States history. The case did not fail because it was brought about hastily, for the trial lasted seven years—another record. The prosecution's case did not fail due to a lack of evidence. The trial generated over a hundred thousand pages of transcripts alone as hundreds of children were interviewed at length. The case against the McMartin Seven ultimately failed due to a lack of *concrete* evidence.[51] Even today, at the dawn of the twenty-first century, it is hard to believe that such a gross injustice could have occurred. It is important to remember that this was not an isolated episode. Even more striking are the parallels to the Salem witch trials.

In 1692, Salem Village was the scene of a great fear that spread throughout New England involving claims of real witches. At least 200 people were imprisoned and twenty were executed. All of those accused of being witches were convicted on flimsy "spectral evidence" involving claims by their accusers that the specter of the accused had accosted them. As in the McMartin case, the principal accusers were children whose testimony was widely believed. The adults saw what they expected to see. The McMartin Seven initially *looked* guilty, and interviewers asked the children leading questions on the assumption that they *had been* molested at the preschool. In Salem, a mole or birthmark was seen as a "witch mark" and a sure sign of guilt. The lesson of the McMartin saga is clear: focus on the facts and do not let emotions influence your judgment. Child molestation is one of the most heinous crimes imaginable. It is a crime against the innocent and vulnerable who must live with emotional scars for the rest of their lives. One can think of few crimes that are more atrocious. Among them is falsely accusing someone of molestation who then must live with this stigma.

The preschool scare was a form of national scapegoating. All cultures have a concept of evil, and in modern Western countries with Christian traditions, Satan epitomes it. From the late 1940s until the breakup of the Soviet empire, communists conveniently filled this niche. The preschool scare rose conspicuously with the decline of communism.[52] Sociologist Jeff Victor believes that the creation of Satanic cultists violating the youth of America and other Western countries was a reflection of parental anxieties. "There is a great deal of parental guilt today; many parents feel guilty about leaving their children at day-care centers or about having little time to spend with them or about being reluctant to use their authority to guide their children's choice of entertainments and friends or about feeling unable to guide the moral values of their children."[53]

The most disquieting aspect of the McMartin saga is that it is but one example of similar scares that have long plagued humanity. Yet the lessons go unheeded. Other modern examples include the internment of Japanese Americans after the bombing of Pearl Harbor and the profiling of Muslim Americans as terrorists after the September 11, 2001, attacks on the United States. Historian Dorothy Rabinowitz observes that every so often society is afflicted with an exaggerated fear of some evil, such as communists in the early 1950s. "After the McCarthy era, people would ask: But how could it have happened? How could the presumption of innocence have been abandoned wholesale? ... How was it possible to believe that subversives lurked behind every library door, in every radio station, that every two-bit actor who had belonged to the wrong political organization posed a threat to the nation's security?"[54]

This chapter has looked at two types of hysteria. The first is mass hysteria (conversion disorder), which involves the rapid spread of illness symptoms: twitching, shaking, convulsions and trance states caused by anxiety that was generated by various social pressures. The earliest known school example occurred in Holland in 1566, when students experienced convulsions, spasms and trance states. The second type is social hysteria: community panics based on the fear of witches or other evildoers for which the inhabitants began searching for scapegoats in order to account for inexplicable events. The earliest known examples date from the fourteenth and fifteenth century Europe (modern-day France and Sweden), where children were accused of consorting with the Devil and were coerced into naming other innocent victims. Often, as in the events at Hoorn, Amsterdam and Salem, mass hysterias and social hysterias have overlapped.

What is so remarkable and alarming about these accounts that occurred hundreds of years ago is that while the false accusations of witchcraft are no longer plausible, similar outbreaks of false accusations involving child abuse continue to occur in modern times because fear clouds judgment. Future witch hunts are inevitable. As new scapegoats are created, the form of the scare will change to reflect the social and cultural context. The challenge is to identify these panics as soon as they appear and recognize them for what they are: creations of the human imagination.

CHAPTER 2

Twitching Epidemics and Pregnancy Panics
Historic Tales from Europe and America

Every man is the creature of the age in which he lives.—Voltaire[1]

By the late nineteenth and early twentieth century when outbreaks of mass hysteria began erupting in European schools, the explanation shifted to reflect the enlightened times. Instead of witchcraft, the emerging field of psychology was used to explain bouts of violent trembling, twitching and shaking, as scientists focused on the role of stress on the subconscious mind. Convulsions and trance states were also common. Outbreaks were clustered around the strictest schools in Germany, Austria, Switzerland and France. What were these institutions doing that would evoke such reactions? Foremost was the new teaching method of "mental discipline," developed in the writings of German philosopher Christian von Wolff in 1734 and popularized in the late 1700s by Scotsman Thomas Reid. This approach, widely accepted in Europe during the nineteenth century,[2] held that the mind was a muscle in need of exercise. Teachers using this method forced their students to endure torturous sessions of monotonous repetitions in math, science, spelling and writing. Teachers saw themselves as coaches whose job it was to make students practice each and every school day in order to strengthen their minds. Students were also forced to learn subjects that were not immediately useful, since most of the population were laborers. Educators thought it was time well spent because it would help the students excel in other areas. For instance, learning Latin was thought to improve one's recall in history; studying geometry was held to strengthen the ability to reason. While the theory behind this new method seemed logical, there was one major problem: it wasn't true.

Experimental studies by the likes of American psychologist Edward Lee Thorndike (1874–1949) soon refuted the idea. When math students were tested for their ability to reason against equally successful pupils with inferior math training, there was no difference in the two groups' reasoning capacity.[3] Thorndike realized that drilling and memorizing was largely a waste of time. While recalling names, dates and formulas has a place in education, during the nineteenth and early twentieth century, "memory work" *was* European education.[4] Creativity was in short supply, and schools of the period were largely regurgitation factories. In the wake of compelling evidence put forth by Thorndike and others, the fad of "mental discipline," which had waxed so brightly for decades, began to wane, and by the start of World War I in 1914, it had been eclipsed by less draconian approaches.

During its heyday, several schools practicing "mental discipline" recorded an array of strange reactions that correspond to what British psychiatrist Simon Wessely terms "motor hysteria." The condition is common in repressive settings and is so named because the slowly accumulating stress disrupts motor neurons that cause muscles to contract and control coordination.[5] Occasionally it interfered with signals to the brain, resulting in trance states. Outbreaks were once common in intolerable settings such as strict schools where students who received poor grades faced a heavy stigma. Like prisoners, they felt trapped and powerless. But theirs was a fear of expulsion, not incarceration. There was no negotiation, and protests were unheard of. In those days parents and school officials were all-powerful, and students did not question their principals or teachers. It was within this backdrop of chronic stress and frustration that hysteria outbreaks became common.

Motor hysteria appears gradually and may take weeks or months to subside after the stressful trigger has been eliminated or reduced. In rare instances it can take years. Students often convulsed in their seats.[6] Sometimes their limbs seized up and became rigid, their bodies falling to the floor, twisting in odd, unnatural ways.[7] These episodes of twitching, shaking and trembling often persisted in a waxing, waning fashion over a period of days, weeks or months.[8] Fellow students could only look on in amazement as their classmates engaged in the most remarkable behaviors. In one episode a group of girls wept uncontrollably, only to follow this with outbursts of nervous, convulsive laughing.[9]

Outbreaks afflicted students who were under pressure to perform monotonous drills. A 1908 British inquiry on European education found that French primary schools had curriculums that were "too intense" and "far too much composed of memory work."[10] Fear of litigation or losing one's job also played a role. Article 1384 of the French education code discouraged physical activities and games, as teachers were held legally responsible for mishaps occurring under their supervision.[11] Playgrounds were scarce, and during the little time that students were not laboring on their lessons, recreation took on the look of a prison exercise yard. Most instructors played it safe by engaging in games that were more mental than physical. The inquiry noted that in some French schools, teachers and parents put enormous performance pressure on pupils, who knew that if their grades slipped, there was a long waiting list of eager students ready to take their place. One educator said, "With such dismissal constantly hanging over their head, pupils appear to be always at high pressure."[12] French secondary schools were described as "a veritable prison-house for all pupils from the youngest equally to the oldest, with a system of continual espionage known as *surveillance* (every minute of the day being duly apportioned, even recreation policed), relieved ... by scarcely a human feature." One British educator who visited a French school described the teaching as "monotonous and reiterated preaching" during which, at the end of each lesson, a lengthy tract must be committed to memory.[13]

Some elite Swiss and German schools were so strict that even the punishment of elementary students was "harsh and severe,"[14] with administrators obsessing over order, obedience and uniformity.[15] School inspector Joseph Lucas wrote in 1878 that in Bavaria "it truly does not matter if one serves his three years in the army or in the schoolhouse."[16] One German curriculum issued to elementary teachers in 1890 was typical for its uncompromising rigidity: "In order to save time, maintain order and quiet, and accustom the children to uniform activity and to 'obedience and command,' it is recommended that every activity which occurs daily or which is frequently repeated be regulated by orders and done in time."[17]

Under the daily barrage of stress in these academic boot camps, bizarre behaviors broke out. In one girl's school, fifteen pupils developed strange coughing spells, imitating animals as they coughed including "the baying of a hound, others the sounds made by a horse, a parrot, and a goose."[18] In 1892 a peculiar case of mental contagion struck a Catholic girls' school at Biberach in southern Germany, a region notorious for its strict schooling.[19] A young girl kept falling into a trance. Her frightened classmates soon "fell into such condition themselves that they could not be awakened by shaking, calling or even by pricking with pins." Some of the girls talked while in a trance; others went into violent convulsions. American child psychologist William Burnham viewed the episode as a form of group hypnosis.[20]

In 1893 Dr. S. Rembold investigated an outbreak of mass hysteria at a girls' school in Stuttgart, also in south Germany.[21] Upon arriving and glancing down the corridor, he saw a procession of weeping girls making wild, exaggerated gestures. At times they would break into uncontrollable laughter. "They were in groups of two or three, in each of which one was led by another or dragged along by two. Those who were dragged usually hung unconscious in the arms of their companions, head sunk upon the breast, and the legs dragging upon the floor," he wrote.[22] About forty girls were sitting on benches in the drawing room; several were slumped over and passed out. Others were sighing and crying. Soon the healthy students were ordered back to classes, while those who were unwell were taken to an open window, reassured that they would soon feel better and told to take deep breaths. Their upper eyelids trembled. Ten of the girls were lying on the floor, unconscious. Rembold tried talking to them but got no response. He then began shaking them; still no response. He then took their pulses, which were weak but otherwise normal. Twenty-five girls in all were affected. His treatment was politically incorrect by modern standards. He threw half a liter of water into the face of each victim, who was ordered to immediately stand and "quit such nonsense."[23] The outbreak lasted less than twenty-four hours. The next day at school the students showed no signs of illness or unusual behavior; it was as if the wild spectacle of the previous day had never happened.[24] That same year seven girls at the People's School in Valle, Austria, were stricken with convulsions and seizures. The students would complain of dizziness and a buzzing in the ears before passing out,[25] after which their bodies would heave and convulse and they would foam at the mouth.[26] They also had a tolerance for pain, a classic feature of hysteria.

While less common, these so-called psychic epidemics were occasionally reported in British schools. One such incident took place over several days in May 1905, when forty-five students at a girls' school in Derby in the English Midlands exhibited fits of screaming and fainting. Too weak to walk, they had to be carried home to rest. Enterprising school officials, suspecting a noxious gas was responsible, placed mice in the classrooms and waited. Nothing happened. There was no word on how and when the episode subsided.[27]

Emotional Tremors

There are many nineteenth century reports of tremors in European students undertaking repetitive writing assignments. Between June and September 1892, a writing tremor epidemic struck at a village school in

Gross-tinz, Germany.[28] On June 28 the right hand of a ten year-old girl began trembling. Soon her entire body was shaking. The next day the hands of several classmates began to tremble for up to an hour. With each passing day the malady lasted longer and longer. Soon their entire bodies were shaking. With each new case, the girls, ages five to twelve, were immediately taken from class. Between July 14 and 20, the symptoms peaked: "On almost every seat were patients having convulsions of the whole body. The girls fell under the seats and had to be carried from the room by the boys."[29] Twenty of the school's thirty-eight girls were stricken; eight of them lost consciousness. The fits lasted from between fifteen minutes and an hour. Upon awakening, those who had passed out said they could recall nothing of their ordeal.[30] The principal soon ordered the school closed. Upon reopening on August 19, the trembling and convulsions had stopped, though several girls were complaining of a new ailment: severe headaches with no obvious cause. Those affected were sent home to rest. The drama ended after the autumn holiday.[31]

That same year, trembling spread through a girls' school in Basel, Switzerland, preventing twenty girls from writing. The malady subsided after school hours, only to reappear when students entered the school grounds. The tremor began in one class and spread to nearby rooms. "The disorder frequently appeared among children who had before been healthy when one of the sufferers had an attack in the immediate neighborhood; and when one child had an attack others did so."[32]

The ailment returned to the school twelve years later, striking eleven- to fifteen-year-olds. On June 11, the right hands and forearms of two students began to shake. Apparently the previous occurrence had made its way into school legend, since the outbreak coincided with a rumor that the tremor would force the school to close for six weeks if three hundred pupils were stricken. Crisis talks were held, and it was decided that school would stay open no matter what. The tremblers were put in a special room with one teacher, who would instruct them for a month. Instead of being punished, their workload was cut and they were fed well. Authorities were also careful not to criticize their inability to write. In all, just twenty-seven students were affected. The shaking soon subsided.[33]

One girl, Ellie, was scolded by her mother after coming home on June 17 with a trembling right hand. The stress also caused her face to twitch. The next day Ellie was put in the tremor class. "She trembled so violently that writing was impossible for her. She was unable to answer the easiest questions and could not work with one-place numbers in arithmetic." But on June 24, after being smothered with love and encouragement, Ellie was symptom-free.[34]

A "trembling disease" also swept through several schools in Meissen, in east-central Germany, between 1905 and 1906, afflicting children with heavy writing loads. The outbreak began in October when the hands of a thirteen-year-old girl began to shake and twitch. Gradually, more students succumbed. By February 21, 134 students were trembling, and by March 20, a whopping 237 students were afflicted. With all of the time off from writing, the pent-up tension appears to have dissipated, and by late March the numbers fell with each passing day. By mid–May, it was over.[35]

In 1906 at the People's Elementary School in the industrial city of Chemnitz in east central Germany, a little girl's writing suddenly turned to scribbles as her hand began to shake violently. In the coming days and weeks, more students were stricken. One girl after another fell victim and was taken from class. In all, nearly two dozen nine- and ten-year-old girls succumbed. The pupils trembled only when it came time for writing drills. There were other oddities: only the arm and hand that each girl wrote with would shake. Students were able to carry out all other aspects of their schoolwork normally, including gym class. With only one exception, those affected were average or above average students. These bright, imaginative pupils were under pressure to get good grades, yet found it difficult to sit through tedious writing classes under the baleful eye of a dominating instructor.

School physician Johannes Schoedel took measures that today would seem barbaric. He gave the students electric shocks, not as a punishment, but believing it would render them more open to his suggestions. After the treatment, during the next writing session it was announced: "Since you are not able to write, you must unfortunately have mental arithmetic again." The tremors soon subsided and eventually stopped. Newspapers may have been instrumental in spreading the symptoms to Chemnitz. The first victim said that he had read about the "tremor disease" at Meissen in the paper.[36]

These outbreaks are examples of conversion disorder. Pupils felt they must stay in school and get good grades, yet they were in conflict with the workload, especially the tedious tasks. Pent-up anxiety appears to have been converted into hand tremors, which disappeared when the students received sympathy for their plight and a temporary respite from their dreary exercises.

A Tale of Two Continents: American Fainting Outbreaks

A survey of nineteenth century North American newspapers reveals a conspicuous absence of the twitching, shaking, convulsions, and trance states that were so prevalent in Europe at the time.[37] While "mental discipline" was used by the early pioneers, it was diluted as it did not suit their needs. It was impractical for frontier conditions, which required settlers to wear many hats: trader, farmer, butcher, tax collector, judge, mayor. Education historian Arthur Pinsent writes that in the New World the classics might guide a local leader in political and legal principles, but "if his cows suffered from contagious abortion, or his sheep from footrot, he would need some knowledge of animal husbandry *applicable in North American conditions*. He was not likely to find it in Virgil's *Georgics*."[38] American schools focused on teaching information that was "directly applicable to agriculture, manufacture, and trade in frontier conditions."[39] In schools where the rare outbreak of fits and seizures did occur, discipline was strict, as in a young ladies' seminary school in Montreal where sixty Canadian students were stricken in 1894.[40]

Most outbreaks of unusual behavior in American and Canadian schools during the late 1800s reflect stereotypes of girls as emotionally immature and inferior, as evidenced by numerous mass fainting episodes in response to unexpected events. The triggers were varied, ranging from hair curling to thunderstorms, and reveal how girls of the time were conditioned to believe that they were psychologically fragile. Consider the following incident that took place at a small boarding school in New York City during January 1899. One evening two girls were in their tiny dorm room when they "took the globes off the gas fixtures for hair curling purposes" and forgot to put them back on. A short time later the curtains caught fire. The girls let out piercing shrieks and promptly fainted. Their dorm mates rushed to see what the fuss was about but quickly lost their nerve. Of the girls who arrived on the scene, one fainted, several stood around weeping, and some ran out of the building, while the rest shouted for the only man in the dorm to do something. The lone male arrived at a chaotic scene: three girls were lying unconscious on the floor, others were screaming, and by now both the curtains and the adjacent woodwork were ablaze. Maneuvering over the girls, he ordered everyone else out of the room to lessen the confusion. Meanwhile, a girl from Texas went to fetch water, but "returning in mad haste with a pitcher full of water borne triumphantly aloft, she collided with the retreating forces at the door. The pitcher struck the leader of the retreat squarely in the face and knocked out two of her front teeth, where upon the injured girl made the fainting trio a quartet and the water carrier dropped her pitcher and went into violent hysteria." The fire was extinguished by the time teachers arrived.[41]

There were many cases of American schoolgirls fainting during school fires at this time. Some triggers were novel. In May 1897 a lightning bolt struck East Denver High School in Colorado, giving many students an electric shock, after which several girls fainted. In June 1897 four girls fainted on a boat ride during a Sunday school outing. The first girl to collapse had a history of fainting spells. The others grew anxious, perhaps overexcited by the trip, and soon collapsed.[42]

Modern Outbreaks: Pregnancy Panics and Drop Attacks

Rare, sporadic outbreaks of motor disturbances continue to strike students in Europe and North America, such as a mysterious wave of fainting spells that swept through a class at a London girls' school in the early 1970s. The outbreak lasted for much of the year. Even when conscious, students complained of walking around in a mental fog. The episode began in November when the class was taking practice O levels — notoriously stressful exams that British students must pass to graduate from high school. Louise, age seventeen, began to have fainting and falling spells in class. By late February, Margaret began to faint. Shortly after, Rosemary was stricken. Before long, five more classmates and their teacher began to have falling or fainting spells. The class was then sent home a week early for the spring break. Louise was the worst affected, as she would curl up on the floor in a ball and appear to sleep; at other times she would roll her eyes and fling her arms about. She claimed amnesia during the attacks. The outbreak ended in July with the summer recess.[43]

The saga began when Louise heard that her best friend Anne was pregnant. Anne gave birth in February but died when a blood vessel burst in her brain. That's when Louise's condition grew worse — perhaps from anxiety over the potentially disastrous consequences from having sex. A psychiatric team went to the school to investigate. They later observed: "If one assumed that Louise's falling was a form of identification with her pregnant friend, Anne, one would not be surprised at the epidemic ending after a period of nine months!" Louise was a charming young lady with a magnetic personality and a complicated, stressful personal life. In fact, her personal life was nothing short of remarkable for a girl of seventeen. Louise had an affair with a brother-in-law, an incestuous relationship with her bisexual brother, and after that ended, an affair with his bisexual partner, whom she eventually married. To raise anxiety levels even higher, Louise even had to fend off sexual advances from one of her female teachers. Later, Louise told psychiatrists that soon after the onset of her fainting spells, she found she relished the attention and began to fake attacks: "At first, I would not admit to myself that it was not genuine: I was convinced that, because I really had fainted several times, that I was still doing so. When I did face up to the fact that it was false, I still couldn't stop."[44]

During one psychiatric admission, Louise triggered a pregnancy panic after suggesting to her fellow patients that she was pregnant. Within days, several patients, "at least one of whom had no sexual experience, began to complain of the same symptoms and needed to be reassured that they were not pregnant."[45] Through simply chatting with others about the possibility of pregnancy, Louise's charismatic personality appears to have caused a domino effect in the ward. Psychiatrists refer to this condition as false pregnancy or by its formal scientific name, *pseudocycsis*. False pregnancies often involve women who desperately want to bear a child and feel physically and psychologically as if they were pregnant. Yet when the time comes to deliver the baby, there is only an empty uterus. Those experiencing false pregnancy can show all of the outward signs of pregnancy: an absence of menstrual periods, vomiting, feeling the baby moving. Some even suffer pains as if delivering a baby. While many cases of false pregnancy have been documented, an epidemic of pseudocycsis is extremely rare.

A Twitching Epidemic in the Southern United States

In twentieth-century America, outbreaks of motor disturbances have taken the form of twitching epidemics and pregnancy scares in traditional schools in the Deep South. We begin with the story of Helen, who, in the spring of 1939, was a popular seventeen-year-old high school senior in Bellevue, Louisiana. By all accounts, she did not like to dance. She was popular and bright, but a poor dancer: tentative, nervous, and awkward. Her boyfriend, Maurice, was an outstanding dancer, and this was Helen's dilemma: How could she keep her boyfriend from ending their relationship while she was unable or unwilling to dance with him? It seems that Helen's subconscious was able to resolve the problem: her legs began to twitch. Soon Helen was excused from dance classes and Maurice was again showing romantic interest. The twitching spread to several of Helen's girlfriends, who, investigators surmise, were subconsciously identifying with Helen in order to get attention themselves.

The episode began on Saturday, January 28, at the annual homecoming dance. Because of her aversion to dancing, Helen went only to socialize. After watching the dance, her right leg began to twitch and jerk. Over the next several weeks, her attacks got worse. While playing basketball at school, Helen sometimes had to stop as her leg began to twitch. As news of her twitching spread, several students urged Helen to stay home, fearing they could catch it.

On February 21, Helen's friend Millie was attending Mardi Gras celebrations in nearby Ferryville when her stomach, chest, and neck began to twitch. At age sixteen, Millie came from a poor, troubled family, and before her attacks she had been seeing a doctor for "nerves." Two days later, a third girl, Frances, 16, began to twitch during French class and was sent to the nurse. During this time, Geraldine, who sat next to Frances, started twitching. She later said: "And then I started jumping. Then they carried me upstairs to the infirmary, and I started crying. They gave me ammonia but that didn't help. Plenty [of] girls tried to hold me down, but they couldn't."[46]

While the twitching girls were being taken to the infirmary, an angry mother made a dramatic scene, loudly demanding that her children be let out of school, fearful that they might "catch" the twitching. Rumors began to circulate of strange goings-on, and soon other parents arrived to withdraw their children for the day. As students gathered in the halls and went to their lockers before departing, tension grew and word spread that something was up. The principal called an emergency assembly to reassure students, only to have it backfire. As pupils began filing out of the room, the hallways became chaotic:

> With the break-up of the assembly ... the children scurried around and pressed forward in an attempt to see and hear what they could of the hysterical subjects. Some were to be seen in the principal's office; others were being administered ammonia-water ... in the infirmary; still others, who had not developed the motor disturbances, but who contributed even more largely to the general confusion because of their uncontrolled fearful crying, had been taken to the nearby teacherage."[47]

One observer quipped: "You've seen a stampede? That's how it was. The children were running up and down and all around trying to get a wiff here and a wiff there." School closed early, but on the bus ride home, students made light of the day's events, and the driver joked: "If you want to talk about the jerks, why don't you practice them." Shortly after, Mildred, age seventeen, began to twitch and jerk. When school reopened on Monday, the girls were reassured that the twitching wasn't contagious and there was nothing to fear. Students and parents were skeptical. Nearly half of the student body stayed away. It took a week for the school routine to return to normal as the twitching slowly subsided.[48]

Investigators found several causes for the malady. Several days before the dance at which Helen first began to twitch, mandatory dance instruction had started in gym classes. Because of her illness, Helen was excused from dance instruction, and at the same time she was able to rekindle Maurice's waning interest. The investigating social scientists observed that Helen was being forced to take part in an activity she neither liked nor was good at, noting: "The jerking of her leg muscles obviously made it impossible for her to dance, so the painful conflict situation was resolved with no discredit to the subject." By this time, the fleet-footed Maurice was getting friendly with Gretchen, an attractive, energetic freshman and skillful tap dancer. Despite her youth, Gretchen's spirited attitude and dance prowess had caught Maurice's eye. He found himself drawn to her and gave her his class ring. Maurice and Gretchen were on the verge of dating. Helen needed to act quickly but was too shy to approach Maurice, and she couldn't win him over through dancing. Helen's twitching may have been a subconscious attempt to hold on to her boyfriend by gaining his attention and sympathy. Investigators concluded, "Helen was both by temperament and training entirely incapable of consciously making a bid for the attention of her boyfriend, but ... unconsciously and involuntarily she may have been achieving precisely this end through [hysteria]." But high school students are notorious for being cruel and intolerant of anything different. Why weren't Helen and the other twitching girls seen as peculiar or strange? The investigators surmise that as Helen was popular and a local, there was little or no stigma for her or those unconsciously imitating her twitching and it served a purpose — getting attention.[49]

A Pregnancy Scare in Cajun Country

Pregnancy. The mere mention of the word once instilled fear in American schoolgirls, who often risked banishment from school and their community to spend the duration of their term "visiting a relative." Today, pregnancy is more common and accepted among American high school girls. Most no longer try to disguise the fact, and during commencement it is not uncommon to see a conspicuous bulge beneath the midsection of a graduation gown. In conservative Louisiana during the 1960s, premarital sex was a major moral infraction, and getting pregnant was even worse. The embarrassment, scandal, and repercussions often created a lifelong stigma.

In 1960, a girl at the all-black Bethume Negro School in the small town of Welch in rural southwest Louisiana became pregnant. It did not take long for authorities to identify the boy responsible. The two were sent away to reform school.⁵⁰ The repercussions were swift and made a lasting impression on the student body. Against this backdrop of intolerance and fear, in early 1962, rumors began spreading that more students were pregnant and that once identified, they too would be sent to reform school. Sexual activity among students had been rampant, and the rumors set off a school-wide crisis. Investigators later learned that a series of sexual rendezvous had been taking place in the photography darkroom during lunch. Investigators believe that one girl had engaged in sex with thirty different boys on various occasions. At about this time rumors spread that *all* of the girls were going to be given pregnancy tests, and those with positive results would be sent to reform school. Strange behaviors swept through the school: seizures, shaking, dizziness, headaches, catatonic posturing, and overwhelming drowsiness. Most of the spells lasted a few minutes, though a few persisted for an hour. Doctors tried sedatives, but they had little effect. Visits by outside authorities made matters worse, further heightening fears.⁵¹ Twenty-one girls and one boy in grades six to eleven were stricken over the next six months.

The first outbreak began at a nearby Methodist church during an evening choir concert on February 14. A thirteen-year-old girl complained of shortness of breath, grew dizzy, and fainted. While it was determined that she had hyperventilated from nerves, the incident was dramatic, and she was carried from church unconscious. The next day a classmate who had watched her friend faint the night before had a "blackout spell" at school. Her attacks became a daily fixture at the school, and she was soon ordered to rest at home for a month. On March 6 a third pupil was stricken. By late March, eight girls were having blackout spells, and by early April an alarming twenty girls and one boy were afflicted. Theories abounded as to the cause: a gas leak, a tainted water supply, drugs, toxic poisoning, even an infection. The Louisiana Health Department investigated, eliminating each of these possibilities and concluding that stress-induced hysteria was the culprit. The exams were thorough, with doctors even conducting painful lumbar spine punctures to try to identify any exotic abnormalities. While each of the girls was given sedatives, the fear of being tested for pregnancy remained and the attacks continued.⁵²

A psychiatrist from Tulane University in New Orleans, Dr. James Knight, led an investigation into the episode and reported that soon after the outbreak appeared in the press, most of the town's white population felt that the affected black students had been "acting foolish" and behaving in a "childish" manner. At this time, African Americans were commonly viewed as emotionally immature and mentally inferior, and racial segregation was common, with blacks forced to use separate movie theatres and restaurants; they even had separate drinking fountains and bathrooms. Other whites said they thought the girls were on drugs.[53] One woman claimed that a doctor told her that "some kind of humbug was apparently responsible for the attacks," suggesting that those involved were engaged in an elaborate deception.[54]

A boy named Jerry was made a scapegoat by many parents and teachers. He had transferred to the school just before the attacks. It was widely rumored that Jerry was selling drugs. Stories also circulated that he was spiking chewing gum at a nearby store, causing the girls to act strangely. In a sign of deep anxiety, and without a shred of evidence to go on, the Louisiana Health Department moved in, testing the gum and other candy. Investigators found nothing unusual, though the tainted candy rumors continued.[55]

Some of the parents thought that the girls' fits were caused by "black magic," though most students scoffed at the idea. At first, many parents and teachers blamed an infection. This seemed logical, since most of the stricken "were those who touched, supported, or carried to the lounge some girl who had had a 'blackout spell.'" This is not implausible, since the sexually active girls tended to hang out with each other. They were also under the most stress and subject to the same conditions, living under the constant fear of getting pregnant or being tested for pregnancy. But if the outbreak was driven by a fear of getting pregnant, how can we explain the one male student who was stricken? It may have been a fear of being the boy responsible for one of the pregnancies. When this student suffered a blackout spell, his classmates began to speculate as to whether he would be the father of a girl or a boy. By early August, the fits subsided as a new, more lenient principal took over. Because the principal was understanding and supportive of the girls' anxiety, they no longer lived in daily fear of being tested for pregnancy and their stress levels dropped. Life soon returned to normal; the pregnancy scare was over.[56]

Signs of the Times

Outbreaks of motor dysfunction in American schools are rare. When several girls in Mount Pleasant, Mississippi, began to act strangely in April 1976, school officials had one thought: drugs. Narcotics agents swarmed the building after fifteen students fell to the ground, "writhing and kicking before passing out."[57] Police found the girls to be free of drugs and concluded that hysteria was the culprit. Many students and parents blamed voodoo. The girls would suddenly fall to the floor, kicking and screaming:

"Don't let it get me!" or "Get it off!" before passing out. The attacks lasted up to fifteen minutes. The trigger turned out to be a schoolgirl rivalry over the affections of a boy. One group of girls said that a jealous classmate had put a voodoo hex on them. The fear of magic spells spread quickly through the group after the first few girls suffered fits, which only confirmed their classmates' suspicions of sorcery and fueled their own fears that they would be next. By the week's end, one-third of the school's 900 students were staying home because of the fear of being hexed.[58]

Mass Hysteria and the Social Network

In 2002, a mysterious malady swept through a rural high school in North Carolina. Ten girls exhibited strange seizures at the start of the school year, often accompanied by fainting, shortness of breath, headaches, lightheadedness, muscle twitching and jerking, tingling, and numbness. The school nurse noted that the fits were unlike any epileptic seizures that she had seen before. When she placed smelling salts near the noses of a couple of the girls, they cringed, while the mothers of two girls said that when their daughters began to have fits, "they could 'talk her out of it' as the episode started to develop."[59] There was another oddity: the malady rarely occurred in class, but struck students in the hallways between classes, in the cafeteria, or in the schoolyard during recess. This feature is highly unusual and does not fit the historical trend.

The first stricken was a cheerleader, and the fear of "catching" her seizure may have made her fellow cheerleaders and other classmates nervous, triggering their blackout spells. It may have also been some kind of identification with a school role model, as four others who were stricken were either cheerleaders or former cheerleaders. This case is odd for another reason — three of the students were eleventh-graders, three were tenth-graders and four were in the ninth grade. In most outbreaks of mass hysteria in schools, the students share classrooms, but not so here, as just two were in the same class. While most had just a few attacks, one had thirty. It took four months for the symptoms to subside. Doctors Steven Roach and Rick Langley investigated the episode and reviewed the tests on the girls. After examining their brain wave results, the doctors were certain that their seizures were hysterical.[60]

Five years later, a similar episode took place in nearby Vinton, Virginia, when an outbreak of twitching arms and legs, headaches and dizziness swept through William Byrd High School. At least nine girls and a female teacher were stricken. Once again, there was a conspicuous oddity:

the girls were scattered throughout the school and did not share the same classroom. The episode lasted several months and occurred during a spate of public health crises that had been reported in the local media, including an asbestos scare and warnings that a drug resistant strain of golden staph (Staphylococcus aureus) had resulted in the death of an area student.[61]

In 2011, another rare outbreak of motor hysteria was reported among a dozen girls at Leroy Central School in western New York, and for the third time since 2002, the way the symptoms spread was highly unusual, as they were scattered among students throughout the school instead of being confined to a single classroom. The girls were suffering from facial tics, twitching muscles and garbled verbal outbursts that resembled Tourette's Syndrome. Some of the girls could not complete a single sentence without severely garbling their words. After examining ten of the victims, neurologist Laszlo Mechtler announced that having conducted a series of tests and eliminating other causes, he was confident the culprit was conversion disorder. Of course, there was an immediate outcry from parents, some of whom allowed their kids to appear on national TV to refute the diagnosis. Presumably this generated even more stress.

The New York State Health Department made matters worse by failing to release their hysteria diagnosis to the public, claiming patient privacy laws and suggesting that it was not a public health issue. However, their secrecy only served to create widespread fear that a "mystery illness" was loose in their community, and it fostered conspiracy theories and much bitterness from many parents when the diagnosis was made public by Dr. Mechtler in late January 2012. This led to a perception that state health officials had been engaging in a cover-up and could not be trusted. Before the official diagnosis was released to the public, the refusal to render a public diagnosis created a media frenzy. On Fox News Dr. Marc Siegel said he was almost certain it was PANDAS, caused by strep throat infections, while others suggested a reaction to Gardasil, used in human papillomavirus (HPV) vaccinations to protect girls against cervical cancer.[62] Neurologist Rosario Trifiletti agreed with Dr. Siegel's diagnosis and conducted his own tests. On February 7, he announced that eight of the girls had a "PANDAS-like illness." However, the woman who identified PANDAS Syndrome, Dr. Susan Swedo, refuted the diagnosis and noted that just because high levels of strep antibodies were found in the patients, it did not necessarily implicate PANDAS, as the same antibodies are very common in students of the same age.[63] Dr. Siegel was correct on one key point: given the fear generated by not knowing the cause, it *was* a public health issue — and such issues should have overridden the privacy of the 12 girls. It is also curious that many of the girls' parents only learned of the mass hysteria diagnosis through media reports. What was really going on here is obvious: State health officials were afraid of the public backlash they knew would ensue once the "H-word" was used and their hysteria diagnosis became public. While the pronouncement was always going to be met with resistance, withholding it was a mistake and made matters worse. With 12 families involved and the media placing the issue in the national spotlight, the public was always going to find out.

A parent of one of the girls was incredulous at the hysteria diagnosis. James Dupont said: "For us to try to buy that our girls all seem to have a traumatic experience within a couple of months ... and all seem to have handled it the same way with the same symptoms, that don't even know each other, it's just unbelievable."[64] Dr. Mechtler later refuted the claim and noted that the girls were not exactly strangers to one another: "Some of them were friends, some played on the same soccer team and all are in the same high school," he said.[65]

Researcher Paul Cropper believes that one of the functions of mass psychogenic illness is to act as a force for instant social networking. He observes that in Leroy the girls may not have known each other well, but they "may have unknowingly shared the fact that they felt 'invisible,' excluded, neglected (maybe only in a minor way), stressed, etc., but once Case 1 arrives it becomes a public invitation for all the others to join this exclusive club or protest—'the tic sufferers.'" Cropper believes that the attention drawn to the girls subconsciously underscores their status as special, different, and suddenly "visible." As a result of their illness they even received specialist care; one of the doctors treating some of the girls described them as wonderful and unique. He speculates that perhaps this was "the kind of individual focus they weren't getting in either their school or family lives before the outbreak."[66]

Cropper defends the health department's strategy of keeping the hysteria diagnosis under wraps, even though it created communitywide—even nationwide—anxiety. They were in a damned-if-you-do, damned-if-you-don't situation. Cropper states: "MSI is a public health issue that is created and perpetuated in a social space, but not in the same way that a traditional infectious disease is, and its treatment has to be far more personal than simply giving vaccine jabs." He notes that each of the girls may have vastly different individual pressures and stresses, but the first case signalled that it was OK to let the tics be the acceptable way to release the pressure and send a public signal out that there were problems. "Saying it's all conversion disorder as a mass explanation for such a personal issue is not a sensitive way to treat the patients. You also have the massive stigma attached to MSI language as words like 'stress' and 'hysteria' are very loaded words," Cropper observes.[67]

The public reaction was clearly stoked by the health department's initial cloak of secrecy. When the *Huffington Post* published an article online about the outbreak on January 17, 2012, they recorded over a thousand blog postings to their site in less than a week. People suggested dozens of pet theories ranging from Lyme disease to pesticides. One person wrote: "Mass hysteria? I call BS. Mass cover up? Most likely." Another suggested the likelihood of copper poisoning from the girls' placing pennies in their mouths to mask the smell of alcohol! This far-fetched notion is even more unlikely given that since 1982, pennies contain just 2.5 percent copper; the remainder is zinc, and the symptoms were not consistent with zinc poisoning. Other explanations included Ritalin or Ecstasy abuse, exposure to fertilizer or electromagnetic fields, and magnesium deficiency. Some even suggested that the girls were part of a secret government experiment. There was seemingly no end to the exotic theories put forth to explain the outbreak.[68] The most popular belief among locals was that the cause was toxic chemicals from one of the many dumpsites in the area, in particular a nearby cyanide dump. However, extensive tests of the area by both the Environmental Protection Agency and the state health department could find no evidence of contamination. Furthermore, if chemicals were involved, why did they almost exclusively affect adolescent girls? Why weren't their siblings and parents affected? Many teachers would have been on the school grounds for longer periods than the students, yet they were unaffected. Why would symptoms have appeared after decades, and then in such an abrupt manner? It is clear that the distrust of the state health department fuelled the list of possible theories and led to the formation of a local parents group, ensuring that the issue would remain in the public eye for the foreseeable future.[69]

The outbreaks of this rare type of motor hysteria in North Carolina, Virginia and in western New York, all within a 10-year span, are significant and unique in the annals of psychogenic illness because of the unusual way that these symptoms spread. The common factor linking these episodes is the role that social media appears to have played. This is most clearly evident in the case of LeRoy, as the students used Twitter, Facebook and Youtube to communicate about the outbreak, not to mention blog postings, text messages and e-mail. Dr. David Lichter observes: "It's remarkable to see how one individual posts something, and then the next person who posts something not only are the movements bizarre and not consistent with known movement disorders, but it's the same kind of movements. This mimicry goes on with Facebook."[70] Another odd dimension to all three twenty-first-century American cases is the absence of a clear singular stressor. It may be that interpersonal conflict — a staple of the adolescent world — played a major role, and once the initial symptoms appeared, an array of folk theories, from toxic chemicals to exotic illnesses, fuelled the initial anxieties.

One of the most commonly observed patterns in the mass hysteria literature is that episodes are typically spread through sight and sound. The technology revolution has placed inexpensive telecommunication devices in the hands of most students, devices that are essentially extensions of our eyes and ears. It would now appear that social media is eliminating the necessity of being in direct visual or verbal contact with other victims. This has implications for the potential of future outbreaks, as students no longer need to be in close physical proximity to the perceived harmful agent. This helps to explain why in recent years, American cases have not been confined to a single classroom but have spread throughout the schools in question. This may be a milestone in the history of psychogenic illness because for the first time, the primary vector or agent of spread appears to be the Internet and social media. The neurologists treating twelve of the LeRoy victims support this view. They write: "As soon as the media coverage stopped, they all began to rapidly improve and are doing very well." By June 2012, they report that all but one of their patients were "free of tics and vocalizations."[71]

Since the sixteenth century, observers have noted a fascinating array of strange behaviors among students in European and North American schools, adolescents enduring long-term stress being especially susceptible. Their pent-up emotions eventually burst forth, resulting in disruptions to their motor function and triggering coordination problems, convulsions, twitching, shaking, and trance states. From the fear of witchcraft to reactions to drills in repetition and memorization, to more recent episodes involving a fear of toxic chemicals and mysterious illnesses being spread through the social media, each of these episodes uniquely reflects its time.

CHAPTER 3

Fear 101— Fates Worse than Homework
Modern Tales from East and West

Of all our passions, fear weakens judgment most.— Bertrand Russell[1]

Since the 1950s, health conscious Americans and Europeans have heeded reports of toxic food and unsafe products. Each year the mass media produce a new list of hazards. Most prove untrue. In 1959, many Americans avoided cranberries after claims by scientists that use of the weed killer aminotriazole caused thyroid cancer in rats. After sales were banned in several states, it was determined that one would have to eat thousands of pounds to be at the same risk as the rats.[2] Twenty years later there was a fear of "killer apples" as scientists made the alarming claim that apples sprayed with the growth hormone Alar could cause childhood cancer. Again, it came to light that the threat was exaggerated. A child would have to drink thousands of glasses of juice daily to be at risk. More recent scares include genetically modified foods, various chemicals, and terrorists. Since the 1960s, European and North American schools have been dominated by short-lived health scares, with pollution fears fueling overbreathing, fainting, dizziness, nausea, stomach pain, and headache— classic indicators of stress. This shift reflects a loosening of strict attitudes and a greater student voice in school issues. Meanwhile, watchdog groups such as the Parent-Teachers Association began holding teachers and administrators more accountable. As education was growing more liberal, *Silent Spring* by biologist Rachel Carson led to the birth of the modern environmental movement in 1962. Exposing the threat from pollution, Carson's book led to many new laws protecting the environment. As awareness of the threat grew, so did the preoccupation with the quality of water, food, and air. It is no surprise, then, that the most common mass hysteria trigger in the late twentieth century was the detection of strange odors. Rumors of food poisoning were another source of dread. We begin our survey of modern outbreaks in the southeastern United States.

Phantom Gas in Florida

Monday, May 13, 1974, began as a typical day in southern Florida — sunny and warm — when sirens pierced the calm, humid air. The local dispatcher received a report that a student had fainted at an elementary school in Dade County. The worried voice on the phone said she was unresponsive, even to smelling salts. It was 9:30 A.M. An ambulance was soon rolling to the scene, where 169 students from the fourth, fifth and sixth grades at Bay Harbor Elementary were huddled in the school's "cafetorium" (a large room used as both a cafeteria and auditorium), unaware of the unfolding drama. They were rehearsing for a musical. The students were twenty minutes into singing practice when "Sandy," a fifth-grader, began to have a headache and feel woozy. While the music teacher wasn't looking, the eleven-year-old slipped away to the nurse's office down the hall and collapsed. The teacher and most of the singers were oblivious to Sandy's distress.

Just as rehearsal was breaking up, paramedics were wedging through the hallways with a look of urgency on their faces. It wasn't long before they emerged from the nurse's office wheeling Sandy, looking like a rag doll, limp and unconscious, on a stretcher for the whole school to see. Soon after, several students exiting the rehearsal began to feel unwell. Rumors that a "gas leak" was poisoning students spread like wildfire. Within an hour scores of students in different parts of the school were feeling ill: headache, nausea, stomach pain, chills, difficulty breathing. Soon police, fire, and rescue personnel arrived at the school. Adding to the confusion was the presence of parents, politicians, community leaders, curiosity seekers, and a small battalion of reporters.[3]

By 10:30 A.M., Dr. Joel Nitzkin of the Dade County Health Office was asked to go to the school to help treat the children who had apparently been sickened by a "poison gas." It took him forty-five minutes to reach the school, at which point thirty four pupils had been deemed sick enough to be sent to the hospital or home to recuperate. "The scene was complete pandemonium. It had the *look* of a disaster," he said later. The school was mobbed. Nitzkin and two colleagues had to park nearby and walk in, as the parking area was overflowing with vehicles. Nitzkin had difficulty believing what he was seeing: "Ambulances. Fire equipment. Police cars.

All with their flashers flashing. And the media — they were swarming. Newspaper reporters and photographers. Radio people with microphones. Television cameras from four local stations.... Members of the Dade County School Board. Members of the Bay Harbor Town Council. And neighbors and passersby and parents all rushing around. I had never seen anything like it."[4]

When Nitzkin got to the school he began to assess the gravity of the situation. He wondered how the students who had been taken to the hospital were faring. Phoning the attending doctors, he learned that the children's urinalyses, electrolytes, blood counts and blood gases were all normal. What's more, the children seemed well, except one who was clearly hyperventilating and another who seemed to have a mild virus. Unfortunately, in the confusion and chaos at the emergency room, given the presence of nausea and headache with reports of a strange odor, a doctor hastily concluded that the victims "must have been exposed to a toxic gas."[5] In reality, it turned out that there was no gas.

Like a general in the heat of battle, Nitzkin was assessing the situation on the run, making mental notes and going through different scenarios in his head. After a quick survey of the building, there was no obvious sign of anything that would have made the students sick. He reasoned that bacteria and viruses could not have been the culprits on the basis of the short incubation period and symptoms.[6] The strange odor reported by many students — the apparent cause of the illness — was carpet glue in the library. Although it gave off a solvent-like smell, Nitzkin learned that the distinctive odor had been in the school since the carpet was laid, two weeks earlier; yet over the previous fourteen days, no one had become ill from the smell. Why now on the morning of May 13? As more details came to light, Nitzkin grew more curious. He had a hunch: Everything he was seeing sounded suspiciously like mass hysteria. But did the facts fit? He soon found out that none of the ill children had visited the library that day, and those who did were *not* among the ill:

> Minutes after dismissal of the class in question from the cafetorium, another group of children entered through a separate door and spent the next thirty to forty minutes in musical rehearsal similar to the class before. No one in this second group, including the teacher, was aware of the commotion from the previous class immediately outside the door. No one in this second group experienced illness despite exposure to the room in question.[7]

Nitzkin believed that what he was dealing with was essentially a large-scale panic attack, and set out trying to restore calm by reassuring the students and the community. He composed himself and began radiating a sense of outward calm and confidence. At 11:40 A.M. he walked up to a scrum of reporters and announced his assessment: "mass hysteria with hyperventilation."[8] In other words, the students had become anxious and began to overbreathe. Nitzkin was nervous about making the announcement but felt that someone had to take charge. It was a gamble, as he knew he could be discredited if others began to openly challenge his views. The immediate reaction was silence. Nitzkin said, "The public health nurses looked stunned. I saw Dr. Enriquez smiling and nodding. The parents of the sick children looked horrified and insulted — I was telling them their children were crazy. But most of the others — the teachers and school board people and the firemen and the head secretary — just stood there looking thoughtful." Nitzkin observed that as he carefully explained his rationale, a sigh of relief seemed to sweep over the crowd. "The firemen and the police just sort of disappeared. People began to turn to each other and talk. The sick kids stopped looking so sick." Incredibly, by noon, two and a half hours after it had begun, the crisis was over and no more pupils were sent home sick. The next day, tests of the building yielded no evidence of toxic gas. In the days and weeks that followed, attendance rates were normal.[9]

Dr. Nitzkin's bold diagnosis and decisive action put a quick end to the crisis, but the episode was not over. A new drama was emerging among furious parents, who believed he had made the wrong diagnosis. How dare he suggest that their children were victims of their own imaginations? Mass hysteria might happen to other children, but not theirs. Some, while admitting he was right, were critical of Nitzkin for making such a quick diagnosis before thorough tests of the premises could be conducted. Nitzkin steadfastly defended his actions, noting that the telltale signs of hysteria were everywhere. He simply fit the pieces together — the normal lab tests, except for values that were altered by overbreathing; the rapid cessation of vague symptoms; the absence of illness in adults sharing the identical environment; a preponderance of symptoms among young girls; and the spread of symptoms by sight or sound.[10]

Nitzkin later studied the eight most severely affected students, who were hospitalized for a time. Of the five girls, he concluded that one was a hypochondriac, while another often complained of vague ailments. Another had chronic anxiety and a history of hyperventilating under stress. Of the remaining two girls, one was a close friend of Sandy's and the other had come to school that morning feeling vaguely ill. Of the two boys, one had a long history of getting into trouble at school; the other was "highly excitable."[11] As for Sandy, she fit the profile of a classic trigger person in hysteria outbreaks. She was a leader: popular, attractive and precocious, and a good student. She was someone the other students looked up to and wanted to emulate. Nitzkin believes that like the pied piper leading the children into the sea, Sandy's collapse and dramatic exit from the school on a stretcher struck a responsive chord in her fellow chorus members, who had just finished a tiring rehearsal only to see rescue personnel carting off one of their own. It was unnerving. The stage was set for the children to be led astray by their own imaginations.

"We've Been Gassed!" Malathion Hysteria

Malathion is a highly effective insecticide. It has been used for decades in the war on bugs, from the Mediterranean fruit fly to the pesky mosquito. When mixed properly, it poses little danger to humans. Malathion is one of the world's most widely used insecticides. But everything has a downside. In the case of malathion, it has a pungent odor. It is easy to see how a group of students who were suddenly exposed to such a strong smell could believe they had been poisoned. Just such an incident happened at an Arizona elementary school in the spring of 1987.

On Friday morning, April 24, a Tucson man, determined to win his annual battle with bugs munching on his trees and shrubs, began spraying his yard next to the school. A short time later, at 9 A.M., two teachers in separate parts of the building called the main office on the school intercom. Something was wrong: There was a strong odor wafting through the hallways. The office worker announced that there was a foul smell outside the school and that doors and windows should be shut until it went away. Despite being told to stay inside, one teacher took her class outdoors and walked right into the foul odor. Retreating to the school, they found themselves in the cafeteria, where they began to complain of nausea, dizziness, and headaches.

Seeing the group's distress, an office attendant became fearful for their well-being. As luck would have it, the principal was away, so she took matters into her own hands, grabbing the phone and raising the alarm. As emergency personnel began trickling onto the scene, they came upon the twelve students who had walked into the mysterious cloud, all sitting in the cafeteria and looking unwell. When the fire chief arrived, he made a quick assessment and called for reinforcements. Within minutes, additional paramedics, firefighters, and HazMat teams were speeding to the school "on the basis that an unknown and possibly toxic substance was causing illness." As the number of unwell students grew, emergency responders went into each classroom to see if the students and teachers were well. Meanwhile, other squad members were fanning out to find the source of the odor.[12]

With more and more students feeling unwell, authorities declared a major emergency and set up a lawn triage. An urgent disaster call went out to local doctors, who rushed to treat the "poisoned" students who were by now littering the grounds. The scene was dramatic. Before long, the head paramedic, unsure what substance he was dealing with, ordered a full-scale retreat, transporting all 296 students to area hospitals. The campus looked like a set from a disaster movie. No fewer than one hundred emergency responders were at the school, and nearly a dozen fire departments. Police were everywhere. Adding to the confusion, reporters, film crews, and parents were scurrying about, checking on the children's welfare.[13]

The atmosphere at the school was chaotic and tense. The principal and the triage nurse began arguing over the nurse's decision to change the school evacuation plan, at which point it is alleged that the nurse threatened to arrest the principal for interference. It was high drama. This public argument between the head nurse and principal must have been unnerving for the students. Several doctors on the scene commented about the presence of anxiety responses that may have been prompted by the heat of the moment. Interviews with other observers suggest that "emergency responders did not consider the effects of their actions on the children," notably, that the "shouting of orders" had unduly frightened the children.[14]

At the hospitals, the students' symptoms quickly subsided, and it was soon evident that no one was seriously ill. Symptoms included stomach upset, headache, runny eyes, weakness, sweating, difficulty breathing, dizziness, and blurred vision — all typical of sudden stress. When the doctors finished examining the students, not a single case of insecticide poisoning was verified.[15]

Meanwhile, the man spraying the pesticide was being vigorously questioned. He swore that he had followed the instructions just like he was supposed to, diluting twenty-two milliliters of malathion into fifteen milliliters of water. On checking the residue in the bottle, investigators concluded that he had done just that.[16] To be certain, samples were sent to two independent laboratories — the manufacturer and the Arizona Agriculture Department; both confirmed that he was telling the truth.

So what happened? Malathion gives off a strong odor, but it is widely used across the United States and is very effective. It has even been used as a body lotion to control lice. How likely is malathion to cause breathing problems like those at the Arizona school? Just how harmful is it? The scientific answer is clear: not very, unless you're drinking it. In one study subjects were placed in a sealed room with no ventilation while concentrated malathion was sprayed into the air for two hours a day for forty-two days straight. There were no observable effects. Each subject was found to be in perfect health, with no hint of breathing problems. While there are warning labels on malathion, they advise against misuse. Of course, too much of anything can be harmful. Consuming an entire shaker of salt could prove fatal. Even drinking too much water in too short a time can kill a person. Investigators found that the malathion *had* been mixed properly, but even if it had not been, much higher concentrations should not have caused the students' symptoms, which were typical of anxiety.[17]

The malathion scare is reminiscent of an incident four years earlier involving parathion, another common insecticide. There was an air of nervous excitement in east Texas on the evening of June 15, 1983. Dozens of eleven- to fourteen-year-old students from a summer camp were on a major university campus for a big dance. Meanwhile, next door, two college students were conducting a routine fumigation of a biology department greenhouse. The evening calm was shattered when passersby noticed smoke pouring from the greenhouse vents and sounded the alarm. Emergency personnel quickly evacuated the area, fearing a massive case of organophosphate poisoning from the "toxic smoke." Firefighters began dispersing the fumes with fans and urging those in the area to go to the hospital for treatment. Back at the dance, students were becoming aware of the "smoke cloud." While standing on the dance floor, one girl began to feel woozy and teeter. She was helped to the side to recuperate. Rumors flew through the group that "the cloud got her." Before long, other students felt ill. Worried chaperones took about thirty of the children to the hospital. The victims were treated at two hospitals where doctors were looking for signs of parathion poisoning: restricted pupils and respiratory distress. Dr. Gary Elkins was curious about the students' reactions, as he noted that parathion poisoning symptoms "were absent in the vast majority of victims who felt sick; fully 99 of the 119 persons evaluated ... showed no clinical evidence of organophosphate poisoning." It was evident that many were overbreathing as a result of the excitement. Stomach pain and headache were common, as was a burning sensation of the skin and eyes.[18]

The blaring sirens and flashing lights of arriving rescue workers only added to the confusion and tension. Civil defense personnel even told bystanders that the smoke was toxic. Staff at one hospital gave worried patients "a list of symptoms" that they could expect to have as a result of parathion poisoning. Some personnel began to label the victims with triage tags that would have been more appropriate for a major trauma disaster such as a plane crash. It *looked* like a mass poisoning. In his report on the episode, Dr. Elkins said: "The language used by emergency and hospital personnel while assessing and treating patients ... can be a powerful source of counter-suggestion." In other words, if an emergency worker or doctor tells you you've been poisoned before conducting a full patient exam, it's likely to make matters worse.[19] The malathion and parathion poisoning scares underscore the power of suggestion, though neither incident could rival the events in Europe during the summer of 1999, when a relatively small number of schoolchildren spread fear through the countryside and, for a short time, brought one of the world's largest corporations to its knees.

The Great Coca-Cola Scare

On June 8, 1999, the innocuous "phffttt" of an opening soda can became a sound to be feared. Our story begins in the most unlikely of places—the picturesque small town of Bornem, Belgium, near Antwerp. What happened that day triggered a series of events that would eventually send shock waves across Europe and beyond. Thirty-three pupils at a secondary school were rushed to a hospital upon feeling ill after drinking cans of Coca-Cola. In hindsight, the Coke was harmless, and the students were simply suffering from anxiety after noting a funny taste and smell. But at the time, it appeared to be a disaster. The real casualty was the Coca-Cola Company, whose sales temporarily slumped.

After the first ten students were stricken, the school nurse quickly made inquiries and found Coke to be the common denominator. Concerned staff went room to room, asking students leading questions: "Did you drink Coke?" "Do you feel sick?" Soon, another twenty-three students reported feeling ill, complaining of headache, nausea, stomach pain, breathing troubles, and dizziness. At the hospital, doctors found nothing physically wrong. Urine and blood samples were normal. The only thing out of the ordinary was that the patients seemed nervous; some were huffing and puffing, appearing to be overbreathing from excitement. None of the students were treated with medication, though some were given oxygen. As a precaution, fifteen were kept overnight. The next day, four more students from the same school were taken to the hospital with similar symptoms. Again, doctors found nothing unusual except anxiety.[20]

As the Bornem incident made headlines across Europe, other students began complaining of symptoms, with 75 more Belgian children suffering similar ill effects after drinking Coke at four other schools; in Brugge, eleven were affected on June 10; seventeen became ill at Harelbeke on June 11; thirty-five felt sick on June 14 at Lochristi; and on the same day in Kortrijk, twelve reported soda-related illness. The patterns were similar to the

Bornem outbreak. Meanwhile, Coca-Cola announced a recall of quarantined Coke and Fanta containers on June 11, and by the 14th, with the two new school outbreaks, *all* Coca-Cola products were taken off the shelves in Belgium.[21]

These beverage scares had their origin in an earlier Belgian contamination crisis. In early 1999 a tank of fats used to make animal feed was polluted with a toxic brew of cancer-causing chemicals: dioxins, dibenzofurans, and PCBs. The accident led to many cases of chicken poisoning when farmers gave their hens the contaminated feed. Despite government attempts to hush the news, word of the incident leaked to the Belgian media in May, fomenting a political confidence crisis that cost the jobs of the ministers for agriculture and health. The fear and anxiety began with a massive recall of chicken and eggs. (For those wondering which was recalled first, the chicken or the egg — it was a tie.) Soon most dairy and meat products were pulled from the shelves. By the time of the Coke scare in early June, the food contamination crisis dominated Belgian life. Food safety was on everyone's mind, and experts worried that even small amounts of chemicals could seriously impact people's health.[22]

With headlines crying "Poison!" the soda scare quickly spread across Belgium, exploding into a panic. Over the next eighteen days the Belgian Poison Control Centre logged 943 calls from people feeling unwell after drinking Coke and other drinks made by the giant corporation: Fanta, Sprite, Minute Maid, Pepsi, Lipton Ice Tea, Nestea, and Aquarius. Things were getting out of hand. There was no rhyme or reason to the reports; calls were scattered from across the country.[23] It was clearly a media-driven scare.

On June 15, Coca-Cola officials made a dramatic admission: *they* were at fault. First they blamed transport pallets treated with fungicide for tainting the outside of cans. Then suspicion fell on "bad carbon dioxide." These findings were sent to Belgium's top toxicologist, Professor Dominique Lison at the Catholic University de Louvain in Brussels. After careful analysis, Lison came to a stunning conclusion: the real culprit was mass hysteria. Hydrogen sulphide was present on the cans in quantities high enough to cause a noticeable odor, yet was harmless to humans at a mere ten parts per billion. He continued: "Small amounts of 4-chloro-3-methylphenol were found on the outside of some cans (about 0.4 μg/can). In both cases, it is unlikely that such concentrations caused any toxicity beyond an abnormal odour. No other notable chemicals had been found." A similar conclusion was reached by a second body advising the Belgian Health Ministry.[24]

The ban on Belgian Coke products was lifted June 23. By the end of

June, the episode was over. The recall had cost Coca-Cola as much as $250 million. On March 31, 2000, a Belgian government commission issued its findings: mass hysteria. Reports of similar symptoms were noted in France during June, and it is thought that these were incidents of mass hysteria in the wake of the Belgian media publicity. Coca-Cola shot itself in the foot. It was embarrassing, but not fatal. Company officials contributed to the scare by overestimating the seriousness of the first illness reports by the schoolchildren.[25]

Post–September 11th Terror Scares

September 11, 2001. Mere mention of the date is enough to raise the blood pressure of many Americans. The worst terrorist attacks in U.S. history on that day were closely followed by the mailing of anthrax-laced letters. These events terrorized a nation and generated widespread discussion about the likelihood of further chemical or biological attacks. In 2008, the FBI concluded that an American microbiologist named Bruce Edwards Ivins was the sole culprit. But in 2001, the anthrax was widely believed to have been the work of foreign terrorists. Media speculation prompted heightened anxieties and alertness and a surge in false reports. On September 29, 2001, in Washington state, harmless fumes from oil-based paint set off a bio-terrorism scare at Canyon Creek Middle School. Sixteen students were sent to the hospital and an army of rescue personnel rushed to the scene, believing a terror attack was under way.[26]

A few days later, on October 2 and 3, a bio-terror scare swept across the Philippines when 1,400 students from Manila schools flooded local clinics, reporting mild flu symptoms such as coughing and slight fever. Some students were confirmed as having Type A H1N1 influenza, but many were diagnosed with anxiety after rumors spread among jittery parents and pupils that the cause was bio-terrorism. The bogus story was spread rapidly by students using hand-held text messengers.[27]

CNN reported that there were no fewer than 2,300 anthrax false alarms during the first half of October alone. Almost any powdery substance was enough to warrant a mass evacuation, and stress was heightened by emergency personnel, often dressed in space suits, entering buildings in dramatic fashion and removing the suspicious powder for testing.[28] The anthrax scare appears to have given rise to what historian Elaine Showalter calls "the Bin Laden Itch," which swept through dozens of U.S. schools.

Between October 2001 and June 2002, a mysterious rash was reported by thousands of students in twenty-seven U.S. states and parts of Canada.

From Alaska to Florida, students were scratching. The rashes would last anywhere from a few hours to two weeks. There were no other symptoms, and no evidence of spread from person to person. Fearing the worst — a terror attack on American children — the Centers for Disease Control carefully studied the rashes, ruling out an infectious agent given the absence of fever or headache. The culprit was a variety of skin ailments. According to CDC officials, "With 53 million young people attending 117,000 schools each school day in the United States, it is expected that rashes from a wide range of causes will be observed." Among the causes: bacteria and fungi, physical agents such as fiberglass, chemical agents such as pesticides and cleaning products, allergens, and insect bites. These skin conditions have always existed in schools, but during the bio-terror scare, students began paying more attention to their skin and school nurses were on the lookout for anything out of the ordinary — and were more likely to report such cases. Dry, itchy skin is notorious during the winter months in the U.S. as people spend more time indoors and heating systems suck moisture out of the air. In a few cases, students were caught faking rashes by rubbing their skin with sandpaper in an effort to close their schools. But the post–September 11 itching frenzy was not the first time that anxiety in schoolchildren has triggered terror scares.[29]

Phantom Terrorists

Mid–February 1991 was an anxious time in America. The Persian Gulf War was just three and a half weeks old. The news was saturated with discussion of poison gas attacks on Israel from Iraqi Scud missiles. While no poison gas attacks took place, several false alarms had everyone on edge. The stage was set for an outbreak of war hysteria at a Rhode Island elementary school. It began when a pupil fainted. At the same time, classmates smelled a strange odor. A sudden wave of anxiety swept through the seventh and eighth graders, who assumed they were under an Iraqi gas attack. Seventeen students and four teachers were stricken with dizziness, headache, and nausea. The victims were examined at a nearby emergency room, where they were reassured and quickly recovered.[30]

Two years earlier, in 1989, Soviet Georgia was in the grip of political unrest coinciding with the early stages of the breakup of the Soviet Union. Desperate to maintain control of its crumbling empire, Soviet authorities ordered the use of poison gas to disperse crowds during a protest rally. The incident made headlines across the country, shocking Georgian citizens. The episode had a powerful impact on schoolgirls in the region. Amid rumors that they had been exposed to the potentially deadly gas, 400 adolescent girls at several nearby schools began to exhibit the short-lived symptoms of gas poisoning: burning eyes, skin irritation, dry throat and stomach pain.[31] The girls were taken to nearby hospitals, where they quickly recovered.

The West Bank Toilet Scare

The Rhode Island and Georgian terror scares pale in comparison to what happened in the Middle East during 1983, when a toilet was responsible for triggering an international crisis that nearly led to war. The initial news reports were both stunning and horrifying, even for a place hardened by decades of suicide bombings, rocket attacks, political assassinations, and invasions. Media reports told of a plot by Jewish terrorists to sterilize up to one thousand Palestinian schoolgirls. The claims made world headlines and dominated the media for months. News of the accounts even prompted a United Nations resolution condemning the acts, triggering outrage throughout the Islamic world. This time it seemed that the Israelis had crossed the line between war and barbarity. Had the perpetrators no sense of decency? It was an outrageous and unthinkable assault on future generations of innocent schoolgirls. The trouble was that it was not true.

The world media spotlight quickly focused on reports that the girls had been deliberately poisoned by Israelis. Reports of the poisoning even appeared in major Israeli newspapers, crystallizing the popular notion that Jews were behind the sinister attacks. Between March and April 1983, in the Israeli-occupied West Bank, nearly a thousand schoolgirls, mostly Arab, fell ill, complaining of headaches, blurred vision, stomach pain, fainting, blindness, and limb weakness. Investigations by U.S. and World Health Organization doctors soon concluded that the illness was psychological.

The scare took place amid poison gas rumors and long-standing Palestinian mistrust of Jews. The medical complaints appeared over fifteen days, coinciding with intense publicity that someone was using poison gas on the Palestinians. The episode was mostly confined to schools in several adjacent villages in this bitterly disputed region. The case became widely known as the Arjenyattah Epidemic because panic swept through the nearby communities of Arrabah, Jenin, and Yattah.[32]

The social and cultural climate was important in fostering the hysteria. The Israeli military has occupied the West Bank since 1967, with its presence generating intense hatred. While the occupation is widely viewed as temporary within the Arab world, one observer noted, "Some tend to believe that the Israelis would do anything to perpetuate the status quo."[33] Targeting would-be Palestinian mothers with poison — either Israeli soldiers or civilian extremists, was a natural suspicion within this long-standing climate of fear and hate. The episode spread in three waves.

The First Wave: Arrabah

A mysterious and sickening smell filled the air near the Arrabah Girls' School. The date was March 21, 1983. In the middle of class, a seventeen-year-old pupil felt unwell, complaining of dizziness, difficulty breathing, headache, and blurred vision. Soon fifteen more pupils fell ill. Some of the girls said their symptoms coincided with a smell like rotten eggs coming from a schoolyard bathroom. By the next day, sixty-one students and five adults were in the hospital for tests and evaluation. Doctors were called in to investigate the poisonings and noted that the highest attack rates were in those rooms nearest to the bathroom where the foul smell was coming from; the lowest rates were in those rooms furthest away.[34]

On March 22 the Israeli newspaper *Yedi'Ot Ahronot* reported on the mass illness at the Arrabah school. In the article, the journalist implied the likely presence of poison gas, noting that the pupils "were suddenly afflicted by an attack of blindness, headache and stomach pain." The reporter exaggerated the symptoms, as complaints such as "blurred vision" were changed to "blindness."[35]

Nerve Gas Attack or Attack of Nerves at Jenin?

A second wave of nearly identical symptoms swept through six schools near Jenin on March 26, sickening two hundred forty-six girls and some staff. The next evening, sixty-four residents in Jenin experienced similar complaints when a cloud of gas was emitted from a passing car. By March 26, press descriptions were portraying the events as attempted genocide. Even the Israeli press was jumping on the "Jewish terrorist" bandwagon. Israel's *Ma'Ariv*, for example, said the episode was undoubtedly mass poisoning, running this sensational headline: "The Mysterious Poisoning Goes On: 56 High School Girls in Djenin Poisoned." The only uncertainty was the source of the poison. The report read in part: "The mysterious poisoning of 50 students that took place last week in Arraba ... affected 56 additional students yesterday in Djenin. Currently no definite evidence exists as to the source of the poison. Yesterday morning, 29 schoolgirls were admitted to the hospital from Djenin High School with difficulty breathing, cyanosis, and dizziness." Two days later, a report in the Israeli paper *Ha'Aretz* claimed that preliminary tests revealed that nerve gas had made the Djenin students sick. While the cause of the symptoms was not known at the time, both *Ha'Aretz* and *Ma'Ariv* said it was a case of poisoning.[36]

The Israeli Health Ministry sent psychiatrist Albert Hafez to investigate the poisoning claims. Visiting Djenin Hospital on March 31, Hafez noted a melodramatic atmosphere with foreign journalists swarming to interview both the sick girls and hospital staff. Suddenly, an Arab girl was rushed in on a stretcher and immediately enveloped in a sea of doctors and nurses, who pushed her frightened, bewildered mother aside. Almost instantly, an oxygen mask was forced over her face while someone else administered an intramuscular injection. The mother later told doctors that her daughter was playing near their home when she developed a headache and nausea. Due to the publicity about the so-called mass poisoning, the mother grew alarmed and rushed the girl to the hospital. Dr. Hafez provides a sense of the chaos at the hospital:

> While busy examining the girl amid the surrounding crowd, I became aware of a new turmoil consequent to the arrival of a new group accompanying a second patient ... an 18 year-old girl who was quite excited and tried to throw herself off the stretcher while those escorting her tried to restrain her. As with the previous patient, the oxygen mask and intramuscular injection were used instantly. The shouting girl, the excited crowd, the first patient, and her helpless mother together created an atmosphere of utter confusion.[37]

THE THIRD WAVE: YATTAH

Amid a third cluster of reports on April 3, students and parents began to panic. The epicenter was a girls' school at Yattah, in the Tulkarem and Hebron districts, with symptoms quickly spreading to several nearby schools. When the schools were closed the next day the "outbreak" stopped. In an effort to resolve the "poisonings," Israel's top epidemiologist, Baruch Modan, was sent to investigate. Modan and his team soon traced the outbreak to a smelly latrine near the Arrabah school and concluded that mass hysteria was the culprit. Later that day a second, larger wave ignited during recess, when friends of the first group affected spread rumors about their possible poisoning. During the second wave at several Jenin schools and nearby villages, the media and the rumor mill were instrumental in spreading the symptoms. As part of this phase, 64 Jenin residents were reportedly gassed by a speeding car. Investigators were able to later determine that the "poison" was nothing but thick black smoke belching from the vehicle's faulty exhaust system. The final wave of illness reports was, according to Modan and his team, triggered by the continuous spreading of poison gas rumors by the media.[38]

Modan's report was dismissed as one-sided in the Arab world.[39] What followed was a public relations war between the Israeli government and the Arab leaders, conducted through the United Nations. On March 30 the Commission on Arab Women, meeting in Tunis, Tunisia, sent an urgent message to the UN director-general, complaining that Israeli authorities were responsible for the "poisoning" and asking the UN to stop the "genocide."[40] Israeli authorities branded the claims as propaganda fueled by pro–Palestinian forces.[41] In an effort to resolve the issue, several top U.S. doctors were asked to conduct an independent probe. Their conclusion: the outbreaks were triggered by the smell of hydrogen sulphide gas escaping from the Arrabah latrine. Mass psychology and the media did the rest. In other words, it was mass hysteria. American doctors Philip Landrigan and Bess Miller concurred with Dr. Modan's findings, blaming the media for fueling the crisis. They said that without any clear evidence to support their claims, the local media published and broadcast reports that a toxin was the likely cause of the outbreaks. The Americans left no stone unturned, taking air, water, and soil samples and finding "no evidence" of any toxic agent. They noted the curious pattern in which the illness struck certain groups: "Support for the diagnosis of psychogenic illness was provided here by the preponderance of female patients, particularly of adolescent girls. The relative sparing of infants, adolescent boys, and older adults argues against the presence of a toxin."[42]

Fertility Fears Flourish

Across the Arab world at this time, rumors and media reports circulated that a group of Jews had perpetrated the poisonings to counter the Palestinian birth rate, and that they "specifically targeted young girls approaching the age of marriage. Supposedly, the poisoning was done to harm this most fertile age group in order to limit Arab demographic growth. They [Arab authorities] even said they had found medical proof, claiming that urine tests showed a high protein level, which means that something is abnormal in the fertility system."[43] Such test results later proved false. The Palestinian schoolgirl poisoning claim of 1983 is just one in a long list of false reports of Jews poisoning their "enemies."

In April 1993, another scare involving schoolgirls being poisoned swept across the Middle East in Egypt and Palestine. The Egyptian government convened an emergency investigation into a wave of nausea and fainting fits that closed 32 schools. The previous six days had seen the collapse of some 1,300 girls aged from 9 to 16. The panic began in a village school 75 miles north of Cairo, when a teenage girl, reading aloud in class, fainted. Witnessing that, some of her classmates also swooned. As news of the event spread to Cairo, Alexandra and Ismailia, the numbers of collapsing girls increased rapidly. A rumor that a girl had died after fainting caused 150 girls to faint while waiting at a railway station at Damanhour on the 6th. Further outbreaks in the three days following the establishment of the committee brought the numbers up to 1,500. Senior officials and other pundits exacerbated the situation by blaming, without evidence, everything from food poisoning to nuclear contamination; even a plot to render Egyptian girls infertile.[44]

Chewing gum laced with aphrodisiac was also blamed as rumors spread through the Egyptian town of Mansura, northeast of Cairo, in July 1996, of orgies among the students at the town's university. According to local parliamentarian Fathy Mansour, the gum was peddled to the students by Israeli agents in "a huge scheme to ravage the young population of Egypt." An engineering student told a reporter that at first they thought it was a joke; then "we began to hear rumors that a girl had sex with seven boys on campus and another had sex with several men in a car." Loudspeakers on the town's mosques began broadcasting warnings against chewing gum — a topic that had occupied Friday prayers for several weeks — but this only seemed to make matters worse. A member of staff at the Youth and Sports Affairs Department told a reporter that girls had confessed to her that they had had sex with several students after chewing the gum. Yet another female student, identified only as Amira, admitted that she had accepted a ride with two male classmates, and after they gave her some gum she "found no resistance. You know the rest." Such was the uproar in the town that the country's ministry of health stepped in. They found nothing suspicious in the brands of gum that were "traced to smugglers in Gaza," said Ismail Sallam, the health minister. At the same time, an investigation by the provincial vice squad found nothing to substantiate Mr. Mansour's claim that fifteen young female students had sexually assaulted their male classmates after chewing gum. Some students were very specific about the packaging of this now-banned gum. It came in the form of brightly colored, candy-coated squares bearing the brand names Aroma or Splay. But when local authorities closed down kiosks and made several arrests on suspicion of selling the gum, nothing of that nature was found. It is clear that rumors came to be accepted as truth because so many people were repeating them and because the authorities were taking decisive action. Unfortunately it is not clear from the reports whether the girls who admitted such loose behavior had any real existence outside the gossip or whether they fell under its sway and became suggestible after chewing quite ordinary gum.[45]

A similar scare occurred in 1997. Raphael Israeli, a professor of Islamic civilization at Hebrew University, describes the affair:

> In 1997 the Palestinians exposed yet another Israeli "plot to suppress Arab population growth." They claimed to have tested packets of strawberry-flavored bubble gum which were found to be spiked with sex hormones and sold at low prices near schoolhouses in the West Bank and Gaza Strip. It was claimed that the gum aroused irresistible sexual appetites in women, then sterilized them. Even Palestinian Supply Minister Abdel Aziz Shaheen believed the myth, saying it was capable of "completely destroying the genetic system of young boys," as well.[46]

In May 1997, the Palestinian Ministry of Supplies said that samples of gum tested in Cairo food labs were found to contain the female sex hormone progesterone. One Palestinian official did not help matters by declaring that seven types of Israeli gum contained "a sexually-stimulating substance" that "may generate sterility in men and women." In June, as general anxiety continued to spread, the ministry went further, sending 40 samples of soft drinks, biscuits, chocolate, beans and sugar to Cairo to be tested "for ingredients that may stimulate the sex drives of women and bring on puberty in teenagers." Then, most sensationally, the newspaper *al-Haya al-Jadida* reported that Palestinian forces had seized 200 tons of aphrodisiac-laced gum allegedly being sold by Mossad agents "so that Palestinian women will become prostitutes and be easily recruited as spies." Dr. Brian Coussin, director of food control services for the Israeli Health Ministry, acknowledged that gelatin, used to make gum, can be found in bones, and that progesterone can be found in the bones of female animals treated with a fertility hormone. "But," he added, "I think it's rubbish to say Israel is trying to change Palestinian society in this way."[47]

During the West Bank crisis of March 1983, people saw what they wanted to see. Doctors treating the girls tended to interpret medical findings based on their politics. Palestinian doctors at Djenin Hospital assumed that different poisons were used on the girls. This assumption was made by doctors who had no immediate access to laboratory facilities and were basing their diagnoses on hunches. In contrast, some Israeli doctors treating victims at Tel-Hashomer Hospital were certain the girls were faking to get Palestinian sympathy. They said the girls were often hostile, aggressive, and uncooperative. Some Israeli press reports even supported this view. According to Dr. Hafez, "Attracted by such a theory, reporters mobilized their resources and ingenuity to bring in evidence to confirm it. They filmed patients during doctors' rounds and alone, demonstrating the change in behavior from one situation to the other. They even tracked cars that were suspected of 'recruiting' new patients and showed these films live on television."[48] It is hard to believe that from such humble beginnings as fumes from a blocked toilet, events could have spiraled so out of control. Every day toilets become blocked up around the world, but they don't usually trigger mass hysteria. The Great Toilet Scare shows that anything can trigger an outbreak of mass psychology given the appropriate context and a plausible idea.

Mass Hysteria and the Balkans

In 1990, an outbreak of mass hysteria occurred in Kosovo. To understand the episode, it is important to examine the context in which it occurred. Ethnic strife in the Balkan Peninsula can be traced to medieval times, but the modern conflicts—involving (at different times) Croatia, Serbia, Montenegro, Bosnia and Herzegovina, Macedonia, Albania, and Kosovo—arose from the dissolution of the Ottoman Empire in the early 1920s, and more recently from the fragmentation of Yugoslavia following the death of its president Marshal Tito in May 1980. Superstition and credulity were openly exploited by the military and the press on all sides. In 1999, a British journalist noted the increasing use of astrologers and their predictions by politicians and an accompanying wave of rumors and baseless claims. Announcements included Yugoslavian assertions to have a new energy source that could "bring down planes" and "assassinate at a distance"; that Serbs had military units using "paranormal forces"; that canisters of deadly spiders had been dropped by planes over Croatia; that Croats were freeing tigers and other wild beasts to attack dissidents; that the Serbs originally came from the planet Sorab in the Pleiades; and that an "army of vampires" would rise up from cemeteries to overwhelm the enemies of Serbia.[49]

Not surprisingly, anxiety levels were high and there were numerous panics against the backdrop of the general terror of war and ethnic cleansing. In March 1990, children in an Albanian community in Kosovo were gripped by a fear of being gassed. Four hundred students collapsed gasping and screaming. After they were ferried to the city's Pristina Hospital, the nurses there feared that police were about to attack the hospital and closed all the windows. Examinations of the children found nothing except that they were exhibiting signs of extreme anxiety. Most children calmed down and were released the next day, just as 240 more teenagers were brought in suffering from a similar panic. The Albanian Kosovars believed that Serbs had sprayed an unknown chemical into the classrooms, which medical spokesmen in Belgrade denied. Soon after, Serbian troops were drafted into five Kosovar towns, leading to two days of intense fighting. Believing they had been poisoned, more than 1,000 Albanians complained of stomach cramps and nausea. On April 3, Albanians in Podujevo were hospitalized. The Serbian federal government accused them of "deliberately stirring up trouble." This was shortly before full-out war broke out. Dr. Zoran Radovanovic analyzed the "poisonings" and concluded that there was no toxic agent involved; instead it was psychological in origin, triggered by poisoning rumors, ethnic tension and mistrust. An increase in respiratory infections during this period further heightened anxieties.[50]

Seven years later, in September and October 1997, about 1,000 ethnic Albanian students in the Macedonian town of Tetovo fell ill with stomach cramps and headaches. They accused their neighbors of poisoning them but an investigation team from the World Health Organization found no evidence of any infectious or toxic agent. Reporting in *New Scientist*, team leader Zsuzsanna Jakab noted that "twice as many girls as boys were affected." A bad smell was noticed before the panic spread and she thought "the incident probably started with a few real cases of flu or food poisoning," but mass suggestion then took over.[51]

The drama was repeated in the Macedonian city of Kumanovo in December 2002, when, on the 11th, about 200 ethnic Albanian schoolchildren thought they were being poisoned. Headaches, cramps and dizziness were blamed on inhaling "a mysterious gas." The head of the city's medical center epidemiology department, Jordan Dzimrevski, could find no cause. The Serbia-Kosovo peace plan had been implemented just four months earlier, but ethnic tensions were still in evidence; Macedonia's leading newspaper, *Dnevnik*, dismissed the scare as "manipulation with children for political purposes."[52]

Like the Balkans, the Chechen and Ossetia regions of the northern Caucasus have an ancient history of ethnic conflict. In the latest war, Russian troops ruthlessly suppressed Chechnya dissidents, leading to the infamous 2002 siege by Chechen rebels of a theatre in Moscow. Russian authorities refused to negotiate and gassed the whole building, killing most of the terrorists and 129 hostages. Since 2005, across Chechnya there have been reports of many outbreaks involving mainly female students and their teachers. It seems to have begun with one girl, 13-year-old Taisa Minkailova, a pupil in Starogladovsk in the Shelkovsk region. On December 7, 2005, she collapsed in class with the familiar complaints of asphyxia, numbness in her limbs, headaches and fits. She was taken to a hospital in

Dagestan, but her condition did not respond to treatment. Two days later, two older pupils from the same school were taken to a hospital in Grozny, suffering similarly. In the following week 19 more children and three adults were transferred from Starogladovsk to Shelkovsk; then more pupils from four other schools in the region. Doctors watched as clusters of girls lapsed into unconsciousness, exhibiting seizures, amnesia, numbness, chills, dry mucous membranes, breathing difficulties and eye pain. Experts from Moscow arrived and concluded that the episode was entirely psychological, triggered by a decade of often brutal warfare that had led to chronic stress combined with poverty and despair. The doctors also blamed the media for spreading "alarmist reports." Musa Dalsayev, the Chechen Republic's chief narcologist, went further and accused the sick children of faking and their mothers of colluding in the hope of getting compensation, even though, as journalist Paul Sieveking observes, there had been no such requests from the families of the victims. It was the view of many parents and some doctors that there was a cover-up under way. If it was hysteria, said the deputy chief of therapeutics at Shelkovsk hospital, the girls' conditions should have responded to the sedatives and anti-convulsives they were given; but they didn't. "I am certain that such a number of children could never enter a state of psycho-motor excitation simply from hysterics," he said. The hospital's chief physician, Vaha Dardeyevich Ehselayev, concurred with Dr. Dalsayev: "We will not change our diagnosis—an intoxication of unknown etiology."[53]

An interesting detail then emerged in September 2005, three months before Taisa Minkailova fell ill. Nineteen children and one teacher from Staroshchedrinskaya village were brought in with similar symptoms, said Jamilya Halilovna Aliyeva, a doctor at Shelkovsk hospital. "We saw the same strange laughter and hallucinations. It was a frightening sight," she added. Dr. Dalsayev confirmed that samples were sent for testing and that a note from the "legal medical expert's office" declared the children had been poisoned with carbon monoxide. This claim appears to be a clear instance of popular opinion being taken as a scientific fact. "How on Earth did that happen during a heatwave," Dr. Dalsayev said, "when the stoves had not been fired up yet?"[54]

Many of the affected schools remained shut, and parents refused to let their healthy children go back until the premises had been "detoxified" and the "true cause" made public. Still the cases kept coming. Just before Christmas Day, 81 more cases were admitted. By March 2006, the admissions passed 100. Some of those affected exhibited bouts of uncontrollable laughter,[55] frustrating those doctors who searched in vain for a chemical or biological cause.

Much Ado About Nothing: Parent Hysteria

Sometimes parents alone trigger scares. In 1988 the Centers for Disease Control investigated a mysterious illness at an elementary school in Georgia. The first hint of trouble came during a routine gathering of parents and students in the school cafeteria in early September. A mother noted that since the autumn term began, her child had been ill and looked pale. Other mothers then recalled similar signs of illness in their children too since the start of term: pallor, dark circles under the eyes, headaches, fatigue, nausea, and occasional vomiting. The parents grew suspicious that the building was making their kids sick. On October 11 their suspicions were seemingly confirmed. During routine maintenance, a natural gas leak was found. The building was evacuated as a precaution, even though the leak was minor. When other minor gas leaks continued over the next month, parents pressed their case by picketing the school and appealing to the local media to highlight their fears. A battery of tests were conducted at the school in hopes of identifying a foreign substance in the air — all negative — leading investigators to conclude that the fearful mothers had seen what they expected to see — a sick school with sick kids. Curiously, the children in question neither sought attention nor were overly concerned with their symptoms, and kept high attendance levels through the term.[56]

In their report, investigators from the CDC and the Georgia Department of Public Health noted that one third-grader had been ill with headaches since the first grade. Another student had complained of nausea and headaches for two months before the gas leak, and still another had a history of headaches for about a year before the leak. Investigators said that exposure to natural gas could not have caused the symptoms, which were vague and common in childhood. The CDC report concluded: "Parental anxiety, interpersonal contacts, and extensive media coverage could have further encouraged this mistake."[57]

Vaccine Panics

Vaccination in schools has also been a factor in outbreaks of mass hysteria. This has been particularly true in the Middle East, where outbreaks have taken place during school immunization drives in Iran and Jordan. These are places that have long mistrusted the West. Their mass media are filled with negative images of Europe and North America — where the vaccines usually originate.

On October 6, 1992, Iranian schoolgirls in the tiny village of Hanza were inoculated for tetanus. Four days later a girl fainted in class, complaining of blurry vision, headache, tremor, and burning hands. Over the next several days, nine of her schoolmates, all of whom had received tetanus shots, began exhibiting similar seizures. An investigation revealed that the first victim had a long history of stress-induced seizures with accompanying symptoms nearly identical to those reported during her classroom fit. At the time of her attack, she was seeing a neurologist, and she was later diagnosed with conversion disorder and depression. The other girls grew anxious after observing her fit, fearful that it was a result of the inoculation.

The symptoms persisted for five weeks amid rumors that a bad batch of vaccine was causing "brain disease." The scare subsided when Dr. M.T. Yasamy invited students, parents and local officials to a dramatic public meeting, during which he had himself injected with a dose of vaccine from the same batch used on the twenty-six girls. He then met with five of the afflicted pupils individually, reassuring them that their symptoms were psychological. The girls quickly felt better. Symptoms in the other five students persisted longer, but soon subsided. Two were treated at home in nearby villages, and three were hospitalized and discharged after being reassured that the vaccine was safe.[58]

Between 1992 and September 1998, there was not a single adverse reaction to the tetanus-diphtheria vaccine (Td) given to all Jordanian students in the first and tenth grades. On the morning of September 29, 1998, the entire class of tenth grade students at the Eben-Al Abas School, 160 in all, were injected with Td vaccine. Two pupils "felt faint" and were immediately seen by a doctor.[59] Their exams were unremarkable and they were soon returned to class. That evening, several students experienced dizziness and headaches, but none were ill enough to see a doctor. The next day, upon arriving at school at the usual time of 6:45 A.M., a boy who had reported feeling sick the previous night fell at the school gates, cutting his lip. School officials sent him to the hospital, fearing that his fall was from fainting. The incident and the school's overreaction sent a wave fear through the school. By 7:30 A.M., twenty students had either fainted or reported feeling sick, triggering more fear. Ambulances and health authorities rushed to the scene, suspecting food or water contamination. After a quick assessment of the situation, they realized that all of the stricken students had been vaccinated the previous day. Fifty-five students from the school, all age fifteen, were examined at the hospital.

TV and newspaper reporters descended on the school like a cloud of locusts on a grain field, focusing on the vaccine. At noon the health ministry halted vaccinations nationwide. At 6:00 the health minister addressed the country, stating that "any student with side-effects from the Td vaccine should be admitted to hospital for observation." He also called for an investigation. Over the next several days, no fewer than 800 students had side effects; 122 were hospitalized for closer examination. Investigators soon determined that the vaccine was entirely safe. The vaccine scare coincided with rumors that it was harmful. In making their diagnosis of mass hysteria in the vast majority of students and ruling out any reaction to the vaccine, investigators noted that the same batch of Td had been dispensed in two other countries without incident.[60]

While there are only a few reports of vaccine-related cases of mass hysteria, this could be expected, as "the majority of vaccines are administered to infants and young children, who are not likely to react in this way given their inability to perceive vaccines as a threat and to interact as a group."[61] What do these vaccination scares have in common? A small number of children exhibit symptoms either during or shortly after inoculation. The appearance of symptoms triggers anxiety among other vaccinated children, their parents, and school officials. Episodes are typically made worse by sketchy, inaccurate media reports suggesting an association between the symptoms and tainted vaccine.

Smurfs and the Power of Belief

A key element in fostering mass hysteria and social delusions is plausibility. Rumors of schoolgirl poisonings in the Middle East were believable because of the long history of animosity and conflict between Israelis and Palestinians. If any belief is plausible, those involved can be susceptible to its consequences. This is especially true of schoolchildren, given their inexperienced and often naïve worldview. A fascinating illustration of this point took place in January 1983, when the Great Smurf Scare swept primary and junior high schools across the city of Houston, Texas. Many students refused to attend classes after hearing rumors that a group of blue Smurfs from the popular TV cartoon were carrying guns and knives into local schools and killing principals. The scare apparently began when a Houston TV station carried a news report detailing the arrest of forty youth gang members known as the Smurfs for a relatively minor crime spree including petty theft and small-time burglaries. From there, reality got garbled as the news passed through the student grapevine. Some accounts held that the Smurfs were wearing blue jackets; others said they had smeared on blue body paint. By some accounts, they were carrying knives; others insisted that they were toting machine guns. The stories were fluid and they raced through the schools like wildfire, sometimes changing from hour to hour. According to one version, the Smurfs would not harm any student who was wearing sky-blue clothing; another account held that anyone wearing sky-blue attire would be a target. In the Aldine School District, which was the epicenter of the scare, some students were in danger of wetting themselves after refusing to visit the toilets amid rumors that Smurfs were hiding there.[62]

The panic abated after several days, helped by the appearance of school principal Franklin Turner of the Johnston Middle School, who was rumored to have been killed by the Smurfs. "Kids wanted desperately to believe — they wanted some excitement," Turner said.[63] Houston journalist John Nova Lomax observed how as the story grew, it "picked up variations and embellishments as it passed over the grapevine at debate contests, sports events and skating rinks — wherever teens and pre-teens gathered."[64] It would seem that rumors at the school slowly evolved into an urban legend — a piece of living folklore. Two years later after further investigations into the existence of possible organized youth gangs in the city, Houston police said that there was no evidence of such gangs. Lt. Bill Sanders said that some kids formed groups that they referred to as gangs, but they basically just hung out together.[65]

Another illustration of the power of belief and fear can be found in numerous outbreaks of mass hysteria blamed on school hypnosis demonstrations. One such episode occurred at an auditorium in Philadelphia, Pennsylvania, during October 1944. A group of students at Springfield High School were watching a hypnosis show by E.K. Ernst. When he asked 35 students to stare at a spot on the ceiling above the stage and waved his hands, 31 of the students collapsed — many laughing or weeping. All but one of the students was female. It took two hours before the hypnotist, working with the school physician and nurse, were able to calm the affected students. Dr. James Ellzey examined many of those affected and later asserted that the students had not been suffering the effects of hypnosis but mass suggestion and their symptoms were a form of mass hysteria. Ipswich High School in Massachusetts was the scene of a remarkably similar incident on Friday, January 16, 1953, when hypnotist James McEvoy gave a talk on Mesmerism. He hypnotized some of the four hundred students who were packed into the auditorium. Just as he was finishing his presentation, at least two dozen pupils, fearing they were under McEvoy's control, began to complain "of drowsiness and emotional upset." School doctor Frank Collins said that medical exams of those taken ill were normal.[66]

The consequences were more dramatic at a school in Maimi, Florida, when a hypnosis demonstration was blamed for triggering a small riot on October 25, 1979. Here is how Associated Press journalist Stephen Smith began his story: "Police say it was hysteria brought on by a hypnosis demonstration. Some students say it was demons. A school official calls it a political dirty trick.... police say something sent students and teachers rampaging through a military school ... smashing windows, ripping a door from its frame and screaming they were possessed by spirits." The mayhem began soon after several students passed out during a tenth grade science project. There had been recent discussions on the supernatural at the school. The president of the Miami Aerospace Academy, Evaristo Marina, blamed the chaos on the journalists who rushed to the school after initial reports of a mass fainting. "When you are a child and the fire, police, health and media people all come at once you can go crazy. It's like yelling fire in a crowded theatre," he said. Many of the students were from South America. Fire official Dan LaMay attributed the mass collapse not to hypnosis, but hysteria, while he said that students had "flaked out all over the place." He said: "I saw three girls. They had fainted.... There was some screaming about 'bloody Mary' and more screaming." LaMay believes that it was a case of mass suggestion and that pupils were induced to join in the chaotic events "by the sight of others who became hysterical."[67]

In early September 2011, about 40 students were watching a hypnosis demonstration at a high school "fun day" in Mocoa City, Colombia, when they reportedly failed to emerge from a group trance induced by a magician named Miller Zambrano Posada. School principal Daniel Mora said, "30 or 40 minutes after the end of the show, which also included clowns and jugglers, the students were back in their classrooms, when suddenly they all started yelling at the same time." Alarmed by the outburst, public health officials dispatched no less than ten psychiatrists and psychologists to the scene and soon concluded that they were not in a trance but were experiencing a type of mass hysteria. About 590 students each paid 700 pesos to attend the popular show. A journalist described what happened next:

> Twelve kids were called to the stage, and then four were returned to their seats; the remaining eight were put into trance by Zambrano with hand movements, deep eye contact and a monotone voice.
> Zambrano made them lift their arms, walk in circles, cry like babies, laugh hysterically, bark like dogs, act like chickens and whatnot. Students laughed and clapped at the end of the show and when Zambrano left the stage, the students were ushered back to their classrooms.
> Suddenly, as the students walked back, several students developed bizarre symptoms. Police at the scene reported some of the students were crying,

others dived into the ground for no reason, others hit their chest with their palms. One girl went as far as to scream that she was seeing the devil, and before too long a larger group of kids went into a mass panic attack.[68]

At least 36 of those affected were girls. Only one of those affected had been called onto stage by the hypnotist; the others remained in the audience. The students were taken to a nearby hospital where they were examined and soon released. An eyewitness said: "I don't know, they were touching their chests and they started to roll around shouting strange things. They all began fainting, crying and one girl was screaming things, nasty things. She said that she saw the devil." Mr. Posada was taken into police custody after the event for his own protection, as parents, teachers and students were accusing him of witchcraft. He told police that he had been doing the identical act for many years but had never experienced such a reaction before.[69]

In June 2012, a private girls' school in Quebec, Canada, was the scene of yet another hypnosis demonstration that reportedly went wrong, supposedly leaving the students in a trance for several hours. The show took place before a group of 12- and 13-year-old students and was billed as an end-of-year fun activity. The 20-year-old hypnotist (Maxime Nadeau) was performing at the Collège du Sacré-Coeur in Sherbooke. After the show was over, several in the audience reportedly did not snap out of the trance when the hypnotist instructed them to. One student said she felt like she was having an "out-of-body experience." Emilie Bertrand said she felt "spaced out": "I don't know how to explain it. It's like you're no longer there." Several other students experienced similar feelings throughout the afternoon. A second hypnotist, Richard Whitbread, was summoned and reportedly snapped the students from their dazed state. "There were a couple of students who had their heads laying on the table and there were [others] who, you could tell, were in trance. The eyes were open and there was nobody home," he said. That suggestion was the culprit became evident when Whitbread reportedly "went through the process of making the girls think they were being re-hypnotized and then brought them out using a stern voice." Whitbread tried to explain the anomaly by observing that as the hypnotist was a handsome young man, it may have influenced impressionable girls to follow his instructions.[70] In each of these cases, the victims did not appear to be in hypnotic trances, but were reacting as if they were in such states, highlighting the power of belief.

We live in an age of media-driven crises and scares, where even genuine threats are often overblown. Schoolchildren are especially susceptible given their scant life experience and tendency to believe much of what they hear. The most prominent threats of the early twenty-first century are terror attacks and pollution. In the wake of such dangers, imaginations can run wild. Our worst fears can become reality in our minds, setting off a self-fulfilling prophesy in what are essentially school-wide panic attacks. Shakespeare said it best: "Or in the night, imagining some fear, How easy is a bush suppos'd a bear!"

CHAPTER 4

The Demon-Haunted Classroom
Tales from Asia

> Interpretive anthropology directly addresses the world in which we humans are. Conventional science, in its search for underlying causes, explains away ... [the belief in ghosts and demons] and in doing so alienates us from it and destroys its magic. When we are possessed, we do not exist within the category of psychological defense mechanisms. Instead, we are in the company of the gods, who are all the more real for being human creations.
> — Miles Richardson[1]

A young girl collapses on a classroom floor and enters a trance-like state. When her principal arrives she unleashes a torrent of obscenities towards him and complains that the school is too strict. Her voice turns deep and gruff, as if a strange force is controlling her. Students and teachers struggle to hold her down and restore calm. Soon another girl collapses and the scenario is repeated. As more girls collapse, the school is closed. Scenes like this have been common in Malaysia since the late 1950s.[2] Even more fascinating is the link between outbreaks and shopping.

In Malaysia, shopping is an art form. In most Malaysian markets the price is open to negotiation, and a sale tag is just a starting point. Bargaining is part of everyday life, and Malaysians love to haggle over the price of everything from fish to taxi fares—even traffic tickets.[3] It is not surprising, then, that bargaining finds its way into the classroom, through outbreaks of demonic possession during which the students negotiate for better conditions.

Malay parents are known for pampering their daughters. But when some girls reach age twelve or so, life takes a radical twist. After spending a sheltered existence at home during their early years, they are suddenly pushed from the nest and sent to elite boarding schools hundreds of miles away, where they will gain an edge in the competition to get into a university. At these schools, students have little say and keep their frustration to themselves, as they are taught from an early age to obey authority.[4] At these schools contact with boys is forbidden, and there is an extreme emphasis on Islam and schoolwork. There is little time for games or entertainment. Under these circumstances in the stricter schools, strange behaviors may emerge. A similar pattern occurs to the north in Thailand. What is so extraordinary is that these shy, seemingly naive and politically powerless schoolgirls usually get their way, with outbreaks of mass hysteria drawing attention to what they see as unjust rules and poor living conditions. Episodes give a voice to the voiceless as community leaders and government officers soon press school officials to ease rules.

Negotiating with Spirits

Outbreaks of strange behaviors in Malay schoolgirls have been common since the 1960s, coinciding with the Islamic revival and the growth of strict religious schools. Muslim by birth, Malays comprise just over half the population. The victims are almost always Malay girls who have been sent to Muslim boarding schools. They are reluctant to attend such schools, where overcrowding is rife and privacy nonexistent. Even basic decisions such as which school to attend, careers to pursue, and friendships to develop are made by parents and administrators. A typical day reads like a page from George Orwell's novel *1984*, where every aspect of living is rigidly controlled and people are treated like numbers. One cannot blame these girls for feeling paranoid, as they must account for their whereabouts at all times. School officials even monitor visits by friends and relatives in special rooms that resemble fishbowls.[5]

Frustration and anger build over weeks or months. Eventually a single student becomes "possessed" and is a seed or catalyst for the unfolding drama. The school is abuzz with talk of demons roaming the hallways. Anxiety rises further and more girls enter trances. Classmates react by screaming, crying, and eventually fainting as they get dizzy from overbreathing. What follows is a ritual of rebellion that is part hysteria, part melodrama — a subconscious bargaining between the possessing demons and school officials. Malaysian psychiatrist Jin-Inn Teoh has observed several outbreaks: "Some would fall on the floor in a trancelike state, as though in a stupor. Occasionally one or two of the subjects would speak up on behalf of the group, voicing their misdemeanors and frustrations.

Very often they became abusive. They characteristically took hints and cues from one another."[6] When the fits are over, most say they have no memory of the episode.

Spirit possession and trances are age-old occurrences. Culture and beliefs color their form. When Christians enter a trance, they invariably meet Jesus, the Virgin, angels, or Satan. Muslims talk to the Prophet Mohammed or Islamic angels. Hindus meet one or more of an array of Hindi gods. While trance and possession states may reflect mental disorder, more often they affect healthy people who are under severe long-term stress. The mind deals with the strain by acting like a circuit-breaker, switching into subconscious mode. During the trance, a student's voice and posture may change to indicate that another personality, in this case a spirit, is in control. In truth, her subconscious is in charge. Displays of exceptional strength are also common during trances, regardless of the student's religion, beliefs, or gender. One such outbreak of demon possession and emotional upset occurred in Malaysia during the 1970s.

The Evil Spirit Hostel

Forty miles north of the bustling metropolis of Kuala Lumpur, Malaysia's capital, lies the sleepy town of Helang, population 1,100 in 1971, the year of our story. On Sunday, February 21, Sarah, a popular Malay girl, was going about her daily routine in a hostel at the Murai Secondary School, three miles east of town.[7] At age fifteen, by all accounts, Sarah was happy. She was popular, attractive and described as having film star charm. But on this day Sarah was in distress. She was having trouble breathing. Her muscles began to twitch. She began to moan and groan, crying out that a voice of someone or some*thing* was beckoning to her from the bathroom. The incident made a lasting impression on her friends. Instead of calling a doctor, authorities summoned a *bomoh*, or Malay witchdoctor, who offered prayers to ward off the evil spirits that were thought to be attacking her. She was soon feeling better.

On March 3, Sarah was again struggling for breath. Later that day, her father came and took her home to rest. On March 15, two of Sarah's hostel mates, Jill and Eva, were stricken with similar breathing troubles. Eva's voice and persona began to change. In a scene reminiscent of *The Exorcist*, she began to scream and shout, complaining that the hostel grounds had been tainted by insensitive mortals. Eva revealed that there was "bad blood" between some of the girls. When the *bomoh* arrived, Eva verbally attacked her hostel mates, charging that they were tossing their dirty sanitary napkins over a fence, polluting the territory of the *jinn* spirits whom she said lived there. Most Malays believe in the *jinn*. The Koran, the Muslim holy book, discusses these supernatural beings. Eva also said that her hostel mates were unhappy with the headmaster, insisting that something be done to rectify the situation. The *bomoh* nodded in agreement. Before long, Eva and the other girls were free of any demonic attacks. But their relief was short-lived. Following the girl's return from April vacation, another flare-up hit the school. This time the hysteria spiraled out of control.[8]

The hostel was a hotbed of stress. It was clearly inadequate for the needs of the fifty Malay girls living there. There was no electricity, so they were forced to huddle around one of two gas lamps at night just to study. The girls dreaded the night, when the hostel became dark and eerie. They felt nervous just going to the bathroom, as the toilets were in a poorly lit and foreboding area. Another issue was even more troubling than the physical discomforts: the school's headmaster, who enjoyed prying into the affairs of the hostel.

Soon after the school opened in June 1970, a female instructor supervising the girls had quit over the headmaster's meddling in hostel affairs. The headmaster saw himself as a father figure to the girls and was constantly watching over them. He loved to offer unsolicited advice, dispensing what he thought were pearls of wisdom. The girls considered him to be mean, aloof, and out of touch with reality, and they took little notice of his advice. He thought nothing of embarrassing the girls by discussing feminine hygiene and ordering them to toss their sanitary napkins over a nearby fence into an old mine shaft. He justified these instructions by telling them that he worried that the napkins would block the sewer and create a stench. The headmaster's actions clearly crossed the line of Malay decency. An investigating team of psychiatrists would later describe him as "a short, nervous, obsessional" man who was thoroughly incompetent and could not even get along with his assistant.[9]

The headmaster began to conduct surprise inspections of the hostel, even at night. The girls were angry but were powerless to stop it. Malay custom dictates that elders must be obeyed — especially by girls. In Malay society, girls are to be seen and not heard. The headmaster's intrusions created tension among the girls and their parents. His actions were taboo in rural Malaysia. Fearing being caught in an indecent state, the girls were under constant stress and began to dress and undress in the dark, dank, foul-smelling bathroom. Though the headmaster had a key, the girls began to lock their doors, hoping that the sound of a key turning in the lock might give them a few seconds' warning. The headmaster also violated other Malay customs. He instructed them on such deeply personal matters as how to properly wear a feminine napkin — a topic reserved exclusively for Malay women to teach their daughters in privacy. As a result of these actions, the headmaster was loathed and feared. To appear all-knowing, he claimed to have knowledge of "secrets" passing among the girls, implying that his spies were everywhere and that it was impossible to keep secrets from him.[10]

The headmaster was also arrogant and stubborn. In January 1971, floods swept through the region, and a river behind the school began to overflow its banks, causing concern for the welfare of the hostel girls. Though unlikely, there was a possibility that the rising waters would reach the hostel and put the girls in danger. The district officer ordered the school's evacuation. The headmaster stunned and infuriated the town when he canceled the orders. The outraged district officer pulled rank and the evacuation went ahead. After the waters receded, the Education Ministry ordered all headmasters to distribute relief funds to students in the schools affected by the flooding. To the further outrage of students and parents, the headmaster asserted his misguided sense of power and control by withholding the money, vowing to distribute it only when he decided the time was right. It was within this climate of social and political turmoil that Sarah and her classmates began to exhibit their strange malady.[11]

On Thursday, April 22, five girls were stricken with mysterious fits. Among them were Eva and Sarah. Eva fell into a trace, her voice taking on the tone of a tribal chief. In this state, she "ratted" on the other girls, blurting out over and over that her hostel mates were not getting along and were jealous of one another. She then revealed their closely guarded secrets — that some of the girls were writing to boys, a serious infraction at Islamic boarding schools, and that there had been many thefts. Eva then began naming names. The headmaster took down each name with glee, calling the girls to his office, one by one, to face the consequences. He told them to confess their misdeeds, publicly apologize, and return the stolen items. Eva was now the most despised girl in the hostel. The next day, Eva's popularity plummeted to a new low. Several hostel girls were singing together, trying to forget their problem, when Eva had another attack. This time she accused the girls of opposing the headmaster. He again summoned the girls to his office, forcing them to apologize. The next day several of the same girls were fuming with betrayal and went into fits of hysterics. Among them was Eva, who entered a trance and claimed that some of the girls were still holding stolen items that must be returned. That evening, a big pile of stolen goods was deposited on a table. Eva told the headmaster to burn any unclaimed goods. He did. The next morning the same five girls were again stricken with fits, during which Eva complained that some girls *still* had stolen goods. A new pile appeared and was later burned on Eva's orders. Eva was growing bolder and more powerful by the day. Soon the headmaster himself would feel her wrath.[12]

Two days later the school held a track meet, during which Binama, a seventeen-year-old mother figure at the hostel, went into hysterics. This was her first attack. Binama and many other girls thought that a spell aimed at the five girls had been deflected by accident onto her. While she quickly recovered, the situation at the school grew increasingly dire by the day as the outbreaks continued. Education authorities knew they had to act.

Deliver Us from Eva: The Hostel Explodes

On Wednesday, April 28, the state's chief education officer came to the school to see what was going on firsthand. It was to be a remarkable day that none present would soon forget. Upon his arrival, as if on cue, five different girls went into hysterics—screaming, crying, and hyperventilating. It was a wild scene. Among them was Eva, who spoke for the group as she had during past fits, in a foreign voice and persona, as if a spirit was controlling her. The headmaster was quickly losing control. To make matters worse for him, there was a huge turnout for the visit, including journalists, townsfolk, and students. The scene was tense and electric. Eva had worked herself into an emotional frenzy, lying in bed; tears were streaming down her face. Her speech grew fluent and dramatic, and she spoke with wisdom and insight beyond her years. Observers noted that her words and demeanor were both mesmerizing and poetic. Eva told the witchdoctor that she would accept nothing less than "a human blood sacrifice" to appease the angry spirits. The crowd gave off a collective gasp. The jittery headmaster grew humble before Eva and the huge audience in this community drama. He began pleading, eventually managing to bargain her down. Eva soon agreed that a goat would be an acceptable substitute, but the theatrics were not over. She scolded the headmaster, ordering him about in front of the crowd for all to see, as an angry mother might do to a naughty child. The witchdoctor was unhappy with the bargain; he fell to his knees and begged Eva to change her mind about killing the goat. After an emotional half hour of pleading and negotiation, Eva relented, agreeing that a "white cockerel was to be sacrificed in a selected place" and that a *bomoh* from *her* village would perform the ritual in order to pacify the spirits that were harassing her fellow hostelites.[13]

4. The Demon-Haunted Classroom

A major announcement was made that Friday, the Islamic Sabbath, a holy day of reflection and prayer. An exorcism would be held at the school to appease the spirits and get them to leave the girls alone. The day of the ceremony, hundreds of students and townsfolk swamped the campus to witness the supernatural battle. The stakes were high. If school officials failed to rid the campus of the angry *jinn*, the school might be shut down. The townspeople could not afford to lose this battle with the spirits. As Eva had commanded, the hometown witchdoctor was brought in to conduct the casting-out ritual. But this was not just any witchdoctor. It was a *pawang*, a witchdoctor of extraordinary abilities. In this case it was an elderly father-figure who met the crowd. The smell of burning incense wafted through the humid tropical air. This was meant to get the attention of the *jinn*, so the *pawang* could communicate with them. He took a knife and slit the throat of the cockerel. With the blood continuing to flow, he recited passages from the Koran.[14]

With great respect and dignity, he asked the *jinn* to forgive the girls for dirtying their territory with their sanitary napkins, giving his personal assurance that it would never happen again. He walked through the school and hostel, visiting every room while tossing about uncooked white rice in hopes of pleasing the *jinn*. He made a proclamation: For the next three days anyone who had wronged the *jinn* must undergo a *pantang*, a 72-hour abstinence, in order to make amends with the spirits. During this period, they were not to utter a word, had to live in peace and harmony with nature, and were forbidden to harm flowers, leaves, insects, or animals. Lastly, everyone on campus was to stay indoors for the three days and could not leave.[15]

There was some historical background that may have set the scene for the outbreak. Almost everyone in town believed that the school, built on the site of an old tin mine, had been home to a family of royal *jinn*. When the mine opened, many strange things were reported there, such as machines mysteriously stopping. Eventually the area was cleared to build the school, angering townsfolk, as a *pawang* had not been called first to pacify the *jinn* living there. It was also believed that the *jinn* were living near the mine where the girls were throwing their napkins. The *pawang* said that the real culprit for the outbreak was not the girls, but the headmaster who ordered them to dispose of their napkins in the mine, upsetting the *jinn*. The witchdoctor said that the *jinn*s had contacted him through a series of dreams, expressing displeasure with the situation and asking the girls to follow several rules: keep their hostel and the surrounding area clean; don't be jealous of other girls; stop saying bad things about others; don't steal; live in accordance with the Koran; and remain virtuous.

The witchdoctor said that since the girls were not living in accord with these rules, the *jinn* had decided to possess them.[16]

The hysteria outbreak at Helang was a veiled attempt at leveling the playing field against the powerful headmaster. The outbreak forced education officials to take notice, pressuring the headmaster to be more accountable. The public exorcism appeased the girls and their parents in what was essentially an exercise in collective bargaining. The headmaster was told of his failings and to change his controlling ways or lose his job. A woman was appointed to care for the hostel and watch over the girls. The headmaster said he would do his best to stay out of hostel affairs. The girls grew closer, putting aside their differences. Meanwhile, the headmaster underwent psychotherapy to help him better understand how he had angered the community. In the end, the girls got what they wanted.

The Malay Underworld

Such dramas may seem bizarre or pathological to outsiders, but interpretations of these events by all of the parties are consistent with popular Malay culture.[17] In addition to belief in the *jinn*, many Malays have an unshakable faith in the reality of other supernatural beings, such as diminutive fairy-like *toyl* creatures and *hantus*—the ghosts of Malay folklore. There is a widespread belief in supernatural forces such as magic potions, spells, charms, amulets, and curses, which can be obtained from witchdoctors, who remain popular. One can easily find witchdoctors in the Malaysian telephone directory and, more recently, on the Internet.

The outbreaks of mass hysteria among these Muslim schoolgirls are similar to hysterical fits and accompanying trances among nuns secluded in European Christian convents between the fifteenth and nineteenth centuries.[18] Melodrama and role playing were a big part of these episodes. In both cultures young girls were often sent away against their will. In the European case they were forced by elders to join religious orders in cramped, female-only living quarters. Male companionship was forbidden. Hysteria appeared under the strictest administrations. Instead of witchdoctors, priests were summoned to exorcise the demons, and unpopular girls were often accused of casting spells. In both instances, those trapped in the situation released their frustrations by uttering disrespectful and blasphemous remarks and engaging in strange antics. Their status as possessed gave them impunity, getting them off the hook for punishment, as the demons were blamed.

Where the Malay schoolgirls might call for the dismissal or transfer of their restrictive headmasters, the nuns accused despised colleagues or convent priests of causing their possession through witchcraft. In short, it was payback time. Malaysian episodes usually subside when school figures relax rules or the offending official is fired or transferred, while in convents symptoms disappeared soon after the accused was removed, banished, imprisoned, or, more commonly, burned at the stake. While Malaysian episodes typically persist for months, convent outbreaks often endured for years, since lengthy church inquisitions were required and exorcisms were performed in order to remove the offending administrator and mete out punishment.

One extraordinary mass hysteria saga involving thirty-six Muslim girls at a Malay hostel in Alor Star, in the remote northern state of Kedah, endured for five years. The behavior involved shouting, running and mental confusion, crying, bizarre movements, trances and spirit possession. The girls, ages thirteen to seventeen, complained of too much religion and study, and too little recreation. School officials brought in witchdoctor after witchdoctor, to no avail, as underlying dissatisfaction continued to brew. The struggle between the students and administration waxed and waned for years, climaxing in 1987, when several desperate girls took hostages with knives and demanded changes. Their "hysterical" status deflected blame, and no criminal charges were laid. The fits ceased soon after former Malaysian prime minister Tunku Abdul Rahman went to the school and saw to it that the hapless girls were transferred to a more cheerful, liberal school.[19]

The Helang college affair is far from isolated. Scores of similar incidents have been reported across Malaysia. However, outbreaks are rarely recorded in such detail. Two other episodes have been investigated, the first on the southern tip of the country in Johor Baru, the other to the north along the eastern seaboard.

"Ghost Nests" at an Islamic School

Malaysian psychiatrist Eng-Seng Tan had seen a lot of strange scenes in his practice. But the events that unfold on September 25, 1962, would remain permanently etched in his memory. Tan was going about his daily routine seeing patients at the Tampoi Mental Hospital in the southern city of Johor Baru when the phone rang at noon. There was a ghost scare at a nearby Islamic school for young Malay boys and girls. The situation was described as tense and deteriorating rapidly. Upon arriving, Dr. Tan was told that a schoolyard rambutan tree was the center of the outbreak; nearly a dozen girls had fainted after seeing a ghost nearby. Rambutans are popular, sweet fruits whose skin resembles a spiky red ping-pong ball. The girls were carried inside where several recovered, but at least eight were still slumped like rag dolls, lying on the laps of classmates who were vigorously fanning them in the tropical heat and humidity. They were conscious and soon moved to benches for examination. Except for a rapid pulse, neither Tan nor his colleagues could find anything physically wrong.[20]

Other psychiatrists went to the school and tried talking to the girls to find out what had frightened them so, but the girls were rambling and incoherent. While doctors were trying to assess the situation and decide on a plan of action, there were occasional flare-ups. One girl started screaming and crying, beating her breasts and tearing at her hair. Soon after the first girl went berserk, one or more of the other seven joined in. Scores of other students were crying, upset by what they were seeing and caught up in the emotion of the moment. Tan describes the scene as something out of a theatrical drama: "The atmosphere of the schoolhouse was tense and electric. There were pupils of the school, some nursing their fainting schoolmates, others milling around quite bewildered. There were the school officials rushing about excitedly trying to pacify the screaming girls, and there was before long a big number of curious spectators crowding in to see what was going on."[21]

With the situation threatening to get out of control, the psychiatrists ordered the crowd to disperse, and they cleared several classrooms of students. They put each of the eight sobbing girls in a separate room along with one or two schoolmates to comfort them. Over the next twenty minutes, the tension faded. Soon the girls were sitting up, feeling well enough to be taken to the Johor Baru General Hospital, though when their parents arrived, they were taken home. After talking with teachers and students, it was learned that the episode began during recess when one girl, Sariaton, said she saw a ghost near the rambutan tree. She said that when the ghost threatened to harm her, she screamed and fell unconscious. Soon other girls said that they too saw the ghosts, though their descriptions varied; no two were the same.

Later that day saw the dramatic entrance of a middle-aged *bomoh* clad in yellow. Most Malays live in two seemingly incompatible worlds—the scientific and the supernatural.[22] When the hysteria broke out, school officials hedged their bets and made two phone calls. One was to the nearby psychiatric hospital, the other to the *bomoh*. The old man grabbed a heavy iron nail with his right hand, a hunk of clay in his left, and began stabbing the clay with the nail. He then walked around to each of the afflicted girls, holding their palms and lightly stabbing them with his nail. This was intended to exorcise the ghosts from their bodies. Later he escorted the psychiatrists to the rambutan tree where the ghosts were first sighted. The witchdoctor told Tan that "it was the nest of a mother — and 44 children-ghosts. He said that the girls had trodden on the toes of some of the children ghosts, so that the mother ghost retaliated by haunting the girls. He then stabbed the tree with his big iron nail, by which means he said he had killed a few of the children ghosts and assured us that the incident would not be repeated."[23]

The *bomoh's* antics did not "cure" the girls. The outbreak endured for several more days, always starting with the same pupil, Sariaton, who began to scream and then faint. Many of her classmates would follow suit. In all, twenty-nine girls were stricken during the week-long drama. In addition to fainting and screaming, the affected girls reported vague feelings of discomfort in their heads, heart palpitations, weakness, difficulty sleeping, and hallucinations such as seeing a ghost beckoning to them. The psychiatrists were ineffective, since only one of the girls ordered to seek psychiatric treatment ever showed up. The one who did was given a sedative and recovered. Many of the girls sought further help from the *bomoh*, though their problems continued.

The attacks stopped after the school was shut down for several weeks and Sariaton was told not to return. But was Sariaton the sole culprit in triggering the outbreak? What had caused her to become so distraught? Dr. Tan said that just before the events began, "there was an emotional storm brewing in the school"—a storm stoked by claims of behind-the-scenes shenanigans. There were allegations that a school official was showing favoritism, specifically, "of promoting some pupils who had failed their examination, and, in a few cases, who had not even sat for their examination."[24] After the hysteria died down, the official was fired. Consciously or subconsciously, these seemingly powerless girls had succeeded in getting their way.

Trouble at Timor College

On Malaysia's rural east coast, teeming with lush, green jungle and pristine beaches, lies the small, picturesque fishing town of Timor. It was in this seemingly tranquil setting that, in early 1978, the curtain rose on a peculiar drama. Timor was a conservative community, and at the time there was great concern over the moral impact of tiny Timor College with its 377 students, half of whom were girls.²⁵ An ugly rift broke out between the townsfolk and the college. The campus became a hotbed of tension that would soon incubate an outbreak of strange behaviors. Many locals were fearful that the school's presence would usher in a catastrophic decline in morality and lead Timor's youth astray. To make matters worse, the school was a magnet for students from liberal, urban areas across the country. Many students avoided certain parts of town, complaining that local youths were harassing them. At the time the strange behaviors broke out, the greatest stress on the girls came from themselves.

Just before the outbreak, the seniors were putting the freshmen through initiation rituals, trying to scare them with ghost stories and rumors. The freshmen were soon terrified. One story had it that the school had once been used as an execution site by Japanese soldiers during World War II. As a result, it was said to be haunted. Another tale held that a student had drowned while swimming at a nearby beach the year before, and their restless spirit was wandering the campus at night. If this were not enough to rile the girls, the seniors told stories of spirits inhabiting a stretch of nearby beach and a clump of campus trees. The scene was set for a wave of hysteria to sweep through the freshmen.

The trouble began early one Friday morning at about 3:00 A.M., when a first-year student, Rita, awoke from a nightmare. She was so scared that she climbed into bed with her roommate, where she eventually fell back to sleep, only to reawaken in terror a short time later. Suddenly, Rita screamed and fainted. Five hours later she regained consciousness and decided to rest while her roommates went to classes. As they left, she again grew frightened and fainted again. She was found and rushed to the hospital, where doctors could find nothing wrong. Meanwhile, that night, a senior girl, Wati, "freaked out." Peering into a bathroom mirror, she saw her face appearing distorted and ugly. Then an overwhelming feeling swept over her. She was sure that a presence was watching her. She dashed from the dorm to a nearby guardhouse. Tears were streaming down her face. She was adamant that she would not return to her room that night. Wati had worked herself into a state of great distress before looking into the mirror that Friday night. On top of worrying about ghosts, she was in constant, throbbing pain from a toothache, and she had been staying up late studying for a test the next day. Wati had had similar episodes in the past.²⁶

That night more strange things happened to other freshman girls. Roni was strolling with her boyfriend, Aori, when she suddenly felt unwell and was seized with bouts of laughing and weeping. Aori and several nearby students carried her back to the dorm, where a senior boy who may have seen too many Cary Grant films tried reviving her by slapping her across the face several times. When that failed, someone suggested phoning a native healer. No one thought to summon a medical doctor.

Later that night another freshman, Zani, became upset when someone told her that Roni had fainted. She went to a nearby room to check on her friend's condition. Soon Roni was well enough to walk into the TV room, a move that frightened Zani, who said that Roni had a "creepy look" on her face. Zani suddenly collapsed and was unconscious for two hours. When she awoke, she didn't utter a single word for hours. Several friends stopped by to see how she was doing. One of them was Roni. As soon as Roni appeared, Zani began to clench her teeth and scream. One of the boys walked over and slapped her in the face and made her repeat several Islamic prayers. Still no one thought to call a medical doctor.

By 4:00 A.M. Saturday, yet another girl succumbed to the hysteria. Newey, a senior, "became disturbed and bruised her neck in the process of trying to strangle herself." She was sent to the hospital. Meanwhile Aori, who saw the incident, was tense and upset, but tried to calm the other hostilities and then went to bed himself. It was about midnight. He couldn't sleep. At 3:00 A.M., still wide awake, he saw a mysterious object begin to circle above his head: "It was the head of a human being with long hair and it warned ... that he would suffer the same fate as the other victims.... [Aori] screamed, cried, and became unconscious. At daylight, he recovered and attended classes, but became hysterical again in the middle of a lecture." He later met with different native healers for help.[27]

That morning, while Aori's drama was unfolding, Roni was also attending lectures when a sudden chill sent shivers through her body. Her stomach began to ache. She collapsed. Her friends picked her up, placed her on a desk and began chanting. The religious teacher, or *ustaz*, came over and began reading verses from the Koran. At one point Roni began to scream and moan. The commotion was upsetting to onlookers, and soon another freshman in the lecture hall cried out and fainted. The screaming and crying caught the attention of a nearby class, where teaching came to a halt as students began to eavesdrop on the strange goings-on. It wasn't long before that class also descended into chaos. First one student screamed and fainted, then another. Soon the entire class was in a panic, including the female lecturer who fled the room with other students, instructing some male pupils to go back and try to calm the rest of the class alone, especially the girls. More and more freshman girls soon exhibited fits of hysteria. Each new outbreak created more tension. The cycle of fear and hysteria was broken only when officials were forced to temporarily close the college.[28]

In Malay culture, elders and those in authority are all-powerful. You do not challenge their word. An outbreak of hysteria is one way to get around this extreme obedience to authority. Ordinarily, students could not express their feelings about the teasing and the cold shoulder from locals. During the outbreak, many conservative students felt the possessions and spirit attacks on the freshman girls were deserved. The "freshers" were said to be provoking the campus guardian spirits (*penusggus*) with their flashy dress and make-up. They were also seen as too "uninhibited in their speech and behavior and too Western in their outlook." The girls were unhappy with the way they were being treated. Yet, any expression of those feelings would surely have been met with punishment or expulsion. Their emotions built up. School officials could not take action against the students, instead blaming the hysteria on the spirits. Another inhibition created by Malay society is the reluctance to discuss one's troubles publicly, because of the fear of embarrassing others. In some cases the students may have been feigning or exaggerating; at other times they seemed to be genuinely having "fits." In either case, the effect was the same. Anthropologists Raymond Lee and Susan Ackerman, who investigated the outbreak, remark, "Voicing one's grievances through references to the supernatural is acceptable since it is the spirit, and not the individual, which is responsible for revealing the person's problems in public." In this way, students can express guilt or remorse, but the evil spirits get the blame.[29]

Outbreak at a Thai School

In the fall of 1993, evil spirits reportedly took over girls at rural Thasala Elementary School in a woody, mountainous section of south Thailand. Exams were canceled, the school was shut down, and parents threatened to take their children and leave the region for good. The strange events that would follow began after a tragic accident. Seven months earlier, two Thasala boys died when their vehicle crashed while traveling to a scholars' competition. An obsession with dying soon swept through the students.

In keeping with Thai custom, a spirit house was built at the school entrance. Spirit houses are tiny buildings where the souls of the newly departed are thought to dwell. An integral part of Thai culture, they dot the landscape. Buddhists believe that these spirits wander the countryside, awaiting reincarnation as other earthly creatures. Many Thais build tiny houses on their property as a place for spirits to reside during this waiting period. With the construction of the spirit house for the two boys, the students were beginning to accept the loss. But all was not well.

Tensions at the school soon rose as a bitter dispute erupted when government officials ordered the demolition of an old schoolhouse, a cherished community symbol, in order to make room for a new school. The officials never asked the townsfolk what they thought of the idea. The decision to raze the school and move the spirit house sparked outrage. A fight even broke out between a teacher and a parent over the issue.

Then one day in September, students noticed that a third-grader had a strange look in her eyes. She told onlookers that her body had been taken over by a spirit who ordered a new spirit house be built near the new school. The girl displayed a remarkable ability to enter trances and speak with the spirit world. She told psychiatrists: "It is easy. I just go into a place in my mind. I think about a peaceful place such as the beach or the forest and then I'm there." She said it was often difficult to tell the difference between reality and fantasy, noting, "It feels as though it were really happening to me."[30]

Soon thirty-two classmates were stricken with mysterious fits. Some girls had thirty or more. Before the attacks, they would get headaches and feel woozy. Some felt "shaky" or that their heart was racing or weak. Most said that during their trances, they met an elderly woman in traditional red clothing, who commanded them to follow her. When the epidemic first broke out, authorities organized a public prayer ceremony to cast out the demons. Mediums were asked to meditate and pray for a prophetic vision that would help them find a way to get rid of the spirits. But instead of getting better, things got worse. During one trance, a girl said that the old woman dressed in red threatened to abduct "students as revenge because the school had destroyed her spirit house."[31] The story sent waves of fear through the schools.

Government psychiatrists soon arrived. One of their first decisions was to find an open classroom and meet with worried parents to explain that the strange behaviors were the result of stress. The affected students were herded into a room next door. As the psychiatrists were explaining that there was nothing to worry about, one of the girls suddenly screamed and collapsed on the floor, her arms and legs flailing about in violent spasms. Suddenly another girl screamed and fainted. Her arms and legs also began to twitch and shake. Panic quickly swept through the room. Within ten minutes, four of the girls were screaming and flailing about. Before long, the entire class was in a state of panic, unnerving their parents next door.[32]

Psychiatrist Umaporn Trangkasombat of Chulalongkorn University was summoned by the mother of one of the stricken girls. She said that her daughter looked strange. Trangkasombat tried talking to her, but she stared blankly into space. Eerily, her eyes were wide open. The girl was helped to a nearby room and eased into a soft armchair where she burst into tears and wept for twenty minutes. Snapping out of her daze and trying to stand, she was wobbly and had a confused look on her face. Meanwhile, in the same room, another girl suddenly slumped over, her face hitting the table. She began to move her body as if she were fighting someone. "No. No. I won't go," she cried. Over and over she wept and cried out: "No. No. I won't go." People tried talking with her but she gave no response. Her struggle with the "invisible force" went on for fifteen minutes. When her eyes opened, her only memory was that of "an old woman, dressed in red, trying to get me," she said.

By late November, the "spirit attacks" were over. The psychiatrists had broken up the group and held counseling sessions in which they explained the outbreak in terms of long-term psychological stress. They were careful not to challenge the students' belief in spirits. It was clear that many of those stricken were fearful that they would be kidnapped by angry spirits, unhappy at the demolition of the spirit house and out for retribution. The pattern was repeated with several students who fell into trances, saw visions of a woman in red, and struggled as they perceived she was trying to capture them. Upon coming out of their daze, they could not recall any of what had just happened but for vague descriptions of their encounter with the old woman in red. One of the most effective measures in ending the attacks was the instruction by psychiatrists not to touch girls during an attack. Teachers, parents, and other students would often try to comfort them during the fits. While well meaning, this may have been more of a hindrance, because the girl was likely to misinterpret the feeling of being touched or held as "the act of the spirit trying to abduct her. This advice proved useful since the attack stopped more rapidly than when the child was touched."[33]

The psychiatrists believed that several factors led to the extraordinary tension at Thasala Elementary, culminating in the bizarre fits. The death of classmates had created a tense backdrop, and stress was increased by the destruction of the spirit house that might have been used by the dead students' spirits — or so many at the school thought. These events created frustration and anxiety. Within this volatile cauldron, rumors spread through the school that angry spirits were possessing the girls.

The psychiatrists later made a startling finding: Those most affected led incredibly stressful lives filled with trauma. The Thasala region is one of the most crime-ridden in Thailand, notorious for its violence and military conflict. Amid this atmosphere of terror, the death of the students and the destruction of their spirit house pushed their stress levels even higher. Just how stressful were their everyday lives? The psychiatric team noted: "Many children had reported encountering dead bodies on their way to school. Some had witnessed the death of their neighbors or loved ones. A sister of one of the girls was shot to death a few months prior to the epidemic." Everyday fear, coupled with their friends' deaths and the destruction of their spirit house, created unbearable tension.

Thai Ghost Attacks

During mid–January 2001, Thailand was also the scene of a series of "ghost attacks" when about one hundred students at a school camp in Nakhon Ratchasima province suddenly fell ill for no apparent reason. An investigating physician said the students were exhausted after a long day of exercise and grew fearful that ghosts haunted the camp. Dr. Somchai Chakraphand said the exhaustion "built up on top of the general belief that spirits and ghosts haunted the area. The students' fear increased and this led to hyperventilation and eventually to breathing problems." The episode began when a girl who was singing around a campfire screamed after she thought she saw a ghost. Most area residents have a strong belief in ghosts and malevolent spirits.[34] The ghost fears in Thailand that generated hyperventilation seem to represent the same phenomenon (anxiety hysteria) that is so common in modern Western schools, only in a different social and cultural context.

In August 2003, Buddhist monks were called to a Thai school to drive out evil spirits reportedly possessing pupils. On August 7 an exorcism ceremony was held at the Baan Thab Sawai School in Huai Thalaeng. During the previous three months, students had been acting out of character for Thai culture, uttering rude words and threatening to harm themselves. Some appeared to be in a trance, as if hypnotized. Others were having "attacks" two or three times daily over the three months. Medical exams of the pupils surprised doctors, as they found no signs of health problems.

In a bid to appease the ghosts, a merit-making ceremony was held. Even the provincial governor, Sunthorn Riewleung, took the story seriously. Unable to attend, he sent a letter offering his apologies "to the spirits and asking them to stop haunting villagers and students, or a spirit house in the school compound would be demolished." Soon after the ceremony was over, an eleven-year-old schoolgirl named Nong Nam began screaming and "went berserk." She was soon able to regain her senses with the aid of two Brahmin priests who managed to calm her.

The fits often started with students feeling lightheaded before collapsing and falling unconscious. When they awoke they said "it felt as if someone was pressing down on their chests. While unconscious, the students claimed, they had seen a bald man wearing black glasses and very old clothes asking them to accompany him."[35]

The Thai Fossil Scare of 2002

Some Thai school scares that seem unique are based in the firm belief that mysterious spirits may haunt grave sites in areas that must be treated with care and respect. Between late June and early July of 2002, a mysterious illness afflicted many students visiting a site harboring dinosaur fossils. Concern began to mount when 180 students went to the site to look at the remains and fifteen collapsed. Instead of taking the girls to a doctor, they were instead rushed to Liam Banusawan, a local *mor phi* (exorcist), who sprinkled them with holy water, which revived them. Only then were they taken to hospital in the nearest town.[36]

A few days later, four students and an instructor — all female — were stricken on another trip to see fossils. The group was visiting Pedan Cave in the Thung Yai district when they began screaming, then fainted. The incident happened in the morning as they were leaving the site. This time those stricken were first rushed to a local medical center; then they met with an exorcist who treated them with holy water. Panya Lertkrai, an assistant professor at the Rajabaht Institute, said, "They [the spirits] could have been upset by the students' behavior. Some might have taken dinosaur remains home."[37]

The fossils created excitement when they were discovered at the cave on June 18, as by some estimates they may have been 300 million years old. Locals said the cave was used by communists as a base and was also a burial site for persons executed in the past for their opposition to government policies. One villager stated, "It could have been the work of those spirits."[38]

Thai psychiatrist Inthira Puasakul thought that fear may have been responsible for at least one incident, as "the students may have collapsed after their group leader became frightened ... [and] others in the group may then have been overwhelmed by their leader's fear and developed their own."[39] Some villagers blamed the collapse on spirits guarding the cave, which they hypothesized may have been offended by the students.

The belief in supernatural spirits possessing people is widespread in Thailand. In June 2003, more than a thousand people disrupted traffic in the Muang district while following a famous local exorcist through the area as he hunted down and cast out ghosts known as the *pee-paub,* who are thought to feed on human entrails. The exorcism was held after several mysterious deaths blamed on the *pee-paub.* The veteran ghost catcher Phra Khru Udom Panyakorn said he managed to catch thirty-nine ghosts during his three-hour search using only chants and hollow bamboo.[40]

Satanic Panic in Beirut

In early March 2003, a woman on a Lebanese TV show made a startling claim: A group of anti–Christian devil worshippers were operating in the country. She said she was an eyewitness to baby sacrifices, the rape of virgins, orgies, and other bizarre rituals. Her appearance triggered a deluge of rumors, forcing schools to convene meetings with students in order to dispel the claims. Among the rumors was a story that mutilated bodies had been discovered in a popular shopping mall. Other accounts told of kidnappers grabbing children, tearing out their hearts, and drinking their blood.

The problems began on Sunday, March 9, when a privately run Christian TV station, Tele-Lumiere, broadcast a program on Lebanese devil worshippers. One mother, Julie Harfoush, said, "They are convinced that devil worshippers are around the corner waiting to kidnap them.... No matter what I tell them, they don't believe me, because they hear their friends saying that they saw a real devil worshipper on television." The dramatic program blurred the face of a supposed former devil worshipper, who said the group sacrificed babies, the offspring from raped virgins.

The next week, station officials advised young people that they could avoid being victims by maintaining a well-groomed appearance, covering tattoos, and not wearing black clothes. At Beirut's American Community School, administrators were forced to call an assembly to counter the rumors, including a story that a teen had been murdered at a local shopping mall. Mall owner Samir Rayess said, "We have closed-circuit cameras everywhere in the centre.... We monitor everything. If these rumours were true, don't you think that the police would have sealed off the centre?"[41]

Strange Scenes from India and Nepal

It was a bizarre sight: medical and biology students and instructors at a major university attending a ceremony to exorcise ghosts. This unlikely scenario happened during the summer and autumn of 2002 at Panjab University in India. Most school scares are provoked by stress, and this incident was no different. Over the course of several months, two of the university's most popular professors, both department heads, died of heart attacks. It was against this backdrop of grief, uncertainty, and fear that students and faculty, who had dedicated their lives to the study of science, organized an exorcism to rid the campus of evil spirits thought to be responsible for the tragedies. The departments involved in the cleansing ritual were Biochemistry, Genome Studies, Microbiology, Biophysics and Pharmacy.[42]

The same year, another ghost scare struck at a primary school in West Bengal. The scare at the Goalsara Primary School began when a pupil kicked a ball, and the ball bounced into the school. A student disappeared into the building to retrieve the ball. A short time later he raced out, screaming, "Ghosts! Ghosts!" Chaos ensued. Students began running in every direction — some bumping into one another and sustaining cuts and bruises in their desperation to get away. The children and parents in this comedy-tragedy were so frightened that they boycotted classes, fearing that the "football ghost" was still roaming the halls. After the classrooms were empty for two weeks, authorities went door to door in an effort to persuade the students to return. The rumor mill began to churn, and before long there were stories that apparitions had been spotted in the school and that the scratches and bruises from the frantic exodus were from ghost attacks. The next morning, teachers were ready to conduct classes, but no students came. After two weeks principal Chittaranjan Bhanja told the *New Indian Express*, "So far only about 30 students of various classes have started coming."[43]

In May 2003, fears of a toilet-haunting ghost forced authorities to close a girls' middle school in the village of Kapurawala, one hundred and twenty-five miles south of Delhi. Three girls suffered mysterious fits after using the toilet. Police inspector Hakim Singh said the toilet no longer existed: "Nobody has seen the ghost, but the school toilet, suspected to be the devil's den, was brought down by villagers." Villagers were planning a *yagya,* or Hindu fire purification ceremony, in hopes of flushing the spirit from where the bathroom once stood, and convincing the girls to return.[44] While teachers tried to be good role models and instill calm, one teacher panicked and fled the school, requesting and receiving a transfer.

At nearly the same time, mass hysteria broke out to the north of India in the mountains of neighboring Nepal. Two dozen schoolgirls would suddenly burst into tears, followed by prolonged laughter. The episode repeated over the course of several months. A team of doctors visited the grounds of the Nepal Rashtriya Secondary School in the Sunsari district. Doctors pinpointed the cause: men. They observed that all of the teachers at the school were male, and concluded that the girls felt uncomfortable and found it difficult to express themselves in front of men. Parents believed the girls to have been attacked by supernatural beings, so they turned to religion. Attempts to appease the forces by sacrificing a goat and praying to the gods failed.[45]

Meanwhile, on the other side of the border, another bizarre drama was unfolding. Fifteen schoolgirls in northern India had to be restrained from tearing out their hair after a mysterious epidemic swept through their school in the village of Lower Koti in the mountainous province of Himachal Pradesh. The girls collapsed onto the floor, pulling at their hair and shivering as if they were freezing. Principal Purshotam Rana said that over a one-week period starting in late August, the girls began "shivering and contorting their bodies and even wailing wide-eyed and flailing their hair." Frightened locals were about to conduct an exorcism to rid the school of the "demons" when a team of psychiatrists arrived. The culprit was widely believed to be a demon who, according to a local seer, had taken possession of the girls. The psychiatrists recommended against the exorcism, instead issuing their own prescription: "Ignore the girls so they do not feel under undue pressure."[46]

Yet another ghost scare shut down schools in the southern Indian city of Tiruchi in September 2003. The episode began when the newspaper *Thanthi* published a picture of a student standing next to a ghostly, witch-like image. Police said the image was a computer-generated hoax and launched a public awareness campaign to alert others to such hoaxes. The article claimed that the student in the photo collapsed after the picture was taken, went into a coma, and died of a heart attack. Parents quickly decided to keep their children out of school, forcing it to temporarily close. It was reported that the ghost was especially fond of little boys. The scare was made worse when other newspapers published the story, giving the claims more credence.[47]

India's Cat Girls

In early August 2004, at least a dozen girls fell into a strange state and began acting like cats, meowing and walking about on all fours, at a school in the remote hamlet of Dolagobind in Orissa, India. The first signs of trouble came in late July, when several students at the school fainted for no apparent reason. When the girls awoke, they began acting like cats.

The community reacted to the strange state of affairs by summoning native healers to get rid of the evil spirits believed responsible. Teachers reported that the afflicted girls, ages six to twelve, were clawing at their faces and shrieking like cats, leaving authorities little choice but to temporarily shut the school down.

The principal, Manjubala Pande, said the episode began on July 26 when Sasmita Mohapatra, a student in Class 10, fainted during prayers. On that day, she said, "three girls fell down when they came to school. We thought they hadn't had food so we gave them something to eat but after that also they were not normal and behaved strangely." The next day, she said, "some six-seven girls started crying, fell down on the floor making sounds like that of a cat. We immediately informed others in the village but after the faintings and behavior repeated, we were forced to shut the school." Prayers were offered in the school over five consecutive days, but they had no effect. When the fits first started the girls simply fainted and began behaving in a cat-like manner, but after the outbreak was underway, Pande told the Indian News Agency, "The girls tremble with a tingling sensation. They also cry and act like cats and then faint. They get normal after a few hours."[48]

All of the school's seventy-five students, including the "cat girls," were taken to the nearby Nigamananda Saraswat hermitage run by a local Hindu wise man, where they were ordered to recite religious prayers. Similar outbreaks were reported at several other area schools. "We are organising rituals to get divine help," said one parent.[49] In modern India, cats are considered symbols of bad luck. In some places they are believed to be the incarnation of a witch. The girls' cat-like behavior may have been a subconscious reflection of these beliefs.

Stress-Reducing Rituals and Reactions

To outsiders, outbreaks of strange behavior in Malaysia, Thailand and other parts of Asia may seem simple: stress builds and hysteria erupts. In reality, it is more complex. The possessing spirit comes from the student's subconscious—which then negotiates with school administrators to loosen restrictions such as by easing homework or providing more recreation time. Once officials ease up, the stress slowly subsides and the hysteria dissipates. The episodes illustrate the power of culture on behavior. For instance, in Malaysia, where shopping and bargaining are national pastimes, it is no coincidence that when students are stressed by school policies that they have little control over, they react using available methods. That is, when the going gets tough, students use basic shopping techniques to bargain for a better deal. A similar idiom of negotiation exists in neighboring Thailand. Even more prevalent are Asian ghost and spirit scares that seem to reflect common fears during times of crisis and bring students closer together. Outbreaks typically occur amid rumors and are fueled by the media; this is also the case for vaccination scares.

These episodes are local ways of adapting to stress in the face of overwhelming fear and anxiety. The ways that the human mind relieves tension will undoubtedly change during the twenty-first century in order to meet new challenges. Naturalist Charles Darwin captured the spirit of this process when he famously said: "It is not the strongest of the species that survive, nor the most intelligent, but the one most responsive to change."

CHAPTER 5

The Students Who Laughed for a Week
Accounts from Africa

> Under certain conditions men respond as powerfully to fictions as they do to realities, and ... in many cases they help to create the very fictions to which they respond.—Walter Lippman[1]

In much of Africa, people believe that spirits of their ancestors roam the countryside to keep tabs on the living. In this tense, shadowy world, invisible spirits of the dead watch over their every move. In the central and southern part of the continent, the belief in witchcraft and ancestor spirits causes residents to live in a state of perpetual fear, afraid of offending ancestors and frightened of witches' spells. This gives rise to a complex system of preventative and appeasement rituals.

The Great Laughing Epidemic

It is not uncommon for a student to exhibit an attack of the giggles, especially near exam time. They typically regain their composure within a few minutes. But what would happen if the pupil kept on laughing for several hours before stopping, only to experience another attack the following day, and the day after? This is not a hypothetical scenario. This scene was replayed over and over in numerous schools in central Africa during the 1960s.

On January 30, 1962, three girls were sitting at their desks at a Christian missionary school in Kashasha village near the west shore of Lake Victoria in the remote northwest corner of Tanganyika (now Tanzania). Suddenly, an unusual feeling of giddiness swept over them and they began to laugh uncontrollably. At other times they wept. Some fits lasted but a few minutes; others endured for hours, only to flare up later. With each passing day, more and more of the girls were afflicted by the mysterious ailment that was dubbed by locals as *endwara ya kucheka*, or "the laughing trouble."[2] Some grew restless and violent, running around in fear that someone or some *thing* was chasing them. Many girls said they felt things moving around inside their heads. The "attacks" would come and go over several days, though some girls were stricken for more than two weeks. Curiously, not a single adult from the village was affected.[3]

As more and more students were overtaken by laughter, teachers and administrators grew more solemn. At a loss as to how to stop the epidemic, they had no choice but to close the school. They locked the doors on March 18 and sent everyone back to their home villages to recuperate. Most of the girls seemed to calm down and recover during the break, so the optimistic headmaster reopened on May 21. The fits of laughing and weeping returned. By late June, with fifty-seven pupils having fits, the decision was made to close again. Desperate to solve the mystery, school officials were ecstatic with the arrival of Dr. A.M. Rankin of Makerere University College and a local medical officer, P.J. Philip. Their first impression was that a virus was to blame, one that could spread by tiny infectious droplets, possibly from sneezing. A cursory survey found that nearly every victim had been in "very recent contact with someone suffering from the disease."[4] Confidently, the doctors began their examinations, only to find that the girls' vital signs were normal and there was no fever. The infectious disease theory was scratched off the list.

The next suspect was food. The girls had none of the classic signs of food poisoning, so the doctors examined the possibility of contamination by more exotic substances. After all, it was tropical Africa, and other epidemics of strange behavior have been triggered by food contamination such as *Datura stramonium* seeds in corn and wheat flour. But if this was true, the girls should have exhibited the tell-tale signs: lack of muscle control, dry mouth, and dilated pupils. None of these symptoms were present. Sticking with the contaminated food theory, samples were taken and sent off for analysis. The tests came back normal.[5]

The two scientists had one remaining suspect on their list: mass hysteria. But what would trigger such outbreaks? Rankin and Philip noted a theory among locals that the strange behavior was caused by "the bomb," a popular bugaboo of 1960s–era B-grade movies and science fiction literature. During this time, American hydrogen bomb tests in the South Pacific were the subject of intense local media coverage. The culprit was not believed to be radioactive fallout, the effects of which were not fully understood at the time, but rather the hydrogen bomb tests themselves, causing the students to become so filled with fear that the result was hysteria.

The Mania Spreads

As the laughing mania spread, the strange fits grew more elaborate. The outbreaks became violent and spread to nearby schools. More than a thousand people throughout the region were stricken over the next eighteen months; almost all were schoolchildren.[6] Locals believed the episode was triggered by angry ancestors.[7] The mania was spread by students who were sent home to recover. For instance, when the Kashasha School closed in March, several students went to their home village of Nshamba in the south. There they triggered an outbreak of laughing and crying among local school children. In June, the Ramashenye Girls' Middle School near Bukoba experienced an attack of "laughing sickness." Nearly fifty pupils, one-third of the student body, went into fits of laughter, coinciding with the return home of several girls from the Kashasha School. Boys' schools were also "infected" and forced to close. The situation was reaching crisis proportions as more and more schools in northwest Tanganyika were overcome.

In November 1963, a strange malady broke out at both Christian and Muslim missionary schools in neighboring Uganda to the north, in the vicinity of Mbale. These outbreaks caught the attention of psychiatrist Benjamin Kagwa, who worked at the Burabika Hospital in the Ugandan capital of Kampala. Kagwa visited the schools and said the mania had morphed into something more than the relatively benign laughing and weeping:

> Those affected ran about aimlessly and slept out of doors near their family tombs. Almost all of them caught a white chicken, or wore white feathers on their heads.... They all looked physically exhausted because of continuous hyperactivity. In addition, they did not take any solid food for some days. Without exception, everyone complained of "headaches" and "pain in the heart." Most of the men carried a circumcision knife with which they struck their chests incessantly to alleviate the pain.

Kagwa said the first phase lasted three to four days. As with the laughing mania, students were seized suddenly, without warning, usually in clusters. They grew agitated, got into fights with other students, and stole things. They refused to eat, wouldn't stop talking, and said they wanted to smoke cigarettes. In short, they were breaking all of the school's taboos. When asked why they were acting so strangely, they said they were following their ancestors' orders. Many said they could see visions of dead relatives. During the second phase, the students grew sad and quiet and seemed to be exhausted. The only exceptions were occasional relapses. After a few more days the students seemed to regain their senses.[8]

Elder witchdoctors went about visiting the burial grounds of their ancestors and weeding the tombs in hopes of appeasing the spirits, whom they felt must have been upset in some way. Near the tombs they built miniature huts for these spirits to inhabit, placing baked bananas, chicken, and gourds of wine inside. White chickens were slaughtered, their blood sprinkled on the tombs as a blessing. Some of the witchdoctors then sipped the wine and spat it at the feet of the afflicted students, often causing them to snap out of their mental daze.[9]

In May 1966 another outbreak of laughing and crying struck forty pupils at a school in Musoma on Lake Victoria, forcing it to close for two weeks. Health ministry official Charles Mywali told the *New York Times*, "It spreads like wildfire among schoolchildren, particularly girls, one girl starts to laugh her head off and all the others follow. Nobody can control them and the only answer is to separate them for a couple of weeks."[10]

Throughout the 1960s, similar bouts of bizarre student behavior in Central African schools continued to wreak havoc. On June 10, 1967, a fourteen-year-old girl at a mission school in Ghana in west central Africa complained of feeling hot and began clutching her heart, which she said hurt. She grew restless and refused to eat. Her restlessness soon turned to hyperactivity. Before long, more students were stricken. Many began to sob; others were overtaken with laughing and giggling. A few showed no inhibition whatsoever and became uncharacteristically talkative; others grew shy. Some complained of burning headaches.

By June 20, a whopping 62 students had been stricken. Alarmed administrators closed the school and sent the pupils home. By this point the affliction took on some truly creative new wrinkles, adding an array of dramatic flourishes to the already rich cocktail of symptoms. Some girls ran into the bush; others began climbing trees. Some threw rocks at anyone who tried to get near them; others hurled verbal epithets and grew confrontational. Those who stripped off their clothing had to be restrained from running around naked; others helped themselves with fancy clothes, stuck flowers in their hair, and wore pretty ornaments. Some refused to eat, while others obsessed over food and could think of nothing else.[11]

While the hysterical nature of the epidemic was obvious to the investigating psychiatrist, there was much press speculation that some other cause was responsible. As a result, the food and water supplies were tested, but they were found to be normal. Many different approaches were tried to help the girls. First, teachers used a heavy-handed approach, shouting at the pupils. This worked, but only for a short time. Next, they tried reverse psychology, being very nice — even to the point of meeting the students' outrageous demands for food. This didn't work either. They then said prayers for a quick recovery and held Bible readings. This neither helped the afflicted nor protected others from further attacks. At the hospital, doctors gave the girls tranquilizers while offering reassurance. While this helped many, it did not prevent the spread to others. One action seemed most effective in halting the epidemic: closing the school and sending everyone home to recuperate.[12]

Theories abounded. It was *juju*, or evil spells cast on the school by a local witchdoctor, said one faction. Another group thought that perhaps one of their own, a fellow student, was bewitching others. Some parents thought that the culprit was heat rising out of the ground. Yet another group of parents blamed the strange behaviors on spirits trying to send a message to the community through the students. This theory may hold a kernel of truth — not that spirits were involved but that the episode seemed to serve as a means for the unhappy students to convey their displeasure with the poor conditions at the school. Out of respect for authority and their elders, and fearing punishment, students were reluctant to complain. During the investigation, a few girls were brave enough to speak of their dissatisfaction with the school. They confided that advertised menu items were often unavailable, and when they did find something that sounded good, it was not properly cooked; the portions of meat were tiny; and there was a chronic milk shortage. To make matters worse, the water supply frequently ran out, and brown sediment could be seen floating in the water when it was flowing. The dorms were crowded. The school nurse added to the rising stress by often ignoring their medical complaints. Even when they were very ill, students said that she rarely referred anyone to the hospital although it was only a short walk next door.

Given that they were poorly fed, drinking dirty water, lacking sleep, and receiving minimal medical care, the students were justifiably angry and frustrated over their plight. But what could they hope to do about it? Over weeks and months, the tension built. A psychiatrist from the University of Ghana Medical School observed that "the students had no open channel through which to seek relief."[13] The result was hysteria, which quickly spread among the anxious student body. The laughing, crying, and more extreme antics finally got the attention of the community, alerting them to the seriousness of the problem, and may have been an unconscious means to get authorities to listen to their complaints and take action.

A Clash of Cultures

A historical example of this process was the Ghost Dance religion that swept through the midwest and western United States during the late 1800s. Defeated by the American military and displaced from their traditional lands, Native Americans were further demoralized by U.S. government and Christian missionary efforts to rid them of their "superstitious" ways and make them "civilized." In 1883 Interior Secretary Henry Teller ordered the distribution of new rules meant to stamp out paganism and "barbarous" customs. At this time, large numbers of Native Americans were starting to accept Jesus as their savior.[14] It was against this backdrop that the Ghost Dance was born and emotional turmoil ensued. A native medicine man claimed to have had a vision instructing him on how to perform a "ghost dance," which he said would usher in a new, harmonious era. It involved wild all-night dance frenzies for five successive nights, repeated every six weeks. The dance spread quickly to many tribes west of the Mississippi River. Dancers acted strangely, shook and trembled violently, fainted, stood rigid for hours, wandered about in a daze, and saw visions. As sociologist David Miller notes, "During their faints or trances, dancers said they were transported to the Happy Hunting Ground, where they visited with their dead ancestors."[15] Like the laughing mania, the Ghost Dance was an attempt by a group in crisis to establish ancient ties by contacting their ancestors. Both episodes were misunderstood by outsiders. Many settlers wrongly thought that the dancing was a preparation for war, and on December 29, 1890, tragedy struck. Nearly three hundred Native Americans were massacred at Wounded Knee Creek in what is now South Dakota. The Ghost Dance quickly faded and Christianity was soon back, stronger than ever.[16]

As we seek to understand the laughing mania, questions arise. Why laughing? Why missionary schools? Why Tanganyika and the spread across central Africa? Why the 1960s? Every behavior has a context, and the roots of the laughing mania are no different. Central and eastern Africa were the scenes of several major Christian revivals in the early decades of the twentieth century — revivals that had as major features bouts of laughing and weeping.[17] Such symptoms were recorded as early as 1914, when a religious renewal swept through the nearby Belgian Congo in west central Africa, which borders present-day Tanzania. One observer describes the scene during the 1914 revival as electric: "The whole place was charged as if with an electric current. Men were falling, jumping, laughing, crying, singing, confessing and some shaking terribly.... As I led in prayer the Spirit came down in mighty power sweeping the congregation. My whole body trembled with the power. We saw a marvelous sight, people literally filled and drunk with the Spirit."[18]

In 1935 the Great East African Religious Revival started in Rwanda and quickly spread west to the Congo (now the Democratic Republic of Congo), south to Burundi, and north to Uganda, eventually filtering into northwestern Tanganyika.[19] This event set off a series of revivals across the region that persisted into the mid–1980s. Laughing and weeping were prominent features of this movement.

The east African revival had a major impact on many cultures in Tanganyika, especially in the northwest corner near the shores of Lake Victoria, epicenter of the laughing mania.[20] Christian missionary schools were popping up like mushrooms throughout the Bukoba District in the decades after the revival. But while the new Christian God was moving in, the old gods had not yet left the premises. The result was a festering spiritual conflict between the old and the new, generating great anxiety and guilt. To understand the laughing mania that ensued, we must understand the beliefs of this region, which were dominated by the practice of ancestor worship.

Religious Conflict

Since the 1950s African religious scholars have been struggling with the challenges posed by ancestor worship in central Africa — a practice that conflicts with Bible teachings. Ancestor worshippers believe that when relatives die, they maintain an active relationship with the living. They are with you every minute of every day; you just cannot see them. They exist in an invisible, parallel world. Dead relatives are the most revered members of society. At meals, small portions of food are prepared or spilled for their benefit. When things are not going well, relatives commonly offer their ancestors expensive gifts in return for guidance or help. During crises, it is not uncommon for people to enter trance states and report seeing ancestors who offer solutions to their problems. Ancestors are intermediaries — the living dead — who are thought to communicate with both the living and the gods.[21] Working oneself into a trance and talking to ancestors is believed to be like having a hotline to the gods, only the ancestor takes the call and speaks on your behalf. Old beliefs die hard, and conflict arises when the locals are faced with the missionary church's insistence that they renounce ancestor worship and embrace the Bible, because their traditional beliefs remain and are often relied upon during times of crisis and death.[22]

During the 1960s, missionary schools were notorious for paying little or no attention to the pupils' cultural heritage, instead focusing on Western religious and cultural practices.[23] The resulting tension between the old ways and the missionary ways is described by theologian Jack Partain, who spent time living in Tanzania: "Many African theologians—themselves highly educated and westernized Christians—speak of their passionate desire to be linked with their dead and of their own inner struggle." The people's belief that their ancestors are watching their every move and judging their morality brings this psychic stew to a boil, especially for students in missionary schools, who are taught to worship their ancestors at home and are steeped in the study of the Bible at school. Each teaches that the other is wrong. According to Partain,

> Church leaders ... agree that some traditional notions about ancestors cannot be accepted by Christians. For instance, Christians cannot accept the view that ancestors have power over living family members, and they must emphatically deny that deaths are caused by ancestors. And divination [the supposed ability to foresee the future by supernatural means], a primary preoccupation of the ancestral cult, is entirely unacceptable.[24]

Tanzanian scholar Gabriel Setiloane uses poetry to describe the conflict that he feels in embracing Christianity and the guilt that arises from accepting a religion his ancestors would disapprove of: "The dead are not dead; they are ever near us; approving and disapproving all our actions. They chide us when we go wrong."[25] While the voices of their dead ancestors cried from beyond, there was more grief to be had. The laughing mania coincided with a period of local unrest that occurred when government officials forced families to move off their tiny farmsteads and onto more "civilized" planned villages in urban areas. This generated great stress as the people were driven away from their ancestors' graves.[26]

Modern-Day Laughing Epidemics

If one looks at the history of religious revivals, all sorts of strange behaviors are on record: twitching, shaking, jumping and so on. Congregations are worked up into emotional frenzies. These states are the product of what psychologists call hyper-suggestibility. During these services, people become temporarily open to suggestion and are prone to imitate whatever they see. If someone begins to laugh, others may also begin to laugh. It is in this way that traditions develop. The two major central African revivals in the first half of the twentieth century featured laughing amid the rapture of the emotional services. It may be that these conflicted students were simply imitating what they had witnessed at their missionary schools or during revival meetings. This is how the modern-day "Laughing Revival" began in North America.

During the 1990s, fits of laughing and weeping became common in parts of the United States and Canada at revival meetings of the Ontario-based Toronto Blessing. The Holy Laugh Movement or Laughing Revival then spread around the world and continues today. The man credited with sparking the movement, Rodney Howard-Browne, arrived in Toronto after practicing in Africa, where he served with the World Faith Movement. One attendee describes his experience with the Toronto Blessing: "Soon, people were falling down like nine-pins, and there was much holy laughter, shaking, and other manifestations.... One could hardly see the carpet for all of the bodies laying thereon! ... My pastor didn't even touch me ... and I was on that ground in no time at all! And for the first time ever, holy laughter came over me, and I was laughing, and shaking, and laughing, and shaking, and laughing ... for at least 30 minutes, maybe for an hour!!!"[27] Like the laughing mania in Africa, symptoms can last intermittently for days. In his video *The Coming Revival*, Howard-Browne describes an episode involving a man who became intoxicated with the Holy Spirit "and laughed uncontrollably for 3 days."[28]

During Toronto Blessing revivals, members made animal noises: barking, roaring, meowing, and hooting. Some began cackling like chickens, others chattered like monkeys.[29] The Bible is filled with all manner of livestock, from the guests on Noah's Ark to sheep in the manger and sacrificial lambs, so imitating such creatures is seen as natural. Here is a firsthand account of a service during which people in the congregation were asked to share their testimony with the group:

> The first person ... went to the front, began to speak and after a few sentences fell to the floor roaring and screeching. The leader reassured us that everything was all right. This roaring, he explained, was caused by the Holy Spirit ... it is the roaring of the lion of Judah. This was apparently a common occurrence in their meetings. The speaker concluded his message by telling us that the Holy Spirit was now moving in our midst and anyone who felt any shaking, trembling, or numbness was to understand that those feelings or manifestations were from the Holy Spirit and those who were experiencing those things should raise their hands and a member of their ministry would come and pray with them. Many people began experiencing this uncontrollable shaking of their bodies. Many fell on the floor roaring and screeching. Some were laughing hilariously.[30]

In explaining the animal noises during emotionally charged meetings, many followers consider it to be prophetic, noting that "a man roaring like a lion is God prophesying that He is coming soon as a roaring lion."³¹ This is consistent with scripture suggesting that there would be strange signs near the End Time. A disciple of the Toronto Blessing describes one meeting: "That room sounded like it was a cross between a jungle and farmyard. There were many, many lions roaring, there were bulls bellowing, there were donkeys, there was a cockerel near me, there were all sorts of bird songs.... Everything you could possibly imagine. Every animal you could conceivably imagine you could hear."³² Once you understand the context in which these acts are occurring, they seem less strange.

Clashes of Old and New

Since the 1970s even government schools that do not actively promote religious beliefs in their students have been the scene of hysterical outbreaks of laughter in central and southern Africa. In July 1971, Ugandan psychiatrist Joseph Muhangi, from Mukerere University in Kampala, was sent to examine students who had seemingly gone berserk at their school. Upon his arrival, Muhangi calmly conducted a series of interviews, piecing together what had happened. The outbreak centered on the school's poorest performing student, a twenty-year-old man named Ugee, who was still in the seventh grade. Though his performance was academically abysmal, he was not a troublemaker, being ordinarily shy and quiet. One day, he began laughing at things that did not seem funny. Soon Ugee was making strange grimaces with his face and cryptic hand gestures, as if he was playing a game of charades. Before long, he was ignoring his teachers and stopped grooming himself. As a result, his appearance became unseemly, he began to use vulgar language, he stopped wearing his school uniform, and he wandered aimlessly about the school grounds and into the nearby bush.

Though Ugee was a far cry from one who would ordinarily be cast in a leadership role, within days dozens of Ugee's classmates were imitating his actions: laughing, disobeying authority, making strange gestures, grimacing, and disregarding their own hygiene. The school was in chaos. By now some fifty students were involved. Some pupils began to elaborate on the original symptoms, acting in ways that the first student had not: throwing stones, threatening violence and demanding to drink soda. Many reported headaches.

While the other students and teachers could not have known it at the time, Ugee would later be diagnosed with acute schizophrenia and be hospitalized.³³ But what of the others who were apparently not suffering from mental illness? Muhangi noted that for many students the school environment was a place of "chronic anxiety."[34] The cause of the constant stress was obvious even to an outsider. Many of the older students age 16 and up had started school late and were in the same classes with much younger students. Muhangi believed this situation sparked powerful "anxiety at the thought of failure. Secondly, ... where the younger children were achieving better academic results, the less fortunate older children were resentful and ashamed of themselves for doing less well."[35] At the same time, Muhangi identified another reason for stress: the school system had recently introduced new ideas that were often in conflict with the teachings of the students. Some of this frustration at being taught one thing at home and another in school may have incited rebellion, including violence and tossing stones.

Five years later, in May 1976, newspaper headlines in Zambia told of a "mysterious madness" sweeping through a secondary school in the remote village of Mwinilunga in the northwestern corridor. Jikita, seventeen, was sitting in class when her body began to twitch.[36] At the same time she began to laugh. The teacher said that Jikita's eyes looked strange. She began to recite poetry in a loud, gruff voice. Shocked onlookers later said she appeared both confused and euphoric. Soon four more girls began to act in a similar manner. A number of students in other classes, upon seeing the commotion, grew anxious and began to act strangely, running around the school aimlessly. By the end of the day, the six afflicted girls were taken to a nearby hospital for evaluation. That night, more cases appeared, wrenching several girls and boys from their sleep. They too had to be taken to the hospital.

By morning of the second day, it was chaos. A "witch-finder" said the "madness" was the result of contaminated food. Soon the finger of blame was pointing at the cook, and the students were transformed into a torch-bearing mob, intent on burning his house to the ground. Fortunately, he got out of the house just in time and fled for his life as police were called in to restore order. While this was going on, the food tests came back negative. On the third day of the outbreak, the school had to be closed and all of the students were told to go home for two weeks. About 120 girls and six boys were stricken. During the episode, many of the students wandered about in a mental fog. Others were twitching, laughing, and running about.[37] Two psychiatrists at the scene blamed the episode on anxiety caused by the new administration, which was cracking down on rules.[38] When classes resumed, the students had returned to normal.

In June 1993, the laughing mania was back, this time in the small southeast African nation of Malawi. On June 14, one hundred students attending a girls' Catholic boarding school in the country's commercial capital of Blantyre were thrust into the national media spotlight after reportedly going berserk. Some were screaming; others laughed nonstop for long periods. Some were weeping loudly, while others fell to the ground and rolled in the dirt. A number of the girls threatened to do violence to one another and had to be separated. Several wandered about speaking in an unintelligible language. Some complained of a pain in the back of their skulls. Curiously, when school was closed and the students were sent home, the symptoms disappeared. Some refused to eat and wanted to be alone; others showed a strange hypersensitivity to noise. Many claimed unawareness of their bizarre actions. In all, 110 students at Stella Maris Secondary School in Blantyre, about one in five, were affected.[39]

Within days of the outbreak, a team of psychologists arrived on campus, concluding that the key trigger was political tension. Just before the outbreak, the girls had been forced to dance at a ceremony presided over by the country's then-president, Hastings Kamuza Banda. Banda's office always requested their presence whenever there were ceremonies in Blantyre. But this performance was different. The invitation came at a time when the government was under great international pressure to do away with its one-party rule and become democratic. A national referendum would soon be held, in which Malawians would decide on which system to chose. A bitter rift split the country. While the girls had no choice but to perform at the ceremony, they were not looked upon favorably. As their bus was pulling away from Kamuzu Central Stadium, it was met with a hail of stones from supporters of democratic rule. Not long after the girls arrived back at their school, people walked up to the campus gates and began tossing stones, this time warning that if the girls performed again, they would be attacked. It wasn't long before the strange fits broke out. The young girls had found themselves in the middle of a political tug of war. There was no way out. The psychological conflict was overwhelming.[40]

The girls were seething with frustration and anger at the hypocrisy of their being forced to perform. One of the government's new themes was empowerment for women, but the girls were forced to comply with the rigid rules at their traditional Catholic convent school. Tension rose. Later that same day, a 16-year-old girl began to dance and scream while complaining of a terrible headache. The next day, a classmate went into a wild, screaming frenzy. She was taken to the hospital and given Fansidar, a drug used to control malaria symptoms, because it was the only drug in the entire hospital. Needless to say, it did nothing to combat her symptoms, and it was not long before she was again screaming, weeping and withdrawn. Before long, while another girl was quietly studying, she suddenly had a screaming fit. When someone managed to get a hold of the powerful sedative Valium, it had little effect and she continued to exhibit bouts of screaming, interspersed with periods of laughter, through the following day. After these first few cases, roughly fifteen students developed symptoms every day for the next week.[41]

On top of this political stress, the outbreak took place just before final exams. Witchcraft, or *fufu,* is an everyday worry in Malawi, and when the first few students began to act strangely, many of their classmates grew anxious, fearing their friends had been hexed or charmed and that they might be next. Many of the afflicted students and their parents were convinced that with exams looming, some pupils had cast spells in order to steal the brain power of fellow students. Witchcraft in Malawi can be a complex affair. Some felt that the first few students to fall ill could have been the perpetrators: Many Malawians believe that if someone tries to cast a spell on another and the other person anticipates it, it can be reflected back to the person or persons originating it and result in strange behaviors.[42] The school reopened after several weeks, but by then, the laughing mania had spread to two nearby Catholic schools.

Reports of laughing mania continued in parts of Africa. On about March 20, 2000, Okavango Community Junior Secondary School in remote northern Botswana was closed for three weeks after an outbreak involving ninety-three pupils. Some press reports described many students as appearing to be in trances.[43] At nearby primary schools in Gumare, students were stricken with fits of laughing, weeping, and screaming. Some talked ceaselessly for long periods. Others grew violent. Journalist Wene Owino noted, "Afflicted students have caused injuries to their teachers and themselves besides destroying school property."[44] School officials first suspected malaria, but blood tests were free of the parasites. Some villagers attributed the episode to witchcraft and demanded that school officials bring in a traditional healer, but the administrators refused to bow to superstition.[45] Violent acts were a major factor in closing the school, as students threw all manner of dangerous objects at their teachers and classmates. During one meeting between worried parents and school officials, a student pulled out a rifle and began pointing it at the gathering, forcing them to scatter like rats at a pest control convention. Police captured the student before anyone was hurt.[46]

Laughing mania outbursts across Africa highlight the remarkable link between culture, hysteria and distress. These could have fostered racist stereotypes in Europe and North America about Africans being innately prone to superstition. It was one of the reasons used to justify colonial intervention during the nineteenth and twentieth centuries: Clearly, such people were incapable of governing themselves. Of course, nothing could be further from the truth. Poverty, lack of education, and Western missionaries and their tent revivals likely contributed to the states of mind that fostered the laughing mania. Religious beliefs, such as the belief in the constant, watchful eyes of ancestor spirits, may also play a key role promoting stress and anxiety. In recent years, mass hysteria in African schoolchildren has taken other forms, from spirit possession to outbreaks of post-traumatic stress disorder (PTSD). These episodes reflect the remarkable resiliency of the human mind.

Hell on Earth: Rwanda

Sometimes life becomes too painful to bear. During times of war, in the wake of unspeakable acts of cruelty and surrounded by the stench of death, survivors are left with psychological scars they carry with them to their graves. Rwanda in 1994 was just such a place. Half a million people were slaughtered over the course of a few months during ethnic unrest. In April of 1997, some thirty teenage students from the Nyanza Secondary School attended a solemn ceremony for the remains of their murdered relatives. According to Rwandan psychiatrist Athanase Hagengimana and his American counterpart Lawson Wulsin, "They developed acute emotional reactions such as agitation, seeing vivid images of genocide" and continued weeping for more than two days after the ceremony had ended. The grief-stricken children, confused and overcome by emotion, fled the scene. The government quickly ordered the school to close its doors. A similar reaction took place during a later reburial service.[47]

Wulsin and Hagengimana report that in the wake of the killings, an epidemic of mental disorders swept across the countryside. As a result, the psychiatrists estimate that as many as twenty percent of all adults in the country may be suffering from PTSD. "The sudden, overwhelming trauma afflicting most civilians and the persistence of unpredictable threats four years after the 'end' of the war (a period now commonly known as 'the insecurity' in Rwanda) have caused an epidemic of PTSD and related psychiatric disorders," they note. In addition, there has been a dramatic spike in the number of individuals with relatively minor physical complaints experiencing conversion disorder. In one case cited, a soldier returned from the front lines after suffering sudden hearing loss, paralysis to his right side, and inability to use his trigger or index finger. In another instance, an unexplained loss of hearing beset a soldier whose parents and siblings were killed in the genocide in January of 1998. Tests of his ear by an expert revealed that his ear was in perfect functioning order. This is not uncommon in cases of trauma and hysteria. It is as if the mind is protecting itself from unspeakable horrors by shutting down the ability to hear.[48] It is also not uncommon in such cases for hysterical blindness or paralysis to occur. Such problems are usually temporary and function eventually returns.

Spirit Possession Among Nigerian Schoolgirls

In 1996, UCLA anthropologist Conerly Casey was in central West Africa when he came upon an outbreak of mass hysteria. The previous December, five girls attending a secondary school in Kano, Nigeria, had been at a dance party when an elderly woman named Sumbuka appeared, asking them to break up the festivities. They swore at her and told her to go away. The woman grew furious, vowing revenge. Pointing toward the girls, she said that they would be cursed for the rest of their lives, then left.[49]

In the following days the girls began to behave in a strange manner, "foaming at the mouth and holding their arms like Inna," a spirit blamed for causing paralysis. Over several weeks, similar symptoms spread to a whopping six hundred girls at secondary schools in the country. In addition to experiencing temporary paralysis, the girls would scream, cry and break into "spontaneous dancing which resembled that performed in Indian masala film." Masala films usually involve plots that emphasize the glories of romantic love, although arranged marriages remain common in India. A similar situation occurs in Nigeria. Curiously, only girls of a single ethnic background — the Hausa — were stricken, and of these, only those with families originating in Kano. This was said to have been the first time spontaneous dancing such as that featured in the Indian masala films was seen by the Hausa. Local explanations for the hysteria included witchcraft and spirit possession. During interviews with Islamic scholar-healers, Casey was told that the cause of the mysterious behaviors was either an invasion of foreign spirits from places like India "or new configurations of known spirits and witches."[50]

Casey set out to answer this question: Why did the hysteria affect only Muslim Hausa secondary-school girls? Part of the explanation may lie in the mental conflict between pressure to conform to local traditions and the desire to follow outside ways. Their desire to emulate foreign ways was a source of great stress. On the one hand, the Indian movies they were watching promoted romantic love. On the other hand, most of these same girls were likely to have an arranged marriage. To make matters worse, the liberal girls who watched the Indian dancing movies were stereotyped by school and religious authorities as criminals, drug abusers, and sexually promiscuous. All of this tension was too great. Hysteria was the result.

The outbreaks of strange behavior also coincided with an epidemic of meningitis that spread across northern Nigeria from November 1995 to May 1996. The outbreak was terrifying, killing thousands and sickening many more. The government responded with a massive inoculation campaign in hopes of immunizing each and every person in the Kano metropolitan area—six million in all. As more and more schoolgirls were stricken during the winter of 1995, stories of spirit possession and witchcraft abounded. It was during this time that many inhabitants began to tell stories about Sumbuka, the old woman who was said to wander through Muslim areas of the city, spreading both the girls' hysteria and meningitis. Soon many locals were placing ashes in front of their homes to keep the evil woman away. According to one account, a police officer had killed the woman just outside the city. During this same period, rumors of teleportation began to circulate through the city. People told stories of having entered taxis or buses that took them to such far off places as Cairo, New Delhi, and Moscow, or of hearing such destinations being called out during their trip.[51]

One religious official blamed the possession attacks on the girls, claiming they were the result of impure lifestyles such as their taste in music: "They listened to music and some sounds and we heard that the source of their illness, Sumbuka, was that the girls were celebrating their success on their qualifying exams so they stayed late in the night beating drums and dancing. These are all what attracts the attention of the spirits, so they came and joined the girls."[52]

An Islamic Hausa teen allowed Casey to read his diary, which was filled with examples of the contradictions faced by the youths, especially their exposure to the media and the guilt and confusion that it generates: "I have the Devil's alter-nature in front of me now.... I am going to listen to the music I like, hoping that it will not be a source of my ruin. It seems to be a paradox, but for the meantime, it seems, I can't help it. Yes, I stopped watching TV, reading some novels. But some of these things give one more experience in life. There is no point in stopping these when the inner self yearns for them."[53]

The Collegiate Life of Demons

The campus of St. John's College, a church boarding school in Umtata, Grahamstown, is situated along the beautiful eastern cape of

South Africa. On May 21, 1999, more than seven hundred students were attending a morning prayer service when a scream pierced the reverie and a single female student collapsed. Within minutes, at least fifty other students lay on the ground. One authority described the scene as "complete pandemonium."[54] What had been a quiet church service assumed the look of a battlefield. Ambulances could not reach the scene quickly enough, so students and teachers began using private cars to transport the stricken girls to local clinics and the nearby hospital. When the girls arrived, puzzled doctors could find nothing wrong. Told of the circumstances of the mass collapse, a diagnosis of hysteria seemed evident and the students were quickly discharged. But the next morning at another prayer service, once again scores of girls began to scream and collapse. This time even more students were affected, some going into fits of jerking, others convulsing. As the incident had begun while the school chaplain was offering prayers, he and other priests tried to exorcise the girls' "demons" by sprinkling them with holy water, but without success.

These fits persisted throughout the month of August and affected more than a hundred students. During the outbreaks some went into trance states and suffered bouts of screaming, crying, and writhing. Some of the girls foamed at the mouth. Although the school was co-educational, with a population of about fourteen hundred students, only girls were affected. The episode forced the school to temporarily close. The symptoms first appeared during an examination period. The fits were especially intense during prayer time and at large gatherings.[55] According to the school chaplain, Reverend Ebenezer Ntali, "Many girls began to scream or run wildly and most collapsed as their legs became wobbly. They were biting on their teeth, foaming at the mouth and experiencing stomach cramps that caused huge lumps just below their chests. There was also the twitching and jerking of their bodies as if they had suffered epileptic seizures, while their eyes rolled backwards until only the whites were visible."[56] Ntali expressed his view that the girls were suffering from demon possession, known locally as *amafufunyana*.

In an attempt to banish the demons, Ntali conducted a mass exorcism on June 9. His weapons were prayer, incense, holy water, and oil. His stated goal was to get the girls to praise Jesus. Once again, this measure failed. Following the exorcism, at least thirty-two of the girls were hospitalized with what medical personnel described as states of extreme hysteria.[57] Many reported terrific headaches. Bongeka Bulo, a nineteen-year-old student who experienced some relief courtesy of the priest's ministrations, recounted, "Many pupils also complained of excruciating headaches, blindness and memory loss. The pain was terrible and it felt as if something from inside my head was going to fall out. But it all stopped once the priest started praying for us." Makhosi Majozi, sixteen, said she could recall only being stricken with a headache followed by the sudden loss of sight: "I have no recollection of what happened next and when I awoke I was in hospital."[58] According to Professor Felicity Edwards of the Department of Religion and Theology at Rhodes University in Cape Town, the incident was likely caused by anxieties associated with rapid social change, such as the shift "from a peasant society to a competitive and confusing western culture."[59]

During their fits of screaming and fainting, many of the girls rolled their bodies on the ground. Some reported seeing visions. Headache and dizziness were also common. Some banged their heads against various objects. Once the attack was over, most of the girls appeared to be perfectly normal. Others seemed to be confused; some said they could not recall their ordeal. Investigators identified several possible factors contributing to extreme stress on the campus. These included exam stress, dissatisfaction with hostel life, and rumors of satanic practices. In the latter case, "there was a church nearby the school where the students and members of the community believed that satanism was being practiced."[60]

Attacks by Ghosts and Goblins

In 2000, anxiety and hysteria in African classrooms took a different form as a series of ghost attacks were reported at primary and secondary schools across Kenya. Rural schools were especially hard hit. At the Kathuma Primary School in the Kitui district, evil spirits reportedly invaded the school and tried to strangle students, who experienced breathing difficulties.[61] At the Kambaa school it was claimed that ghosts had thrown stones onto the hostel roof during the night. Many girls believed a staff member was responsible for conjuring the ghosts up. As usual, the episode forced school officials to temporarily close their doors and send the students home. The co-educational Gitogo secondary school was temporarily closed in mid–July after several boys claimed to have been attacked by ghosts in their hostel. The fear climaxed in a stampede, and some students required hospital treatment.

The use of so-called ghost-busters is common in rural areas to get rid of evil spirits, with some schools even holding fund-raisers to collect money to hire witchdoctors. After a series of ghost attacks at the Itokela Girls' Secondary School in early June of 2000, a Kenyan businessman reportedly confessed to triggering the episode by sending ghosts to the school. He was arrested after many of the girls showed up at the district commissioner's office and asking that something be done. The ghosts reportedly relished pushing the girls to the ground. The businessman's motive was said to have been to avenge his daughter, who had been so unhappy with her treatment at the school that she eventually left. The man ultimately agreed to pay for the spirits to be exorcised from the grounds.[62]

A similar scare was reported in 2001. Concerned by the ongoing presence of a "mysterious illness" striking down students, the Loreto Day Secondary School in Kenya was closed in early October amid a devil-worship scare. The mood at the Catholic school was tense. The school's closing spread fear to the neighboring Loreto-Matunda Secondary School. Uasin Gishu district education officer Julius Bissem said it was imperative to close the school in an effort to reduce the level of stress among students "following claims that some students were engaged in devil worship." When interviewed by journalists in Eldoret town, students said that the problems had begun to surface shortly after the school reopened for the new term. Many students were upset that school officials had decided to admit several Form Three students who had been suspended for allegedly practicing devil worship. "Since we came back, ghosts have been visiting our school," said one of the disgruntled kids, "making students develop mysterious diseases and more than 100 than have been admitted in hospitals."[63]

Not long before officials decided to temporarily close the facility, there were reports that a local prophet was predicting that the building would be destroyed by a fire. By now tension at the school was reaching a crescendo. There were also rumors that the school was "being protected against the Holy Spirit by an angel Rael."[64] The outbreak occurred amid a backdrop of widespread fears within the region that devil-worship was a major problem in many schools.

Goblin Scares in Zimbabwe and Ethiopia

In July 2002 a phantom goblin scare swept through the St. Mark's Secondary School in Mhondoro, Zimbabwe. The headmaster of the Anglican church school fled the campus and hid out amid claims by parents that he was in control of tiny creatures that were sexually harassing female pupils and teachers.[65] The charges forced the school's temporary closure; the community was in an uproar over the accusations and angry parents turned up at the school, trying to see the headmaster.

Students and teachers told journalists that they had been beaten by invisible objects. At least 30 students said they had been attacked. One teacher, who did not want to be identified for fear of being victimized, said that some of the students were possessed by evil spirits: "I witnessed one incident when a student went into a trance.... He was demanding meat, threatening that after finishing with the students, the spirits would attack the teachers next. We are living in fear here." The outbreak coincided with mid-term exams.[66]

With the headmaster in exile, the assistant principal suddenly found himself having to deal with irate parents. He referred all inquiries to the Ministry of Education, Sports and Culture, and issued a statement that said, "Everything is now back to normal," hoping to calm the community unrest. But he reportedly kept his distance from the school in an effort to avoid being cornered by hostile parents; his words were not taken seriously — and the situation was still far from normal.[67]

The first signs of trouble had begun six weeks earlier when some students claimed that "mysterious beings" were harassing them in their hostels at night. The creatures were known as *zvikwambo* and *mubobobo* in Shona, and *tokoloshe* in Zulu.[68] According to one student, "About 30 students have been victims of the attacks and we can't bear spending another night at this haunted place.... A friend of mine was bitten on the arm after she wrestled with a ghost which wanted to sleep with her."[69] Some teachers also claimed they were being sexually assaulted at night by strange creatures. A written statement issued by some of the teachers read in part, "Sometimes we get up in the morning to find the bedding mysteriously wet and we suspect foul play."[70]

During September 2002 another "mysterious hysteria" swept through the co-educational Moleli High School, operated by the Methodist Church in rural Msengezi, southeastern Africa. Symptoms included shaking of the hands, legs, and shoulders, and "sleepwalking." Some students wandered about in a daze, oblivious to the world around them. Some victims appeared to be possessed by spirits and seemed to be hallucinating. The outbreak began on Saturday, September 7, when the first three pupils were affected. Five more cases appeared the next day. By Monday, twenty-one students were afflicted, and the total would eventually reach twenty-four. Only female students, most from Form One and Form Two were involved.[71] According to school officials, concerned parents withdrew fourteen of those exhibiting symptoms from the school.

One student was admitted to the Kutama Mission Hospital in Zvimba after becoming violent. Doctors gave her a sedative to calm her, and she was soon withdrawn from the school by her parents. Some worried parents were said to be consulting with both physicians and prophets. For the other affected girls, doctors prescribed Phenobarbital and painkillers. This practice upset some psychiatrists, who complained that it was inappropriate without first conducting a thorough history of the students. One surprising aspect of the case was the absence of symptoms once the students returned to their homes and its reappearance once they returned to the premises. A possible contributing factor was the rumor circulating at the time that the spirits of twenty-two students who had drowned on Lake Chivero in a 1995 boat accident were haunting the girls' hostel. It was believed that their spirits were targeting those affected. Amid the ghost stories, girls claimed to hear voices at night, as well as the sounds of footsteps and a screaming child.

Ms. Kwadzanai Nyanungo, the chief education psychologist from the Ministry of Education, Sport and Culture, says the episode was triggered by "rumours and fear." She says that every year her department learned of one or two cases somewhere in the country, explaining that part of the blame lies with the teaching staff for failing to address rumors in a timely manner. According to Nyanungo, "Schools should take care of the kids and parents must watch their kids and assist them to get confidence."[72]

However, the secretary-general of the Zimbabwe National Traditional Healers' Association, Dr. Peter Sibanda, disagrees with the government's approach, noting that a similar outbreak of hysteria at the school about a decade earlier was successfully handled using native healers. Sibanda says an exorcist who was sent to the school had learned that a disgruntled former employee who was not being paid his pension had apparently cast a spell. He said the hysteria stopped after locals were summoned "to discipline the man." It is Sibanda's belief that some small-scale farmers in the vicinity of Msengezi harbored supernatural creatures known as *tokoloshis*, which may have been responsible for the school hysteria: "If these [beings] lack socialisation, they go out to prey on females in the vicinity, in this case girls at Moleli High School." Sibanda said the outbreak could be quelled if, with the community's consent, a native healer was sent to the school to capture the *tokoloshis*.[73]

"Ghost Attack" in Ethiopia

We have learned of a great many cases in which it appears that girls are more susceptible to hysteria attacks than boys, but there have been instances in which mass hysteria has occurred exclusively in males. During the first week of February 2003 at Addis Ababa University in Ethiopia, at least 36 male students fainted in the wake of concern over the unexplained deaths of two fellow students the previous week. Rumors circulated that the pair had been poisoned. According to the hospital authorities where the fainting students were taken, "All the students complained of being poisoned, but it could not find any evidence of this." All tests were negative, including X-rays and analysis of urine, blood, and stool. While some students complained of weakness, hospital physicians noted that "all their vital signs were normal." Fearing the further spread of mass hysteria, university officials canceled exams.[74]

Ugandan Running Sickness

A case reminiscent of the laughing mania occurred in the village of Kayayimba, Uganda, in July 2002. Symptoms included running, perceived demon possession, visions, and various aches and pains. Some 30 people were affected, mostly female. At one primary school, 18 stricken students removed all of their clothing and began screaming and committing acts of violence. One young woman, Annette Muhairwe, said, "All of a sudden, I felt pain in the chest. My hand was aching and heavy. Sometimes, I could see snakes, then fire, but I could not touch them. Even if I tried to show other people, they could not see these things."[75]

According to Dr. M. Kizito, health director for the Kiboga district, the underlying stress triggering the hysteria was an epidemic of cerebral malaria that was sweeping through the area. According to psychologist Julius Kayiira, the intense stress triggered mass suggestibility that was incubated in an environment of fear and witchcraft beliefs: "It is a kind of collective consciousness. Something unusual happens and attracts people's attention, then people behave that way because of fear. And that fear develops because of what they believe in."[76]

Demons and Witches in Uganda

Reports of demon attacks on Ugandan school students have become common in recent times. Between May and July 2004, Bisika Primary was closed after students began acting strangely, speaking in a rapid, incoherent manner while running around the school grounds. Some shook violently as if given an electric shock; others stripped their clothes off and foamed at the mouth. In order to stop their children from wandering off too far, some parents resorted to tying them to pegs with ropes. Those affected were under age 12 in grades 4 to 7. The outbreak resulted in the arrest of a local witchdoctor, Isma Sserunkuuma, who had been accused by parents of conjuring up the demons. A well-known traditional healer, Ben Ggulu, was called in to rid the school of the demons, using chants, herbs and a cow's horn. As to why none of the male students were affected, locals speculated that the demons were only interested in virgin girls.[77]

Four years later scores of parents rushed to the Sir Tito Winyi Primary School in the Hoima District after reports that over 100 students had gone berserk. Head teacher Vincent Kitende described the scene as baffling and out of control: "The situation is bad. About 100 pupils are totally mad. They are chasing everybody including teachers and fellow pupils, throwing stones, banging doors and windows. The situation is difficult to explain." It happened during the first days of term for the new school year. Kitende said that a similar outbreak at the school during the previous year had affected 210 pupils. That incident had resulted in the arrest of four residents, who were charged with casting spells on the school. Curiously, each of the suspects had been involved in a land dispute with the school.[78] The 2008 episode also involved a property dispute, as locals were blaming a well-known land owner for triggering the "attacks." According to the newspaper *New Vision*, the outbreak began when a female student "started barking like a dog. Then, others started shouting and pressing their stomachs, saying they felt a burning sensation in their stomachs. Children, both boys and girls, dashed out of their classes. Many were crying. Some fell to the ground and crawled. Others threw stones at people who were rushing to the scene." In order to calm the chaos, teachers and other adults tied up the wayward students and brought them to church, where prayers were offered and they soon recovered. Reporter Pascal Kwesiga went to the school and noted a common belief in both students and parents that a land dispute was the cause. He writes: "As the saying goes, when two elephants fight, it is the grass that suffers. Juliet Katusabe and Lillian Kwikiriza had just begun the new school term last week when they were hit by severe headaches. Then came sharp pain in their stomachs. And then, darkness. Residents believe the children were attacked by demons, resulting from the land wrangles in Hoima District."[79]

In October 2010, another witchcraft scare prompted the closure of Nakasongola Junior Academy in the town of Migeera after an escalation in the number of "spirit attacks" at the school. At least 26 students, out of a total enrollment of 2,000, were taken to the local health center for treatment of "physical injuries."[80] In March of the following year, police rushed to the Kitebi Primary School in the Rubaga Division after a group of nearly 100 students attempted to kill a teacher whom they had accused of practicing witchcraft. The school had to be closed to restore calm. According to the deputy headmistress, Sarah Namutebi, the incident was triggered when a student began shouting that a teacher named Naome Wandera, wife of the head teacher, had concealed magical charms in the compound. The situation soon spiraled out of control. Police managed to rescue the woman, who was transferred to a police station outside of the area for her own safety.[81] In an effort to rid the school of the evil spirits, a series of rituals were conducted by witchdoctors. Two goats, one cow, a pair of chickens and six pigeons were apparently sacrificed during the rituals. An angry mob of students and residents went to Naome's home, broke down the door and searched inside for evidence of witchcraft. Several suspicious items were removed. All of her belongings were reportedly taken by the group, leaving her with nothing.[82]

Elizabeth Ritchie observes that it seems more than a coincidence that these demon attacks "often occur in schools where there is existing conflict within the local community. It is not uncommon, for example, for evil spirits to 'attack' pupils when there are property disputes involving school land. Quite conveniently, they may attack when the school community is in the process of being evicted by an unscrupulous developer." This upsurge in stress, coupled with the widespread belief in ancestor spirits, may channel the form that these hysteria outbreaks take.[83] It is worth noting that many accusations of witchcraft in Salem, Massachusetts, during the 1690s appear to have stemmed from land disputes, and the labeling of residents as witches may have been a way of settling old scores.[84]

Ugandan journalist James Onen believes that the belief in demons is consistent with the worldview of the typical Ugandan: "The majority, being conservative Christians, are quite happy to accept that it must be evil spirits that are the cause of the strange behaviour of the children in these schools. Add to this the fact that in addition to their conservative Christianity, many whole-heartedly embrace the traditional African spiritual world-view, which includes a belief in the existence of ancestral spirits, who require continuous appeasement in order for good fortune to prevail," he says.[85]

Starting in 2009, a series of demonic "attacks" were reported in students attending the Kitebi Primary School in Uganda. The attacks reached a crisis in early 2011. Reporter Elizabeth Namazzi managed to interview a parent of one of the students. The woman said that her granddaughter, who had become possessed by demons at the school, was still being kept away from the grounds. On the verge of bursting into tears, she recalls the recent events at the "cursed school" and a major folk theory for what was causing it. She said that it was thought that head teacher Godfrey Senfuma was in love with fellow teacher Naomi Wandera and a secretary, and that Wandera had become jealous of the secretary and placed charms around the school grounds to harm her. It is claimed that Mr. Senfuma then angered the spirits when he failed to follow the instruction of a witchdoctor as he was apparently trying to defuse the conflict. Curiously, the school was losing money because it was being forced to hire so many native healers to get rid of the spirits. The top native healer in the area, Sylvia Namutebi (aka Mama Fina), was refusing to go to the aid of the students because the school was unwilling to meet her asking price.[86]

During late September 2011, the Mugabi Primary School in Hoima was in crisis following another outbreak of "demonic attacks" that prompted a mass exodus of teachers from the school. Soon after, the students also fled, fearing more supernatural attacks. This placed tremendous pressure on head teacher Lydia Tusingwire, who was left to handle the panic. During a public meeting aimed at addressing the situation, journalist John Kibego reported that people began shouting and collapsing to the ground from "demonic attacks." One of those stricken was Ms. Tusingwire.

After she collapsed, some residents began chasing a prominent, elderly gentleman named Yason Bagonza, who was widely seen as the chief suspect. He was said to have "owned" the demons responsible. Police were forced to fire their weapons into the air to disperse the crowd. They took Mr. Bagonza and a colleague into custody. Bagonza was rumoured to have been interested in acquiring the school's land.[87] In blaming the attacks on Bagonza, one parent remarked: "My child in P. 7 was very bright but she has become dense because of demon possessions. Whenever she is prayed for, she demands to be taken to Yason [Bagonza]. They must be evicted." Bagonza reportedly had been evicted from a nearby village a decade earlier for practicing witchcraft.[88]

Bewitched: "Love Madness" in South Africa

We have saved perhaps the strangest episode of behavior in an African school for last. One of the most striking examples of the power of culture on human behavior is the casting of "love spells" in some South African schools. Love evokes powerful, sometimes contradictory, emotions. Culture can channel those emotions in unusual ways. This is especially true during adolescence. When turned down for a date by a girl, boys from many Western countries will often feel mild embarrassment or depression, which wears off within a few hours or days. But not so in parts of South

Africa. There, where the existence of witchcraft and the casting of spells is taken for granted, some boys refuse to take no for an answer. Instead, they visit a native healer who specializes in concocting love potions. In some parts of the country, the making of these potions is big business and is taken very seriously. In many parts of Africa, witchcraft and the use of spells and charms are unquestioned realities of everyday life. As a result, many people walk around in a constant state of anxiety, fearing that they may be the next victims of a witch's hex — and they may fall head over heels in love with someone whom at present they cannot stand.

In portions of South Africa, especially the region encompassing Natal, the eastern cape, and Zululand, it has long been a common practice for schoolboys who have been rebuffed in their attempts to date or marry a girl to consult a healer to intervene magically and change the girl's mind. Girls who have turned away boys begin to fear that they may be the subject of a love spell placed on them by a disgruntled suitor conspiring with a native healer. In the wake of concerns that she may be the subject of magical warfare, over the course of weeks or months the tension between the girl and her friends builds. Suddenly, she experiences what can be described as bewitchment hysteria. In these regions, such reactions are common among schoolgirls. Stories of girls "charming" boys are unheard of; it is always the other way around. As early as 1900, there were many accounts of South African students being stricken with episodes of strange behavior known as *umhayizo*. It usually begins with fits of crying, hyperactivity, and the irresistible urge to run. It is commonly believed that victims are being pulled like a magnet toward their intended lover. Most girls eventually pass out from the mental stress. Historian Julie Parle and anthropologist Fiona Scorgie note the pattern: "Teaching activities are regularly interrupted by the sound of high-pitched wailing, classroom doors being flung open and the sight of at least one girl running out into the courtyard, screaming and cradling her head in her arms. Usually, she is soon followed by others, for the *umhayizo* is apparently 'infectious': one girl's screaming sets off others."[89]

Making Sense of It All

Hysteria outbreaks in African schools may seem alien to observers in Europe and North America. The recipe for outbursts is stress and belief systems that include the unquestioned reality of witches, ghosts and ancestor spirits. Yet we do a serious injustice to these peoples by underestimating the influence of the culture and context of their behaviors. When faced with overwhelming, unrelenting stress, the human mind finds creative and unexpected ways to adapt to its plight given its unique view of the world. In Western countries, hysteria epidemics are dominated by overbreathing, nausea, headache, and fainting, often in episodes triggered by the detection of strange odors that turn out to be harmless. Such outbreaks and their symptoms are rare in Africa. Conversely, outbreaks of laughing, ghost attacks, and spirit possession are rare in Western countries today.

It is a mistake to use Western frames of reference to analyze non–Western behaviors.[90] African beliefs about the nature of the world are so radically different from those in Europe and North America that they seem abnormal and bizarre. Africans who believe in ancestor worship talk to their dead relatives every day. To them the existence of these ancestors is real. It is no wonder that social delusions and mass hysterias in African students involve the belief that the ancestors are unhappy. Far from illustrating the primitive and irrational side of humanity, these episodes highlight the remarkable diversity of human beliefs. No less remarkable is the impact the beliefs can have in fostering outbreaks of mass hysteria and social delusions. The episodes are cries for help, attempts to relieve stress. Part ritual, part hysteria, they are culturally acceptable, if sometimes shocking, ways to resolve problems created by a clash of cultures—the East and the West—and of generations—the young and the old. They may seem crude and bizarre, but are often effective in bringing about much needed change by signaling to the wider community that something is amiss.

CHAPTER 6

The Meowing Schoolgirls of Fiji
Accounts from the Islands

> We are all tattooed in our cradles with the beliefs of our tribe; the record may seem superficial, but it is indelible. You cannot educate a man wholly out of superstitious fears which were implanted in his imagination, no matter how utterly his reason may reject them.— Oliver Wendell Holmes Jr.[1]

In 1624, the English poet John Donne wrote, "No man is an island, entire of itself." These words are even more true today than in Donne's day. Island cultures—misty, romantic, exotic, and remote—are known for harboring extraordinary customs and beliefs, sheltering their inhabitants from the hustle and bustle of the ever-changing outside world. For centuries the ocean served as a moat against invasion, either from troops of soldiers or troupes of tourists—for cultural invasions have been nearly as devastating as military ones. Yet during the nineteenth and twentieth centuries, no place remained untouched by the hand of civilization. The inevitable contact with outsiders brought new ideas that were often in conflict with native beliefs. In many cases, native groups had lived for hundreds or even thousands of years with little change to their daily routines—then, within a generation, everything changed. The arrival of multinational corporations and a cash economy often meant the locals no longer had to hunt or gather or tend to animals or gardens. Processed foods became widely available. Access to new drugs brought about miraculous cures—and new addictions. Schools with books touting Western practices and beliefs such as monogamy, Christianity, and democracy trapped students in a conflicted, twilight world that was neither Western nor native. The result was an outbreak of strange mental afflictions. Nowhere was the battleground between the old and the new more evident than in island schools. They were the front lines in the war of ideas between island ways and the outside world.

New Guinea Nursing Madness

Papua New Guinea is the island that time forgot. Its steamy jungles are home to the most exotic tribes on earth to a Western eye. Over the past two centuries, this Pacific island has gone from the Stone Age to the Computer Age with the clearing of airstrips, the arrival of cargo ships, the building of missionary schools, and the Japanese invasion during World War II. But this rapid transition from the old to the new has taken a toll on the country's youth.

An outbreak of hysteria at the Australian nursing school in Telefomin, a village in the rustic highlands of western Papua, began with a terrific headache. It was February 22, 1973. Ara, a twenty-year-old graduate of the local mission nursing school, was working at the school clinic when she was overcome by a strange head pain.[2] Her stomach began to churn and she felt like vomiting. Her arms and legs started to shake wildly. Ara was in the right place to be sick, and her nursing colleagues knew exactly what to do. She was rushed to the hospital and given a battery of tests.

The doctors checked Ara for a variety of ailments. Every test was negative and she was released, but the fits continued. During these spells, she grew confused, started shaking, and passed out. Later she could not recall any of the events during her seizure. Ara's fits "made a deep impression on those closest to her — the nurses, for she was the most senior girl in the school, and greatly liked."[3] This was but the first of a series of strange maladies to baffle residents of the region from 1973 through 1974.

On October 21 the strange malady spread. The second victim was Ferah, a fifteen-year-old girl from the local primary school. Ferah knew Ara and had seen her go into her fits. On that day, Ferah was walking home when she was overcome by a headache. She grew confused, was struck deaf, and felt a wave of cold sweep through her. She began striking at others with her fists, throwing stones, and lunging with sticks until bystanders were able to subdue her. No one thought to summon a doctor or even a psychiatrist. Instead, her friends took her to a witchdoctor, who tried to exorcise the evil spirits that were thought to be controlling her. The exorcism failed. Only then was she taken to the local health center, where a twelve-year-old girl named Karolina was being treated for a sprained knee. She watched with curiosity as Ferah was brought in, fussing and flailing about. As Karolina left for home she too began to complain of a headache and confusion. Her eyes had a strange, wild look. Karolina grabbed a stick and started whacking bystanders and had to be dragged, kicking and screaming, back to the health center. For two days she lay in a hospital bed without uttering a word, occasionally striking out, before her father brought her home, where an exorcism was held to cast out the bad spirits.

Over the next few weeks, more and more students were stricken. By November 10, the toll was sixteen girls. The pattern was similar, beginning with *ai raum* (feeling faint), and *tingting faul* (mental confusion), then *hed i pen* (headache). Some reported feeling drowsy (*hed i hevi*). Many said they felt a sudden chill and were struck deaf. In addition to partial amnesia, some became unsteady on their feet, teetering about, while others toppled over.

To most of the girls and their parents, the cause of the strange illness was obvious: spirits of their ancestors (*usong*) or wandering bush spirits (*magarini*) had been offended. Perhaps someone had said or done something to outrage a dead relative. Perhaps one of the students had trespassed onto the territory of the bush spirits. Something had to be done to right the wrong, so exorcism ceremonies were held for most of the girls.

In Ferah's case, the day she was stricken she had been playing basketball at school when a snake slithered across the court. Instinctively, she hurled the ball at it in hopes of killing it. Realizing that it may have been a bush spirit, she tried reviving it with water, but it was too late. It was then that she was stricken. The snake encounter and the conflict between the liberal customs of the school and those of the elders may have been what tipped her over the edge. An exorcism was held that night. To appease both the bush spirits and the ancestors, a pig was slaughtered and the spirits were ordered to leave her body. Another girl — Delunga — didn't get off so easily: During her exorcism, a pig was tied to her wrist. The animal was then shot with a hail of arrows and chopped up. Its liver was ripped out, cooked and given to the poor girl to eat. It is hard to imagine this ceremony would reduce her stress level. Some older men blamed the outbreak on students who ignored female taboos. For instance, women are not allowed to eat many types of bananas and taro roots and certain kinds of game. The spirits were supposedly angry because women were eating these forbidden foods.[1]

Anthropologist Stephen Frankel talked with many of those stricken and saw many fits firsthand, noting that many girls became violent: "Running was common, and attacks were made using any handy objects as weapons; they chose sticks and stones or just fists and feet, but never knives or arrows." Yet something was odd. Frankel noted that the violence "was never indiscriminate despite their apparent loss of conscious control; they attacked close relatives, contemporaries and children most frequently, and avoided authority figures. They inflicted no serious injuries." While some girls shouted verbal abuse, most were silent when they attacked, operating in stealth mode. After being restrained, most of the girls returned to normal within several hours, though two were disturbed for up to two weeks. Weeping and emotional volatility were prominent features in four others. There was no evidence that anyone had ingested any drug including alcohol, hallucinogenic mushrooms, cannabis, pandanus leaves or betel nut.[5]

In all, nearly two dozen females between the ages of twelve and thirty were stricken. Frankel soon realized that those suffering the worst were the most Westernized. They experienced symptoms for an average of twelve days or longer, compared to just over four days for those who had not been as exposed to Western ways. Tribesmen in that region are infamous for their domination of women. Females are restricted to pastoral duties: tending gardens, animal husbandry, child care, and food preparation. They must adhere to female taboos, and their sex lives are strictly controlled. Marriages are arranged, with little means of redress against abusive or demanding husbands. The women are expected to remain quiet, loyal, and obedient to their husbands. They cannot quarrel with their elders and must keep their frustrations inside. Conflicts between these traditions and Western ideas were evident in the nursing students. In one case, Aranga had married the "wrong" man over the protests of her parents. In January 1973, after constant bickering with her parents, she left her home village to live with her husband, Jonah, in his village. Unfortunately, Jonah left Telefomin in February to attend college at Wewak. It was shortly after his departure Aranga had the first of her fits. She was taken to the Wewak Hospital, near where Jonah was studying, and made a rapid recovery. But when she left for Telefomin again, her fits returned. After a time, she made arrangements to live with her husband at Wewak and her symptoms again disappeared. Frankel thinks Aranga could not handle the pressure and conflict in her life without her husband's presence, support and confidence. Hysteria was the result.[6]

Most marriages in Aranga's village were arranged. But some of the women, especially the more liberal, educated ones like those at the nursing school, were able to choose their own partners. Their freedom came at a heavy price—the wrath and condemnation of friends and relatives for not following the old ways. The mental burden was too much to bear, and the young women developed inner conflicts. Frankel notes that two other affected girls, Terena and Deerna, were trying to avoid marrying the partners that had been chosen for them and were having affairs with other men. These and other women who were stricken with the hysteria were under tremendous pressure from their families to follow their elders' decisions.[7]

One women, Juseh, refused to marry the partner chosen by her elders and instead eloped. Her parents eventually succeeded in poisoning the relationship, but she still refused to marry the man chosen for her. Her life became miserable as a result of her defiance, with one quarrel after another with relatives. During one confrontation, "a stick was thrust into her vagina." The daily barrage of physical and verbal abuse became unbearable and she eventually married the man chosen by her parents.[8]

The "nursing madness" took place at a time of extraordinary tension and strife between the young and old. The elders, who exert strong pressure on young people to conform to traditional island ways, came into conflict with modern Australian ways. Many at the nursing school had grown to like Western lifestyles through their contact with European teachers.[9] While Frankel is confident that hysteria was the main culprit for the strange fits at Telefomin, others are not as sure.

Was It Mushroom Madness?

In October 1954 Australian anthropologist Marie Reay was visiting the Southern Wahgi Valley in the Papua New Guinea Highlands when she saw something extraordinary. At least 30 people from one village were acting strangely. The men ran amok, decorating themselves, grabbing bows and arrows or spears, chasing people around and threatening to kill them. Many young adults and children seemed to react to the goings-on as a game, dodging behind houses and peeping out, at times calling out to those affected, seemingly getting them angry on purpose as if to incite them into doing further violence.[10] The women affected stayed in their huts, going into fits of giggling and recounting both real and fantasized sexual escapades. Many of the women had delusions they were not married.

At first, the explanation seemed simple: The natives had eaten a batch of hallucinogenic mushrooms, resulting in an outbreak of so-called mushroom madness. Reay thought the episode was a way for the locals to get rid of their pent-up troubles and frustrations—what a psychiatrist might term a social catharsis. The bizarre behavior even had a name—(*Komugi Taï,* to the locals)—and was attributed to eating a fungus called *nonda.*[11] While the Kuma eat this fungus year-round, on occasion during the late dry season, the fungus appears to have hallucinogenic properties. Reay observed that eleven males and nineteen females out of a village of three hundred and thirteen began acting strangely.

In 1963 two botanists, Roger Heim of France and R. Gordon Wasson of the United States, went to New Guinea and met Reay, and together they gathered samples of *nonda* that she had identified as being eaten during the "madness." They later determined that the "mushrooms—or at least most of them—do not seem to cause physiological effects leading to madness."[12] As a result, Reay felt the temporary madness she saw was caused by mass hysteria.[13] Based on further analysis, Wasson later speculated that one of the mushrooms eaten by the Kuma (*Beletus manicus*) could produce effects similar to those reported during "mushroom madness."[14] But why only during one time of the year? More recently, Australian botanist Benjamin Thomas has argued that acute nicotine poisoning is to blame. Based on the symptoms described during the "madness" and analysis of local plants, Thomas identifies two types of tobacco commonly eaten by the Kuma during the *Komugi Taï* that could account for the strange behaviors.[15] This hypothesis is supported by Reay's observations that many of the Kuma have been seen chewing and swallowing tobacco during the *Komugi Taï* outbreaks.[16] Thomas also suggests that other forms of "temporary madness" in Papua New Guinea, such as the strange events in Telefomin, could be nicotine poisoning.

The similarities between Thomas's description of acute nicotine poisoning (shivering, altered vision, deafness, confusion, tinnitus, and intermittent aphasia) and the symptoms of "mushroom madness" at Telefomin are striking. Lilliputian hallucinations (named for Lilliput, an imaginary country in Jonathan Swift's novel *Gulliver's Travels*, where everything was tiny) are common during nicotine intoxication. Consider the description of a Kuma man observed by Reay. Exhibiting key features of nicotine poisoning, the man "began to experience Lilliputian hallucinations, seeing bush demons flying about his head. The demons were allegedly buzzing about his head when he heard a strange and terrible noise 'inside his ears' which he interpreted as a bush demon boxing his ears. The onset of the noise was like a clap of thunder, but it stayed with him throughout his attack and, being loud, deafened him to the ordinary sounds like human voices and the grunting of pigs." It wasn't long before he had trouble seeing:

> The disturbance of hearing and eyesight was frightening and confusing. All objects a komugl man saw in front of him while running seemed to him to be rushing towards him.... According to men who had been komugl ... [they] saw human beings simply as moving objects unless they were very close. The

visual sensation of movement in a horizontal direction (like people running or walking) angered him because it irritated his eyes.... His eyes were wild and fierce, with a piercing brightness. They began to travel upward until only the whites were showing. The komugl man had periodic rests from his wild running about.[17]

Even so, such explanations appear to have a social and cultural structuring. Determining which symptoms are the result of psychotropic substances and which behaviors result from social and cultural factors is difficult. Both may play a role.

Evil Spirits Invade a Fijian School

On November 13, 1968, a telephone call to a medical officer at Labasa Hospital on the Fijian island of Vanau Levu told of strange happenings at Qawa Primary School. Racing to the school, he found thirteen girls of Indian heritage acting in unison, as if an outside force was controlling them. They were overbreathing; huffing, puffing, and gasping for air. Some were standing, some sitting; others would slump over, appearing to pass out, then quickly recover.[18] Eight of the girls were sent home while the remaining five were taken to the hospital for a closer examination. Except for a slight fever of 99°F — which could be explained by their exertion — doctors could find nothing wrong. Hours later, they were released to their parents.

Fijian government doctor R.G. Randall went to the school, where he found that the "mysterious illness" had begun with twitching muscles and difficulty breathing in a single pupil in early October. On November 8, two of the girl's classmates were stricken with similar symptoms. The next day, more girls fell ill. Before long, seventeen girls between the ages of twelve and fourteen were twitching and gasping. None of the Indian boys at the school were affected.[19]

The twitching struck only Hindu schoolgirls. Their parents were certain the problem was angry spirits. But why? It seems that a nearby pool had been desecrated and the spirits needed to be appeased. The malady eventually went away, but it took a huge community effort.

Randall was able to trace the outbreak to a twelve-year-old girl named Preta who had a long history of emotional disturbance, including hysterical blackouts and overbreathing. The girl had made many visits to doctors and native healers before the Qawa outbreak.[20]

On November 14 most of the stricken girls were taken to an Indian healer by their parents. Randall requested that they meet with psychiatrist

D.N. Snell at the hospital the next day, but only one pupil showed up. During the meeting she reported feeling "dizzy and strange" and soon "began to over breathe and twitch her hands and arms." Calmly, Dr. Snell soothed her agitation, and she began to calm down and recover. The next day, authorities were able to convince five of the girl's parents to bring them to the hospital. Snell found the girls "sitting on a bench on the hospital verandah. Each was hyperventilating with hands and arms twitching and meowing sounds coming from their throats in perfect chorus and identical pitch. Each was sent off singly, their symptoms subsiding as they left."[21]

By November 25, five more pupils were affected, bringing the total to 18. After Snell's visit the school followed his advice and closed for one week. The symptoms gradually subsided and the school soon reopened. Inwardly skeptical of Snell's advice even while following it, most of the parents remained convinced that the cause of the trouble was a bulldozing accident that had damaged part of a sacred pool near the school playground. The parents believed that the girls were possessed by a supernatural force and it was up to them "to determine which power or spirit (*shaitan*) had been roused and how it should be exorcised."[22]

The girls' parents weren't shy in seeking help and didn't care where it came from as long as it worked. The girls were from the Hindu part of town, but the Hindu healer had failed. Ever practical, they next knocked on the door of a Muslim sorcerer called Amina. She had reputedly acquired powers from the neighboring island of Taveuni. She lived in the nearby village of Bulileka. There she met with seven pupils, and during her healing ceremony, she placed her hand behind the head of each girl and rubbed coconut oil on her throat, all the while telling her to be calm and not worry. "Immediately the hysteria left the girls and they calmed down." The parents breathed a sigh of relief. The ordeal of the spirits tormenting their daughters seemed to be over. But the drama was just starting. Within twenty minutes after they left Amina's compound with their parents, the girls again broke out in twitching and overbreathing. They returned to the compound, believing it to be a holy place of protection. Having failed to keep the spirits away, Amina told school officials that they should approach the Fijian owners of the pool to ask if they would let a Fijian healer conduct a ceremony that would appease the disturbed spirits by presenting them with a *yaqona*, the Fijian national drink. For centuries Fijians have offered this drink in appeasement rituals, believing it would help regain favor from the spirit world.[23] Would educated school officials on Fiji take the advice of an Islamic witchdoctor? Absolutely.

Before long a powerful Fijian chief named Poe was conducting the ceremony, offering *yaqona* to the pool spirits. He explained that the damage was an accident and that those involved were sorry and should be forgiven. After the ceremony, Poe told the girls to go home to their parents but as they left they were again stricken.[24] Exhaustion and frustration set in among the parents, and the girls. They had sought help from three separate native healers, a Hindu, a Muslim, and finally a Fijian. Each had failed. The parents decided to try another Hindu healer, but not just anyone. They called on the great Mara Sirdar, the island's top *pujari*, or "man of prayer," who was known for fire walking. Sirdar worshipped Ganesh, the elephant god. The parents pleaded with him to come to the school and rid their children of the haunting spirits. He agreed.

First he made talismans out of white cloth, filling them with holy ash and chopped margosa leaves. Tying them together with yellow cotton string, he took the talismans and went straight to the school, where he checked the grounds in an effort to detect the evil spirits. He said the place was clean and ordered two of his aids to get the girls and bring them there. The girls had been staying at Amina's compound because they felt it offered protection. As soon as they left the compound, the twitching and breathing fits came back. Mara Sirdar's assistants managed to calm the girls by placing a dot or *bhabut* on the center of their foreheads. The girls were taken to the school.

Mara Sirdar again called on Ganesh to help the girls. He told them not to be afraid and walked over to each one, placing a talisman around each of their necks. Walking the girls to the holy pool, he burned camphor at the pool-side, offered the spirits milk, then poured *yaqona* at spots around the pool. He called out to the pool spirits, asking for forgiveness, apologizing for the bulldozing of the stone. He tried to instill confidence in the girls, noting that they had to believe in order for the ceremony to work. He told the girls that since the rites had been conducted, "the spirits had been appeased. There was therefore no reason why the girls' affliction should continue and so they had nothing further to fear from the spirits."[25] To be certain, he ordered a great *Puja* ceremony to be held the following Sunday at the school. When the day came, some of his followers prepared a holy area. They cut the grass, spread cow dung, and dug a pit in the middle, into which they placed mango twigs to be used for a sacred fire.

To an outsider, the ceremony might have seemed like mumbo-jumbo, but to the girls it had the real power to heal them. Said an observer: "All those girls who participated in these ceremonies apparently recovered. The only girl who was treated exclusively with Western medicine apparently did not." When school resumed the following day, five of the original girls got nervous and began to overbreathe. Two were sent home. After that day the school fits never recurred, though Preta, the "trigger girl," was recuperating at home.[26]

The case of the Qawa schoolgirls illustrates how people of diverse backgrounds, living as neighbors, can resolve problems. Indian and Fijian residents "combined their beliefs and rituals to appease the spirits and as far as they were concerned, to cause the girls to recover and to remove the troubles from the school and to prevent further troubles from occurring."[27] The episode appears to be a case of motor hysteria triggered by the buildup of anxiety in those who saw the first girl stricken, compounded by the belief that disturbed spirits were possessing the girls as revenge for the desecration of a swimming pool. Once the girls were convinced that the spirits were appeased and had some reassurance from authorities, their anxiety subsided along with their symptoms.

Fijian Kidnapping Scare

In November 2003, there was a series of alarming reports that students were being targeted by a mysterious squad of kidnappers whose intentions were as unclear as they were disturbing. The young boy whose reports ignited the furor told of his victimization at the hands of a roving band of shadowy conspirators. According to the boy, he was on his way to school when a car screeched to a halt beside him. Leaping from the car, his unknown assailants grabbed him, hustled him into the vehicle, blindfolded him, and sped away. Here details become hazy, as the boy said he was then drugged. When he came around he found himself on a slab in a makeshift operating theater. Somehow, the terrified youngster eluded his captors, and made his way to police headquarters. Word of the boy's harrowing ordeal got out and before long similar reports started to come in. But as the police followed up on the boy's story they grew more skeptical. They began to suspect that the boy made up the story as an elaborate ruse to cover up his playing hooky from school on the day of the supposed abduction. Further investigation of similar reports led authorities to determine that the claims were not true and were instead part of a student abduction scare.

Police Commissioner Andrew Hughes said that there was another possible explanation: pure fantasy. "We have found that the kids who make such claims are disturbed. They come from broken families and they speculate the story of being kidnapped to seek attention and this is dangerous." In another incident, an investigation of a report of masked men trying to kidnap students in a boarding school proved to be without merit. As a result of the emotional frenzy whipped up by the students' stories, two men erroneously identified as abductors were beaten by locals. Fortunately, their injuries were not life-threatening.[28]

Devil and Fairy Scares in the Philippines

An elementary school in Manila, the Philippines, was temporarily shut down in January 1994 when about twenty Filipino students went into an emotional frenzy after imagining they saw the devil standing under a schoolyard tree. Afterwards, six female students fainted, including Joy Bolante, twelve, who kept screaming, "There is no God! There is no God!" as she struggled against several adults who were trying to calm her. The affected students were later taken to a nearby Roman Catholic church, where a priest dabbed them with holy water and said prayers for their recovery. The devil the students claimed to have seen was "a gigantic man who has horns and a tail," according to another twelve-year-old pupil, Marilyn Umpat.[29]

Nine years later, in 2003 a school in Bagabag, Nueva Ecija, was temporarily closed after evil spirits were reported to have taken control of many students. Though the school is co-educational, only girls were attacked. The episode began one day in early July when about twenty-five girls fainted "almost one after the other." When they regained consciousness, the girls began acting strangely. It was widely believed that the girls were possessed by the spirits of soldiers who had died during World War II and were buried nearby.

"[One of] the possessed students displayed extraordinary strength. It took four male students to restrain her," said teacher Joel Fariñas. Another teacher, Gloria Jasmin, said that some of the possessed students began speaking in odd ways, as if someone else was in control of their minds. Some spoke in deep, harsh voices; others spoke softly. Some let out piercing screams. Rumors abounded that the high school was built atop a graveyard used by the Japanese during the occupation. Locals said that the area had remained vacant until the high school was built on the site.

In an attempt to appease the angry spirits of the dead, several area priests were called in from the local Catholic and Aglipayan churches. They walked through the school, sprinkling it with holy water. A local witchdoctor, or *albularyo*, told the teachers that drastic action was needed in order to stop the attacks. He recommended they dig a hole on the school grounds, then kill a pig, cut its head off, and bury it in the hole. For the offering to work, the teachers would have to eat some of the pork. He said the act should make the spirits happy. The advice was followed and the outbreak soon subsided.[30]

In mid–January 2004, a series of fairy sightings at the Rizal Elementary School in Iloilo, the Philippines, made headlines; reporters from at least two different news agencies went to the school to interview the students and teachers. On the morning of January 16, a fourth-grade teacher, Ms. Hermie Orieno, had her students cleaning the schoolyard. During the pickup, students claimed to have seen dwarves about an inch high. One of the students, Carol, said the creatures had talked to her, saying their names were Wenden and Wendy and they wanted to be friends.[31] About half the class said they had seen the fairies. One student went inside to find Orieno, who ran out but saw nothing. According to a reporter who interviewed the girls, one of the girls said, "Do you see this leaf here that is moving while the rest of the leaves are not? Ms. Orieno said yes. That's because one of the dwarves is right now hanging in there and moving it."[32] Orieno still saw nothing, but apparently believing in fairies and to be on the safe side, she apologized to the creatures and said she was sorry if any of the children were bothering them.[33]

The human mind has a fascinating propensity to see and experience what it expects. It should come as no surprise that many Filipinos believe in fairies. Given the tendency for the mind to fool itself, and the imperfect nature of our senses—human perception is notoriously unreliable and subject to the observer's mind set—it may be appropriate to turn the tables on the old adage and say, "Believing is seeing."

The "Devil" Appears in a Trinidad School

During the second week of November 2012, panic swept through the Moruga Composite School on the island nation of Trinidad and Tobago in the Caribbean after reports that students were attacked by a devil. In all, 17 female students were stricken with strange behaviors. The girls experienced nausea and headaches, then rolled on the ground, hissing and conversing in a mysterious language. Some ran around the room screaming before collapsing in a trance-like state. According to the *Trinidad Guardian*, two of those affected had to be restrained as they tried to leap off a railing. One student observer, Kern Mollineau, described a frightful scene: "One girl was blabbering as if in a strange language. I could not understand what she was saying. It was sounding like 'shebbaberbebeb shhhhee.' The girls were unusually strong. We had to hold them down so that they will not hurt themselves. The teachers were right there. I get a kick in my face when one of the girls started beating up on the floor. Many of them had bruises." Mollineau said he had communicated with the "devil" that had possessed one of the girls. "I asked the Devil what he wanted with the girls and the voice said he wanted a life. He kept saying to send the girls in the toilet and to leave them alone."[34]

A number of priests and pastors from nearby schools rushed to the scene in order to quell the situation. Some of them began showering students with holy water and reciting prayers. Police and emergency personnel were also at the school. Tests of the buildings yielded no toxic substances. One of the teachers suggested that the attacks may have been some type of supernatural revenge by a woman who had visited the school two weeks earlier over a dispute. Another teacher suggested that the outbreak was caused by the school having been built on a burial ground. The students were examined at a nearby hospital and quickly released.[35]

In her commentary on the episode, local journalist Marion O'Callaghan noted that a belief in the supernatural was on the rise among the middle and upper classes, lending legitimacy to a variety of beliefs and their consequences. "Until recently, witchcraft and devil possession beliefs were not considered 'respectable' in the Trinidad professional or upper middle class, i.e., the segment of society expected to be exposed to rational explanation. Pentecostalism, with its emotional manifestation of the spirit, was considered a lower middle class or working class religion." She observes that in recent times there has been an increase in "anti-intellectualism" and "a fundamentalist interpretation of the Bible," leading to a tendency for events "to be explained in terms of miracles, the devil, punishment for personal sins, Government sins of omission or commission and, curiously for Catholics, the sins of dead ancestors. Surrounded by evil spirits, we are in constant spiritual warfare."[36]

O'Callaghan notes that the region where the affected school lies—Moruga, one of Trinidad's poorest and remote areas—has been experiencing great economic strain from the collapse of the local fishing industry and plantation economy, forcing graduates to leave home in order to find viable work. "It means leaving Moruga and often separating from family and friends. That the school is a composite school tells the story of an education system which offers little possibility of upward social mobility. For those teenage girls the adolescent transition is one of acute insecurity. Enough to explain hysteria without the help of the devil," she said.[37]

CHAPTER 7

Strange Tales from Latin America

[Believing that] man is an animal suspended in webs of significance he himself has spun, I take culture to be those webs, and the analysis of it to be therefore not an experimental science in search of law but an interpretive one in search of meaning.—Clifford Geertz[1]

Latin America spans an area from northern Mexico to the tip of Argentina and comprises approximately 14 percent of the earth's surface. The largest known outbreak at a school in this part of the world took place in 2007, when media outlets around the world began reporting on a strange illness affecting schoolgirls in Mexico. Between October 2006 and June 2007, a mysterious ailment swept through an all-girls boarding school near Mexico City, operated by the Catholic Church. At the Girls' Town School students reported headaches, fevers, diarrhea — and, most conspicuously, dramatic difficulty walking. Some complained of creaking knees that sometimes throbbed and bent involuntarily, forcing them to "stiffen them" in order to walk. Others described pains in their ankles or hips. Some students had to lean on their classmates just to move around. Occasionally symptoms spontaneously vanished, only to recur. Some were afflicted once; others experienced many relapses. In all, one in eight students were stricken: 512 out of a student population of 4,000, ranging in age from 11 to 19 — most from poor backgrounds.

A Ouija Board Triggers Mass Hysteria in Mexico

An investigation by Mexican psychiatrist Nashyiela Loa Zavala traced the trigger of the outbreak to a Ouija board that was used during a basketball game.[2] An attractive, popular 15-year-old pupil named Maria[3] was playing the game when she asked the board to allow her best friend's team to win — which happened as requested, infuriating many of the students who considered the use of the board to be cheating. Ouija boards (also called Spirit Talking Boards) are thought by some to be a means of communicating with the spirit world. Participants sit before a board that has the words "yes," "no" and "maybe" surrounded by a circle with letters in the alphabet. An upside-down glass is placed on the board and the players place the crossed middle and index fingers of one hand onto the glass, which begins to slowly move — thus seemingly answering the questions asked of it.[4] Word of the incident soon reached the mother superior, Margie Cheong, who was originally from South Korea and was unfamiliar with the game. She was advised that the board "was an instrument of the devil, capable of changing people's souls to make them do evil things." The mother superior expelled Maria, explaining that ungodly games would not be tolerated. Maria was devastated and vehemently protested her innocence, but a search of her belongings revealed the Ouija board, sealing her fate.

Maria was upset by her expulsion and considered it unjust, because the game was commonly played at the school. As Maria was waiting alone to be taken home, a wind gust blew shut a door, pinching her hand and causing her to lose part of a finger. Angry, Maria was rumored to have placed a curse on the girls who had accused her of using the Ouija board. Not long after, the strange symptoms appeared at the school. One of the stories to make the rounds was that Maria's mother was a witch and a devout follower of *Santa Muerte* (Saint Death). This religion has been active in Mexico since before the arrival of Columbus in the 1490s. The central figure of their worship is a human skeleton clad in robes and holding a scythe or globe, reminiscent of the Western figure of the grim reaper. The Catholic Church has condemned the practice, which many Mexicans look upon as a cult, but it remains popular in some areas, especially Mexico City. These stories of Maria's mother being a witch likely generated fear in her classmates, and shortly after she was kicked out, several girls in her dormitory reported seeing a similar image of Maria in their dreams. In each instance she was enveloped by fire and laughing at them, blaming them for her expulsion and saying that they would be next (presumably to burn in hell).

While the first few victims were only among her fellow Ouija board players, the symptoms quickly spread through the school. As girl after girl was stricken and exhibited difficulty walking, many teachers feared that an unknown infection was responsible, and for a time everyone wore surgical masks. The affected girls were separated from their healthy classmates and placed in a special building, where they were often scolded. One of the girls, Zitlali, recalls:

> They took me there because I started to have pains in my knees but I could walk all right; first I felt very badly because it looked like a hospital and the girls were walking around like drunks ... then I started to walk wrongly; they scolded me when they went to see me because I didn't walk that way before.... Time passed and then they said it wasn't contagious and that it was only in the head ... psychological ... but I don't know ... maybe it is a little bit in the mind but it may also be an illness, because they did the Ouija to us ... playing with the Ouija is like being with the devil.[5]

Some of the teachers had lost confidence in the mother superior's ability to deal with the crisis and harbored views that school officials were not being transparent enough, so they began to undermine the team of psychiatrists who came to investigate. They told their students that they thought the affliction was caused by spoiled food. Another rumor held that the religious mothers had slipped a powder into their food to stop them from menstruating. One girl said: "They give us these powders so we won't menstruate; many of us go for months without menstruating and that didn't happen to us outside, in our homes; but we think that this time they went too far with the powders and so they went down into our legs and that's why we can't walk right."[6] Another theory pointed the blame on voodoo; one girl reported finding her rag dolls with needles stuck into their legs.

When the affliction showed no signed of abating, the mother superior became so desperate that she pleaded with Maria to return to school and undo her "curse." Maria refused. She then turned to the Catholic Church for help. Soon priests were praying over the girls and attempting to exorcize demons. Despite this, more girls were stricken. Some girls would make fun of their unwell classmates and imitate symptoms, only to be afflicted themselves. The power of suggestion certainly played a role. One girl observed: "I felt that at any moment I was going to get sick because they all got sick; one day my knee creaked while I was praying in chapel; I asked the girl next to me if it started with creaking in the knee, she said yes and I knew that I had gotten sick too; I already couldn't walk right."[7]

The conditions at the school were challenging. The girls lived in cramped rooms and were forced to shower together. As some of the girls were expected to become nuns upon completing high school, they were under continuous pressure to meet strict religious standards. Dr. Zavala describes a scene that is reminiscent of the strict Islamic schools in Malaysia where similar outbreaks of hysteria have broken out. The girls lived in a pressure-cooker environment of too much work and too little play, and spent so many hours knelt in prayer that some were developing inflammation of their knees:

> Their hours are filled with religious activities such as Masses, Catholic films, Bible study and penance.... When they arrive at the school they are dressed in an identical uniform ... [and] if they are expelled it is taken away from them "for not having been worthy daughters." The phenomenon which most shocked the medical team initially was that the adolescents looked so identical: all dressed exactly the same in a blouse and long skirt, with the same Asian type haircut and no ornaments at all, which made it difficult to distinguish them; they seemed an undifferentiated mass. It was not just the girls who were nearly identical; everything tends to be homogenized: they eat the same food, but none of the dishes that would be served in their homes, which generates frequent eating problems; they all celebrate their birthday on the same day, which is the anniversary of the school's foundation.[8]

Their daily routine was monotonous. Simple leisure activities that most Mexicans would take for granted, such as watching TV or reading the newspaper or magazines, were forbidden. Even listening to the radio was banned. The girls could not even walk across campus but were restricted to certain areas of the school grounds. At times students had to endure lengthy periods without talking. Living with the girls in the dorms were about 40 "religious mothers" or spies whose job it was to keep close tabs on their inmates.

Most of the 90 Mexican lay teachers at the school were young, inexperienced and poorly trained, making them highly desirable because, as one person remarked, "that way they more readily accept what the religious mothers tell them."[9] Topics such as human sexuality were forbidden to be taught, and teachers were required to remain at a distance of at least 6 feet from their pupils at all times. Students were even cautioned not to become too attached to their dorm mothers; close relationships could result in expulsion for both the girl and the dorm mother. They were even cautioned against becoming too close to their classmates. The students saw their families just twice each year, during summer and Christmas vacations; each lasts only two weeks. In many respects, the facility resembled prison more than a school. Dr. Zavala observed: "Parents are allowed to come to the school once a year for a six-hour visit. The girls are not allowed to write letters but they may receive them. The religious mothers open and read letters sent to the adolescents and decide whether or not they are to receive them. Consequently, long months may pass for many pupils without news of their parents and siblings."[10] The school enforced strict rules that included absolute obedience to authority; no fighting, stealing or lying; and giving thanks without complaint. The penalty for breaking these rules—even once—was often expulsion. Students lived in a constant state of fear that they too might be expelled; this fostered a fear that classmates might turn them in for inappropriate behavior. This made all classmates into potential spies.

Dr. Zavala recalls that one of the affected girls typified the students' plight of loneliness and not being able to secure deeper relationships while simultaneously being cut off from their families. When she finished interviewing her, the student made excuses in an effort to stay; she clearly did not to want to leave. The strict religious setting and rules created an atmosphere of extreme anxiety and guilt. This backdrop became a breeding ground for mass hysteria, when combined with the constant fear of expulsion, the widespread belief in the supernatural and the power of Ouija boards, and a belief that ghosts haunted the dorms. Guilt and sinning was a constant part of everyday life; even an ordinarily relaxing activity such as bathing became an event to be feared. One student observed: "Some girls are morbid and look at the girls when they're bathing; we have to be careful with our eyes because with our eyes we can go to hell; the mother tells us that when we pray is when the devil tempts us most and things that we've looked at wrongly appear."[11]

Because the girls were unable to form secure relationships with their dorm mothers, they lived in an atmosphere of suspicion, fear and persecution. Students who were seen as too close to their "mothers" risked not only expulsion but also persecution for being labeled as "pets." Dr. Zavala notes that there were only 40 or so "mothers" for 4,000 girls—girls who were starving for human companionship and attention. The act of falling ill resulted in the students' receiving more attention than they would have otherwise received in school. Dr. Zavala remarks that the school had an unnatural environment where "hundreds of adolescents seem to be one face, one body and one mind. It is shocking to see thousands of Latin adolescents with Asian hairstyles, dressed identically, who think, speak and walk in such an identical way. All differences have been erased despite their both cultural and individual multiplicity."[12]

Invasion of the Fairies

In June 1996, something strange began happening in the Central American country of Nicaragua. The normal routine of the Simón Bolívar School, in the San Jerónimo district of Masaya, was disrupted by sudden screams from the girls' toilets. Several girls rushed out of the bathroom, one so scared that she fainted. According to the *Barricada Internacional* of August 1996, they claimed to have seen three small elves, dressed in red suits, hats and shoes, "coming out of the toilet bowls." Ten-year-old Darwin Altamirano said: "We were playing during the 9:30 A.M. recess, when we saw five girls running out shouting 'There's elves in there!'" At first, he didn't believe them, he added, but when he went to take a look, he saw "the doors opening and closing all by themselves." Another student, Bismarck Altamirano, said he had heard "strange laughter." One of the frightened girls, Alejandra Montenegra, said she watched as the little men "disappeared before my eyes."

A belief in "little people" is endemic in Nicaragua, as many guidebooks and folklore studies attest, and predates the arrival of the Spanish and Catholicism. *Los duendes*, as they are referred to, have a more sinister reputation than the English "elves." Traditionally they dress in red or green, but they specialize in making life difficult by thieving and causing accidents. The majority of country folk believe in them and sightings are commonplace, writes Nicaraguan photographer Richard Leonardi. "Their main purpose, or joy, is to steal yet to be baptized babies or unwed young women.... The unwed post-pubescent girl is lured away by hypnotism, little gifts, and sweet words, never to be seen again. *Duendes* can be heard laughing in the deep forest, but also take time out to visit schools and homes of rural villages."

Leonardi writes, "Nicaraguan newspapers report annually of school children afraid to attend class and farmers who flee ranches thanks to horrifying little *duendes*, who appear, laughing their dangerously contagious *duende* laugh, invisible to most, but completely visible and both repulsive and enticing, to a select few."[13] The Managua daily *El Nuevo Diario* reported that on June 21, 2003, *duendes* could even penetrate the country's capital city of Managua:

> Managua's *Colegio Nicarao* (primary and secondary school) principal reported to the periodical that five students arrived to her office dazed, apparently under a "strange influence." They then described to her contact with a yellow *duende*, who wore a green scarf and had long ears, blond hair, blue eyes, arching eyebrows, a wrinkled white face, red mouth was about a half-meter tall sporting pointy shoes and white socks.[14]

Nicaraguan Grisi Siknis: "Beckoned by Mysterious Forces"

In March 2009, a mysterious ailment known to the indigenous Miskito people of the Rio Coco region of northern Nicaragua as *grisi siknis* ("crazy sickness") swept through several schools. Three schools located between the village of Kamla and the fishing village of Bilwi were forced to close as around 120 teenage girls fell into "fits."[15] A number of female students from the city's National Institute of Technology were also affected. Many of the victims fell into a trance, believed they were possessed by the devil, and acted out violently. Locals commonly believe that sorcerers conjure up the evil spirits. *Grisi siknis* is a common ailment in the region and most often afflicts adolescent girls. Anadina Smith said that one day at school she felt giddy and had difficulty breathing. "Then, I saw something coming towards me—a kind of black man or a dragon that entered me and possessed me." Three of Anadina's classmates were affected on the same day in March 2009. Their headmaster, Reverend Harold Dixon, witnessed many such attacks among his pupils in this latest outbreak. "They get giddy and they faint and fall to the ground," he said. "Then, they start hollering and they hit their heads on the wall or desk." They gain an unnatural strength. "You have to have five or six people to hold down one girl," Dixon added.[16]

"*Grisi siknis* turns people into witches and they go crazy," says Porcela Sandino, a respected *curandera* (traditional healer) in Puerto Cabezas.[17] The *curandera* is in great demand and is called upon to travel widely. The 2009 epidemic was significant. When she goes to see Lola Emberto, in a poor suburb of Puerto Cabezas, the woman is desperate. "I couldn't sleep or eat," she says. Her three children have been affected for the last four months. One daughter "was just running around like a maniac. She tore off all her clothes," said Mrs Emberto. "One time, she fell into the well while suffering an attack. Other times, she'd run into the bush or into the river and people would try to catch her." Her 18-year-old son and 13-year-old daughter were also affected.

Grisi siknis is included in the American Psychiatric Association's list of recognized mental disorders as a culture-specific syndrome, described as "a psychological disorder due to stress, upheaval, and despair." Phil Dennis—a professor of anthropology at Texas Tech University, who did fieldwork among the Miskito people in 1978 for a post-doctoral study in medical anthropology—has called it "a wild, orgiastic rite of sex and violence"; yet, to be fair, not all cases are as orgasmic as he implies. Miskito community leaders, however, blame the outbreak on a curse by black magicians, which no one seems able to identify. According to Dennis *grisi siknis* is unique to the Miskito, but comparable to other conditions—such as anorexia nervosa which is known only in the affluent West; *amok* among the Malays; and *pibloktoq* ("Arctic hysteria"), found only among indigenous people in Greenland. "The culture-bound syndromes force us to realize that health and disease are not simple biological matters, but a complex interweaving of various aspects of being human. [It] is a very serious health problem for families and entire Miskito communities." He says it is characterized by long periods of anxiety, nausea, dizziness, irrational anger and fear, interlaced with short periods of rapid frenzy, in which the victims "lose consciousness, believe that devils beat them and have sexual relations with them."[18]

The last major outbreak of *grisi siknis* began in 1910 and lasted for 20 years, affecting many communities throughout the northern coastal region of Nicaragua, which faces the Caribbean. However, it is likely to be much older than that. There is a reference to an illness like *grisi siknis* in the 1850s, by the English ethnographer Charles Napier Bell, who grew up on the Miskito coast. In his *In Tangweera*, he tells of visiting a Miskito village:

> I have seen a young girl, who was shrieking hysterically in a dreadful manner, carried in a canoe a long distance to consult a celebrated *sookia* [healer-shaman]. All that the *sookia* did was erect round her painted sticks with charms tied to them, to blow tobacco-smoke over her while muttering strange words, to make a bubbling with a tobacco pipe in a calabash of water, which she was then made to drink, and to tie a knotted string round her neck, on every knot of which was a drop of blood from his tongue. For as many days as there were knots she must not eat the meat of certain animals, must suffer no one to pass to windward of her, and must not see a woman with child.[19]

Mrs. Emberto, like many Miskito people, believes that Doña Porcela's treatment — using medicinal herbs and candles — will lift the curse from her children. The healer is proud of her potion: "It can be drunk or bathed in," she said. "Within three or four days, they are normal again." She certainly has more success than doctors using Western medicine. In 2000, about 80 people in the community of Krin Krin were affected. Many were successfully treated by *curanderas*, invited along by health officials. Porcela Sandino was one and Carlos Salomon Taylor was another; they both use time-honored paraphernalia and ancestral rituals. Sandino's assistants also drove off the bad spirits by spreading one of her concoctions in a ring around the village. Based on their success at Krin Krin, both healers were sent, to Raiti, in 2003, where 25 of the 60 sufferers were said to have responded well to their treatment.[20] The remedies of the *curanderas* are said to come to them in dreams that set them on the path of becoming a healer. It seems nothing much has changed in the century and a half since Bell observed his *sookia*.

The outbreak at Raita and neighboring communities near the border with Honduras, in December 2003, involved upwards of 60 girls, apparently all aged from 14 to 18. The Nicaraguan government sent a large medical team which besides doctors and epidemiologists, included psychiatrists, anthropologists and five *curanderos*. The health minister, José Antonio Alvarado, said that the Miskito healers were getting better results than those trained in western medicine. The medical team was led by Florence Levy, the region's health director; she too acknowledged the success of the *curanderos*. "There's not much our doctors can do; we are giving support to the healers as they know the problem better than us," she said. "The illness is more spiritual than physical, so they turn to the healer for the spiritual part," she added.[21] At Uraccan University in Puerto Cabezas, Professor Pablo McDavis, of the Indigenous Diseases Department, has been researching *grisi siknis* for several years. "We have taken samples of blood from patients while suffering an attack and, in a lab, we can't detect anything [significant]," he says. He admits to being puzzled: "Drugs or injections tend to only increase a patient's aggressiveness. Clinically we can't detect anything."[22] Mr. Alvarado said a medical report on an outbreak in the 1950s raised the possibility of "deliberate contamination of wells with hallucinogenic substances." So, at Raita, wells and likely sources of contamination or poisons were sampled, but no sinister agents were found.[23]

The illness seems mainly confined to young women, although a few males and older women are known to have been victims.[24] *Grisi siknis* behaves like a virus outbreak, says Dr. McDavis. "If an attack is not contained quickly, it can spread throughout an entire community." This is an allusion to one of the remarkable characteristics of the affliction; it can spread by line-of-sight, "sending teenager after teenager into a frenzied state followed by long periods of coma-like unconsciousness," notes Fell. Nicola Ross, who travelled up the Rio Coco to interview families and victims of *grisi siknis*, said one girl, Licha, told of a strange ability that came to her in her madness: she could "predict who the next victim would be and was at a loss to explain how this knowledge came to her." She was eight years old at the time and found this particularly disturbing.[25]

Phil Dennis also noted victims' need for there to be other potential victims within sight; on occasion they named other people and if any of those people happened to be present, they too became afflicted. This may be a form of contagious imitation by the secondary victims, but it is regarded by the community as a form of prophesy on the part of the "naming" victim.[26] This seems to confirm a comment by Dr. Elie Karam to Linda Geddes: "We need more data about the way this outbreak spreads. Usually the symptoms start with one person; typically they are reported to occur in individuals who are in the line of sight of the 'trigger' case."[27]

Dennis himself witnessed four attacks during his research and said the victims were "clearly in another state of reality." In this trance state, they seemed to perform a feat that bordered on the paranormal. With their eyes shut, they attempted to flee from their communities, seizing anything they could find to defend themselves, with surprising strength, against attackers only they could see. Anadina's vision of her spectral assailants seems fairly typical. Ross' informant, Licha, a survivor of the Krin Krin outbreak, told her that initially she simply had a headache and felt dizzy, a condition the Miskito call *bla*. As the trance deepened, Licha felt her mouth began to move uncontrollably. Then began a horrible period during which her stomach bulged and churned. According to several eye witnesses, she said, she then vomited a live spider. Her most vivid memory was of visions in which "small, black men riding red horses came down from the mountains to lure her away from the village." This was why it was necessary to tie her up, she explained. "They offered her a cup filled with blood. She was afraid of the *duende*, the spirits from the forest, but felt compelled to follow these powerful strangers anyway."[28] As Nicola Ross put it: "With their eyes closed, and armed with machetes or sticks, they think nothing of attacking whoever or whatever stands between them and the mysterious force that beckons."

A rather lurid report seems to show some *grisi siknis* experiences evolving to resemble the reports seen from the Middle Ages onward in Western culture. Tim Rogers, reporting on the 2009 outbreak around Kamla and Bilwi for the *TicoTimes*—a blog and newspaper on Central American issues—told of the affliction of two sisters, Jose and Rafaela Chao, in mid–May:

> In a scene that must be reminiscent of the Salem witch trials, the two girls, in the throes of their madness, accused a mysterious drifter, who was living in town, of being a witch and trying to kill them. That was all the evidence the townsfolk needed to organize a lynch mob and go after the man. After being beaten for hours, he admitted he was the one causing all the trouble. The villagers burned what they claimed were his spell books and forced him to cure the girls, which he did in exchange for his life. Since that moment there have been no reported cases of *grisi siknis* and authorities think the problem has been resolved for the moment. However, the suspected warlock has escaped and some fear he will seek his revenge through the dark arts.[29]

Demons "Attack" Schools in Guyana

During 2009, the small South American country of Guyana — a former Dutch and British colony — was the scene of an epidemic of demonic possession among secondary school students. One of the worst affected was the East Ruimveldt School in the capital city of Georgetown, where one morning in early November, 15 girls were stricken. Some shouted, while others giggled uncontrollably. Religious officials came to the school to offer prayers. Some could be heard shouting: "Get out in the name of Jesus." The outbreak triggered a renewed interest in Bible classes at the school. Some of the girls who were helping to aid those affected were stricken themselves; they began to shriek wildly and strip off their clothes. Others turned violent. Some remained silent. The strange behaviors began at 9:45 A.M. Before long students from across the school were fleeing the compound, scattering in every direction to escape the "demonic possession." Two journalists described the emotion-charged scene: "As teachers fought to control the girls—who appeared at times to have superhuman strength—some parents arrived and immediately got involved in efforts to cast-out 'spirits,' while others simply wept and ran out of the building asking 'what we must do?' One mother shouted, 'God help me daughter. They got a bag over she face but it ain't helping.'" Parents and teachers were forced to dash across school grounds in an effort to chase down some of the girls who were running around willy-nilly. Some of the victims were later bundled into vehicles and rushed to a nearby religious center, where several pastors from the Assembly of God Church prayed for their recovery.[30]

In March 2012, Georgetown was again the scene of collective possession among schoolgirls. The episode began at St. Winefride's Secondary School on March 14 when six pupils from separate classrooms reported that they were being attached by "unnatural spirits." Leroy Smith of the *Guyana Chronicle* showed up at the school and said he could hear screams and tumbling furniture from a flat where several students had been locked inside while adults conducted a spiritual cleansing exercise using olive oil and Bibles. School officials prevented the affected students from being taken to a hospital for treatment, believing that their symptoms were spiritual in origin.[31]

Later that month on March 26, another outburst of possessed students was reported. The outbreak began at about 3 P.M. when a female student was standing near the washroom and started to act strangely. A local resident who witnessed the incident described what happened in broken English: "She start talk like a man ... with a man voice, and say how it [the spirit] name Augustus, and he come to kill and such. The poor girl pick up a big heavy wood and was waving it around and running [after] children. Some boys take off their belts and hit her hoping the lashes would cause her to catch herself." Another bystander said: "She run up Middleton

Street and was ... chasing other children. And after a while it [the spirit] like left her body and went into another girl and she began to show antics too. The school needs to be shut down until something is done. Burn it or something." Residents were adamant that the school should be shut down, noting that there had been many attacks by demons at the school in the past, attacks that only targeted females. On this occasion the two affected girls were rushed to Georgetown Hospital. At the emergency room one witness described a chaotic scene: "When they put one of the girls on the stretcher, four persons had to hold her down, she was jumping up and moving like a worm. A male voice was coming out of her body saying my name is Elijah and I won't leave this body as long as I don't find Shaneeza."[32]

CHAPTER 8

Strange Schoolyards and Unusual Field Trips
Cases from Beyond the Classroom

> You can't depend on your judgment when your imagination is out of focus.— Mark Twain[1]

Wherever students gather—football fields, class trips, parades, or schoolyards—can be fertile ground for rumors, rivalries and the swirling undercurrents of dread and suspicion that are an everyday part of the adolescent world. These ingredients are the perfect medium for incubating panics and outbreaks of mass psychogenic illness. We begin this chapter with one of the most infamous episodes in the modern-day history of psychological illness, known today simply as the Hollinwell Incident.

"The kids went down like ninepins," said a policeman attending the scene. The date was Sunday, July 13, 1980. It was beautiful summer morning for the annual Hollinwell Show underway in fields near the small Nottinghamshire town of Kirkby-in-Ashfield. This picture postcard scene of rural England would become, in that policeman's words, "like a battlefield with bodies everywhere." Precisely what happened was the subject of endless and acrimonious debate in the following weeks, involving medical and welfare experts, government scientists, local council officials, witnesses and the afflicted.[2]

The day was to feature a competition involving some five hundred children from eleven junior marching bands. They had all been practicing their music and routines for months. Many had gotten up early and were already tired, restless and certainly nervous when they arrived for the 9 A.M. start. Almost immediately they formed up, their leaders fussing over their uniforms. It was going to be a long, tension-filled day and it began with a long wait as the judges made their final inspection. There was no more time for rehearsals, only for last minute checks. Between 10:30 and

12:30, more than two hundred of the children and some adults collapsed. They were ferried by dozens of ambulances to four area hospitals, where about 259 people were examined. Nine were detained overnight. The symptoms included fainting, running eyes, sore throats, dizziness, vomiting, trembling, weakness, numbness and a metallic taste in the mouth ... but not all at once or all in the same person. Besides the felled bandsmen, 15 adults, two babies and two horses were affected. Horses? We'll come to that in a minute.

In hindsight, it is clear that the area health authorities and the police acted very quickly; however, while several theories about what had happened were made more or less likely by the quick accumulation of information, the conclusions of the investigating experts were not always well received. Indeed, the case might well serve as a study of the gulf in interpretation between the authorities and the local public — especially the parents of the children involved — over too prominent and casual a use of the term "mass hysteria." Let us go back to the moment that chaos broke out. An organizer for one of the bands, Terry Bingham, said: "We were ready for the display when one or two children collapsed. Then a few more went, and a few more. We called off the event but others fell as they came out of the arena. Then spectators started dropping." Another witness said: "Some kids were catching their friends as they fell, and then they were falling down themselves.... No one could understand what was happening."[3]

One of the girls affected, Petula Merriman, age 14, said: "We were on the field in full uniform for an inspection.... I've never had to stand to attention that long before. As we marched off I tried to grab hold of my drum but just fell on the floor. My friends were collapsing all around me." Another of the afflicted, Kerry Elliott, age 10, said: "I went all weak and got pains in my stomach and then I fainted. Everyone was falling down and some were crying. My stomach was all tight and aching. I felt better when I came round in hospital." Kerry's 7-year-old brother, Steven, was similarly affected.

Some of the adults fell during the height of the panic, some were taken ill accompanying their children to the hospital, and still others collapsed in wards at bedsides. Terry Bingham said his own eyes began stinging and watering as he drove six kids to hospital in his car: "I had chest pains. It was like nerve gas poisoning," he later told reporters. Margaret Palethorpe, a 37-year-old mother of five children, three of whom were among the collapsed, said she felt pins and needles in her tongue and lips. "I collapsed and lost the use of one arm." Linda Elliott, mother of Kerry and Steven (above), "felt strange" as she comforted her children on the way to hospital, where she too collapsed. "My arms and legs felt like sponges and it was like cramp in my stomach. That's all I remember until I came round." Mrs. Edna Wells, chairman of one band, the Ashford Imperials, said she tried to keep the children talking: "I was helping them but I was taken ill too."

Theories Abound

Food poisoning was the first thought of many who stood around the arena, staring in disbelief at the numbers of children keeling over. Someone — perhaps well-intentioned — broadcast urgent messages over the public address system warning people not to eat the ice cream or drink water until the source of the trouble was found, although no one was certain whether this happened during or after the collapses. A few minutes later another warning came, this time about mineral waters.[4] When the police moved in with health officials a short time later, they took samples of food and drink from all the stalls. Even as they did so, it became clear this theory was not tenable; many of the children had not consumed anything they had not brought with them in their coaches. The results of tests on the food samples became a formality and proved negative in all cases. The Severn-Trent Water Authority, which supplied the area, was also quick to respond. By the end of the day they were able to say the water had no bacterial impurities. The food poisoning theory was the first to be eliminated, but not in time to save the ice cream men, who for several days afterward were subjected to taunts and jeered in the housing estates around Kirkby in Ashfield.

By the time the police and health authorities arrived at the Hollinwell show-ground, a second theory was being favored, and was to prove longer-lasting. The children, it suggested, had been poisoned by an insecticide used by farmers in spraying crops. The front page of the *Daily Mirror* the day after the collapse was in no doubt: "Gas Cloud KOs Children," it proclaimed.[5] Some people imagined a cloud of insecticide drifting across the show-ground; others speculated about the harmful effects of dust raised by the feet of several hundred marchers. The Nottinghamshire Fire Service was able to establish that this was not a possibility. "The wind was in completely the wrong direction," they told the *Guardian*. Meanwhile, a spokesman at the Queens Medical Centre, Nottingham, said that the symptoms of the children taken there "were consistent with exposure to fumes of some kind."[6] However, every lead turned up nothing. Police tracked down the farmer who owned the adjacent field: it had not been sprayed for more than ten years. Someone claimed to have seen a light plane in the area three days previously on July 10, and it was rumored that it had been spraying the course and nearby woods owned by Nottinghamshire Golf Club. This was refuted by golf club officials and a woodsman. Local farmers and the Forestry Commission also denied spraying.

One of the more exotic theories was postulated by a man in Scotland who suggested that people had been affected by high frequency radio waves. A high frequency transmitter was found nearby at a gas board depot. It did not take long for this line of inquiry, like the food poisoning idea, to be eliminated. In the search for a likely source of debilitating fumes, the police sniffed hopefully in the direction of a fire at a plastics factory, some miles away, that caused an estimated £1 million worth of damage. Again, the wind was blowing in the wrong direction for this to have been a factor.

On the 14th, there was speculation that a "mystery bug" was the culprit on the grounds that a number of the children affected were found to have chicken-pox-like blisters, which the locals call "blebs." Enid Holmes, secretary of the Creswell Graglanders, said she had "noticed some children had blebs on their backs and legs" when she loosened their uniforms. Two other bands reported blebs on children's skin.[7] One doctor nominated the Coxsackie virus as the culprit. However, this too was extremely unlikely to have been the cause of so widespread a reaction.

At a press briefing, Chief Inspector Eric Ogden, who led the police investigation, said: "The whole thing is a complete mystery. A horse competition or *gymkhana* was held in the same field later without trouble." Dr. John Wood, director of health for the Kirkby area, said he was becoming convinced that it was mass psychogenic illness as tests had "virtually eliminated the alternatives." "Part of it may have been one or two people feeling ill and the rest getting hysteria." To which C.I. Ogden added: "A large number of small children had been parading and standing to attention for some time. They would also be under some pressure due to the occasion."

The Aftermath

Over the ensuing 24 hours, five of the children released from hospitals were readmitted when their symptoms recurred. On the 16th four people from the Worksop area, a few miles to the north, collapsed with Hollinwell-type symptoms. The following weekend, members of one of the bands involved collapsed again, at separate gatherings in Nottinghamshire. On the 19th, six members of the Ashfield Imperials band fainted during a five-mile charity march at South Normanton. "Traffic fumes and a long march" were blamed.[8] Two weeks after the Hollinwell collapse, 19 children were taken to the hospital after being struck down by the "band bug" in Leicestershire. They had traveled by coach from Lincoln to Leicester, and were treated for "heat exhaustion" at Newark.[9] That same weekend, five young band members were taken to the hospital after they collapsed during a two-mile procession at a fete at Tipton, West Midlands. All were aged 14 and said to have "fainted in sweltering conditions." Two others were picked up by the ambulances.[10] At Manton, south of Nottingham, it was the turn of five girls from the Kilton Concordes band, who had also collapsed at Hollinwell; they fell ill during a charity event.[11] They were the only band affected on this occasion and quickly recovered once off the field.

Reactions

At first parents, looking for a target for their anger, were critical of the show's organizers. The chairman of one band was also critical of the judges for the long period of standing to attention. "It was disgusting the way the judges kept the children waiting so long ... no wonder they passed out," he told the *Mansfield and North Nottinghamshire Chronicle and Advertiser*. "Tests indicate that the cause was nothing more serious than mass hysteria," pronounced the *Daily Telegraph* on the 16th July. "Nothing more serious..."; this denigration prompted angry reactions from parents and organizers, highlighting the general misconceptions about the nature and prevalence of mass hysteria.

In her *Observer* article Denise Winn referred to American studies of more than 1,000 cases of what the American National Institute for Occupational Safety and Health dubbed "assembly line hysteria" (after outbreaks in factories as well as in schools). It was primed, wrote Ms. Winn, by a combination of the anxiety of performing and the tension of waiting for a long period at attention, so that when the trigger came — "Two children collapsed first, then two more..." — the rest followed in a mounting wave of unintentional mimicry.[12]

There was a serious question about the way the "illness" was transmitted from the children in the arena to others outside it. We have to account for the two babies who became ill, the adults, the spectators, and several horses. The horses may or may not have anything to do with the collapse at Hollinwell, but it fit well into the widespread public anxiety and, to some, was "proof" that it was a conspiracy and not "mass hysteria."

A stricken horse was mentioned among the first radio news bulletins; and the *Sunday Times* reported on July 20 that five horses had become ill during a nearby horse competition, and one had to be destroyed. This was later denied by the organizers, and there is certainly no mention of it among the police reports.

Sloppy and excitable reporting dogged the event and undoubtedly contributed to the overall confusion in the wider public. For example, the *Guardian* reported that traces of blood and protein had been found in samples of urine taken from some of the children, possibly indicating kidney damage. Which hospital this information came from is not stated, but it was grist for the conspiracy mill. At a news conference the next day, Dr. Malcolm Lewis, director of Nottingham Public Health Laboratory, said that tests on blood and urine samples for organo-phosphorus poisoning had all been negative. Despite an unsupported claim in the *Daily Mirror* that the health officers found traces of a "cocktail of cleansing fluid and diesel fumes" in marching field, which "might" have contributed to the mass collapse, most newspapers, the next day, reported that "a complete battery of tests" by the Kirkby public health authorities had found *no* traces of agricultural chemicals or toxic agents.

The *Times* said that the findings (or lack of them) by the health authorities were greeted with scorn by offended parents and show organizers. Terry Bingham called the findings "rubbish. There has been a cover-up. Some people are still feeling ill, so how can it have been hysteria?" This opinion was reinforced by an article in the *Western Mail* suggesting that the local authorities were involved in a cover-up and the children had been poisoned by organo-phosphorus compounds.[13]

In 2003, BBC journalists revived the idea that fungicide poisoning was the culprit after finding that Tridemorph had been sprayed on the nearby fields at the time of the episode. Tridemorph was for years sprayed across England and around the world without reports of anyone collapsing. Often applied to cereal crops, it is capable of producing skin and eye irritation.[14] It was eventually banned in England, in 2000, because of its harm to the environment.

In response to the cover-up allegation, the exasperated medics of the Ashfield District Council published their findings (or lack of them). This did not satisfy their critics either.[15] By now, the clamor included people with more political motives; Denis Skinner, one of three MPs who called for a government inquiry, said the "mass hysteria" verdict was "an insult to the intelligence and another cover-up by the Establishment."[16] Arthur Peacock, of the Mansfield Ecology Party, wrote to a number of journals calling for the uncovering of "a major public scandal." "Everyone but

Ashfield Council," he declared, "can see it is ludicrous to put the blame on mass hysteria."

In Search of a Trigger

What triggered the collective panic? Most reports agree that one, perhaps two, girls collapsed first, with the rest following like dominoes. It may be that they simply fainted, which in turn generated anxiety among the remaining band members. There are, however, other possible triggers. Firstly, there were the ill-considered broadcasts warning folks not to consume the ice creams or mineral waters. Tucked away in the acres of local media coverage was a comment that, quite early on that morning, the show's organizers had, themselves, made an announcement about the dangers of eating some "joke jelly babies."[17] This warning could well have set the tone for the day, the later announcements fanning the embers of fear. Police never found out who made the ice-cream announcements; indeed, there was a suspicion that they might have been rumors, or not broadcast at all, simply imagined in retrospect.[18] The second possible trigger has to do with the two very young babies involved. According to the *Sunday Times*, Margaret Palethorpe thought she had been the first person to feel ill. Two of her five children were in the Woodland Gladers band. It is pure speculation, but perhaps her two children became over-anxious on seeing their mother becoming ill among the spectators. The occasion of Mrs. Palethorpe's unease is quite clear; as her children's band was waiting for inspection, she changed the diaper on her three-week-old baby and was startled to find a mass of "blebs" on him.[19] The fact that Mrs. Palethorpe had to remain in the hospital for over two weeks after the birth might yet be a significant factor in her anxiety. Quite unintentionally, she might have been the prime catalyst in the drama. The mother of the other baby involved, Susan Bonsall, had also panicked when she could not rouse her sleeping two-week-old baby; and her panic was made worse by the chaos going on all around her.

History Repeated

Eight years before the Hollinwell incident, a similar event had happened at Hazlerigg, a town in Northumberland about four miles north of Newcastle-upon-Tyne in the northeast of England. On July 8, 1972, an early summer day, six marching bands had gathered for an annual fete.

About twelve hundred people were there to witness the popular spectacle, four hundred of whom were performers. During the afternoon parade as the bands were performing, scores of band members and a handful of adults suddenly felt ill. Dozens of schoolchildren were scattered along the parade route; some bent over in obvious distress, others collapsed completely, and many more cried or moaned, complaining of stomach aches, nausea, dizziness and headaches. Sensations of hot and cold rippled through many as they lay shivering on the ground. Others felt tingling or numbness in their hands and feet. As was noted at Hollinwell, the scene had the look of a disaster film. While the children soon recovered, what happened remains the subject of controversy.[20]

Since the gala organizers offered no food, and before the event got underway most children ate home-packed lunches, food poisoning was not suspected. The hour-long parade along a mile-long route began at 1:00 P.M. The six bands led the way, followed by local children in fancy attire. Band members were as young as five and as old as sixteen, and nearly all were girls. The bands were not lavish: most of the children played kazoos; some had cymbals or drums. Spirits were high as the crowd cheered them on. The youngest children held banners as they brought up the rear. Suddenly a sixteen-year-old bass drummer fell out of formation, crashing to the ground in a heap. Within minutes, six more girls began to wobble, then collapsed; they clutched their abdomens and wept, complaining of dizziness and stomach pain. By 6:00 P.M. four adults and 168 children were being examined at the area's five hospitals, where doctors noted a curious pattern: their patients, after a little time away from the chaos at the scene, no longer showed signs that anything was wrong, and most got better quickly. Said one physician: "They were all ... frightened and bewildered, many of them believing they had been poisoned and several spontaneously said they had thought that they were dying."[21] Several of those treated were clearly over-excited and exhibiting tension-induced muscle twitching; many more were hyperventilating. Another oddity stood out to investigators—not a single adult or child from Hazlerigg was affected.[22]

Immediately after the incident, investigators scoured the area but found no obvious triggering agent. They looked at everything from candy to ice cream sold at the gala and whether a local farmer might have sprayed the area with a toxic substance a week or more earlier. Grazing fields surrounding the gala had not been sprayed and there had been no gas leaks; indeed, there were no pipes under the field. Weather also didn't seem to be a factor as by mid-day the temperature only reached a cool 61°F, and the humidity was a comfortable 57 percent.[23]

In their final report on the case, two local doctors who were on the front lines that day—H.C. Smith of Northumberland and E.J. Eastham of Newcastle University Hospitals—were critical of the local press for refusing to accept their mass hysteria diagnosis. This made their job tougher, they said, undermining their credibility. As at Hollinwell, such statements from experts were dismissed or challenged by parents and others who felt the diagnosis of "hysteria" somehow demeaned them. The doctors were certain that a bacteria or virus was not the cause as the children came from different locations and had assembled less than five hours before the outbreak. Despite the doctors' assurances, the press rejected their views; one headline even proclaimed: "Mystery Bug KOs Children."[24]

Most of those stricken had noticed a foul smell while making their way to the sports field. It was said to have wafted from a recently cleared pig sty. The locals were aware of the odor's origin, and were probably accustomed to it, but most visitors were left guessing as to its cause. Many of those who fell ill described the smell in dramatic fashion. While symptoms cleared up within a day for most of those stricken, in others they subsided gradually over the next week, likely prolonged by media sensationalism. Investigators report that during the incident, a TV film crew arrived on the scene, heightening the drama. Smith and Eastham said that TV and press coverage had stoked the fires of public fear as reporting was "out of all proportion to the medical significance of the event. It was implied that the children had a mysterious illness baffling medical science. It was not surprising, therefore, that in some children the symptoms tended to persist."[25]

A sample of turf was taken immediately after the collapse, to be tested for insecticide, weed-killer or fungicide, but no such indications were found. Nevertheless, Steven Mitchell, a rescue squad member treating victims at the scene at Hazlerigg, supports the fungicide theory: "There were a lot of young people very distressed—their eyes were very sore and had severe breathing difficulties—there was a smell in the air.... With the bands marching up and down, they were dispersing the chemical into the air, and I am sure it was inhaled by the young children." As would later happen at Hollinwell, other explanations put forward for the incident included food poisoning, water pollution, nerve agents, and radio waves, though there is little or no evidence to support any of these theories. Anxiety remains the best explanation. According to one report, one of the attending doctors separated the children from each other and deprived them of vomiting bowls. As he expected, the symptoms rapidly subsided.[26]

More Marching Mayhem

On a hot, humid Friday evening in Alabama on September 21, 1973, nearly half of a 120-member marching band either fainted or felt ill shortly after performing at a high school football game. The contest had been emotionally draining, with the favored visiting team losing 7–6. The band had performed a seven-minute halftime routine, remaining on the field in a kneeling position while their counterparts from the rival school performed. When the rival's drill was over, the visiting band stood at attention, then marched to their seats in the grandstand. Without warning, a girl in the band fainted. Over the next ten minutes, five more girls fainted. The girls were laid on benches and several were sent to the hospital. Within twenty minutes many more band members reported feeling sick. Many seemed to be overbreathing and reported a tingling sensation in their hands and arms, and, for some, a feeling of choking. Some also reported stomach pain or cramps, dizziness, nausea, and weakness.[27]

Doctors later said that a group of students in the wind section had over-dressed for the warm conditions and were overwhelmed by the heat and the excitement of the game. These circumstances triggered minor dizziness and fainting, which, in turn, generated sudden, extreme fear in other band members, who began to succumb after seeing their friends collapse.

A second wave of symptoms occurred as band members were boarding buses for the one-hundred-mile trip home after the game. Over the following three days, ten more girls were stricken, with five of the original victims having relapses. Tests for food poisoning — the first suspicion — were negative. Heat stroke was also eliminated as the cardinal symptom, fever, was absent. While heat may have played a minor role, Dr. Richard Levine of the United States Public Health Service believed the event was mostly psychological. Levine said, "The discipline of a precision marching drill, the discomfort of wearing heavy clothes in a hot environment, the excitement and disappointment at losing a close game — suggests that the setting ... was appropriately tense for mass hysteria to occur." Levine notes that the first group of girls to be affected were all from the wind section and were dressed in the heaviest clothing with high-waisted, one-hundred-percent wool trousers "and an impermeable plastic jacket overlay." He says that with an air temperature at the time of 73°F, it's likely that some of the girls experienced heat-related fainting spells, but then mass hysteria soon took over.[28]

Levine also uncovered a remarkable coincidence. A fainting episode had occurred in the United States under nearly identical circumstances in 1964. While the location was not noted, as in the Alabama incident, the episode struck girls in a high school marching band at an exciting "away" football game. According to one report, "The band had worn heavy woolen uniforms on a hot day, and the visitors, although their team was favored to win, had lost. Except for the prominence of fainting, this reported epidemic shows a striking resemblance to the one described here." There are many similar incidents on record. In 1963, eight girls in a high school marching band in Maine collapsed after experiencing stomach pains and overbreathing at the site of their school's football game. One of the most remarkable of these episodes occurred during the 1950s.[29]

A pitched Friday night battle was taking place under the lights between two rival high school football teams, the Tigers from Neville High in Monroe, Louisiana, and the home team of Natchez, Mississippi. It was September 12, 1952. The 165-member Tigerettes Pep Squad had first paraded along Main Street, whipping up excitement for the coming gridiron contest. As the first quarter ended, the cheerleaders bounded onto the field, mistakenly believing it to be time for their half-time performance, only to be called back to the sidelines over the loudspeakers. Soon, fainting ensued among the girls. One man said they "fainted like flies." The girls, ages fourteen to eighteen, were all taken to the nearby hospital, where they quickly recovered. Doctors could find nothing wrong with them. In an amazing display of athletic determination and despite the presence of ambulances along the sidelines and even on the field, the game kept going. At one point, five emergency vehicles were crossing the field at one time. "It looked like the race track at Indianapolis," said Thornton Smith. At times players had to dodge ambulances. Neville High won the hard-fought game, 21 to 8.[30]

After talking to the girls, the examining hospital physician, Dr. James Barnes, said that the first two victims had apparently fainted, while the rest followed through mass hysteria, prompted by the heat, the excitement of the game, and the stress of seeing their classmates faint before their eyes. Neville High's principal, Paul Neal, said that after the first thirty-five or so girls had fainted, "every available ambulance and scores of cars were pressed into service." It was learned that following the afternoon's Main Street Pep Rally, the girls had taken a break, grabbing hamburgers at the local burger joint before proceeding to the game, so when the fainting spells began, everyone was sure it was food poisoning. But based on the symptoms, which quickly went away, mass hysteria was the eventual diagnosis.[31]

The Falling Chorus Line

School choruses have also had their share of mass fainting episodes. One large-scale incident took place in Santa Monica, California, on the evening of April 13, 1989. About six hundred students were warming up their voices and checking their instruments, readying themselves for a big concert dubbed "Stairway of the Stars." Chorus members from three area high schools were set to perform in the 40th anniversary of a concert tradition. Then a student fell ill. Before long, 247 students were complaining of dizziness, headaches, stomach pain, nausea, and weakness. Ambulances and police were soon converging on the building. Not a single audience member reported feeling ill. Psychiatrist Gary Small said, "Performance anxiety probably contributed to symptoms."[32]

Several years earlier, a similar episode had taken place on the other side of the country in East Templeton, Massachusetts. On May 20, 1981, 102 elementary students took a bus to their central high school to join three hundred more students from nearby schools to rehearse for a big concert that evening that would be attended by nearly a thousand people, mainly parents. After thirty minutes, several members of the chorus fell to the floor, clutching their throats and stomachs, some gasping for air. The stricken students were escorted out of the auditorium to rest and recover, but the situation worsened. A few minutes later another chorus member went down, followed by another a few minutes later. On it went during the rehearsal: itchy eyes, dizziness, fainting, overbreathing, weakness. Soon one of the teachers phoned for help. Of the nine students who had fainted, six were taken to the hospital, where they were checked over and released in time for the evening performance. Curiously, nearly all of those feeling unwell were from the East Templeton school.

That evening, the concert went on as scheduled. It proceeded uneventfully until an hour and fifteen minutes into it, when during a stirring rendition of "God Bless America" a girl in the chorus fainted. Within minutes, four more members collapsed. Several more felt unwell and simply walked off the stage. The organizers struggled to keep order. Parents sat nervously, squirming and craning their necks, exchanging glances. For a few minutes the auditorium teetered on the brink of pandemonium. The music teachers kept control and the show went on. Meanwhile, on the floor of the nearby hallway, were children, panicky and frightened, moaning and groaning, complaining of stomach pain, shortness of breath, nausea, and itchy eyes. Of the twenty-nine children who were stricken, fifteen were taken to the hospital.

Except for signs of anxiety and a few cases of pink eye (common in many schools), the students had normal vital signs. A battery of tests was given, including chest X-rays and blood counts. Two days later, when the lab results came back, doctors were surprised to find that all thirteen urine samples contained n-butylbenzene sulfonamide, a chemical common in plastics, disinfectants, and insecticides. The announcement caused a sensation in the community as it was believed that the children had been inadvertently poisoned. One newspaper proclaimed: "Victims of Chemical." But to everyone's surprise, when a sample of healthy adults gave urine samples, they tested positive for the same chemical. Then some water samples tested positive. Officials were baffled. Had the whole town been poisoned? Further investigation revealed a curious pattern — the positive samples had come *only* from plastic containers. Those samples gathered in glass containers were free of the chemical, which had come from the containers themselves.

Amid the fear, uncertainty, and media hoopla, rumors quickly spread through the town. Some speculated that someone had put a hallucinogenic drug into the ventilation system. Others said it was a gas leak, ultraviolet lights, or gypsy moth spray. At one point health officials suggested that the school janitor was to blame, having disposed of insecticide on school grounds just two days earlier. But based on the wind direction and distance from the disposal area, authorities ruled out this possibility. Besides, the janitor felt fine.

Investigators noted other curiosities. Not a single adult felt ill despite being in the same building. Further, while students from four elementary schools sang in the concert, all but one of the students who fell ill were from East Templeton Elementary. They were a group within a group, close-knit and apparently excited and nervous after seeing others from their school fall ill.

One of the biggest outbreaks of choral hysteria occurred in 1959 in the midwestern United States. It was a perfect recipe for mass hysteria: 5,400 high school chorus members from across Oklahoma, gathered in the huge fieldhouse at Oklahoma State University for the annual Thanksgiving Song Festival. It was Monday evening, November 23. About two hundred buses were parked around the stadium. Being November, the weather was chilly, so many of the bus drivers started their engines about halfway through the program so they could turn on the heaters to warm the buses for the trip home. That's when some of the diesel fumes were sucked into the air intake fans. The smell frightened the students, who started fainting, and the stadium was evacuated. Many students seemed fine and left the stadium in a calm, orderly fashion, only to feel ill outside when they saw their classmates falling ill. Of the more than five hundred students who were taken to area hospitals, all quickly recovered. A handful were kept overnight for observation. G.C. Epperly, the chorus director at Stillwater High School, said the cause was "a combination of too many hot dogs, a little carbon monoxide and a lot of mass hysteria."[33]

An epidemic of swooning chorus girls swept through Ohio in December 1952. For more than a week, the Warren High School's chorus suffered bouts of fainting. Whenever they sang before their classmates, they were fine. The fainting spells only occurred when they sang before "outsiders," noted one reporter: "The choir will be singing along when — plop!— down go several girls with a swoon, sometimes six or seven at a time." On Tuesday, December 9, seven girls passed out while singing at an Exchange Club luncheon. The next day at a Rotary Club gathering, six more went tumbling down. Then on Friday, December 12, members of the Kwanis Club looked on in amazement as five more keeled over. Not a single student in the boy's choir was affected.[34]

A few days later, Cleveland, Ohio, was the scene of a separate fainting epidemic that struck down choir members from Myron T. Herrick Junior High. Seventy girls were singing "The Bells of Christmas Morning" during a packed school assembly on December 19 when one of them fell over. Before long, classmates began keeling over "in a wave-like reaction."[35]

How Not to Handle a Fainting Epidemic

October 6, 1965, was a big day for schoolgirls in Blackburn, England. It was the day they were to meet members of the royal family. Even though the occasion was to be a stolid church service, on the inside the girls could barely contain their excitement which grew to rock star intensity. But the royals were late — very late. For three long hours the girls stood and waited. Wilting from fatigue, their excitement turned to disappointment and, finally, anger. While the royals did eventually arrive, during the wait twenty girls fainted.

The next day, the fainting episode was the talk of the school. As the morning assembly got underway, a girl fainted. This was not uncommon at the assembly. Ordinarily that would have been the end of it, but through a series of inept decisions by school officials, by the end of the day 30 percent of the entire student body was stricken. As the assembly broke up, four more girls felt dizzy. Teachers quickly sat them on chairs. The trouble was, their seats were center stage, so to speak, along the main corridor in the middle of the school. Over the first two class periods, six more girls said they also felt faint and were asked to sit in the hallway with the others. Now ten girls were seated in chairs along the hallway.

School officials became worried that if one of the girls did faint, she might smack her head on the hard floor. To be on the safe side, the ten girls were asked to lie on the floor in the corridor, making for a dramatic scene, especially considering that none of the girls had fainted—they only said they had *felt* faint. To make matters worse, during the morning, most of the other students had the opportunity to walk by the woozy ten. It was against this backdrop that with each passing period, more and more girls—eventually 141 in all—felt unwell, complaining of dizziness, headache, shivering, abdominal pain, nausea, breathlessness, backaches, facial numbness, and muscle spasms.

An emergency was soon declared. Ambulances and rescue personnel converged on the school and in the ensuing chaos took 85 girls to the hospital. Media reports only fueled community fears by describing the cause as a "mysterious illness." However, a battery of tests on the girls were all negative and gradually over the next two weeks the cases tapered off. The Blackburn affair is a case study in how not to handle a fainting epidemic. If the girls had not been placed in such a high-profile area, the epidemic would likely never had spread.[36]

The Great Train Scare

It began innocently, in a quiet Montreal train station on Friday, May 29, 1981. Summer was coming early to southeastern Canada. The day was exceptionally hot and humid across the region. About 500 seventh and eighth graders piled into a passenger train that would take them home to southern Ontario. The weary students were happy to be heading back after an exhausting four-day cultural exchange in Quebec City, a part of Canada where French language and culture remain strong and French is the primary language. The group didn't mind the heat outside, as the cars were air conditioned. But when they pulled into the train station in Montreal at 8:40 that evening and began to disembark, the Montreal Central Station was oppressively hot and humid. The plan was to eat supper during a three-hour stopover, then get back on the train and finish the final leg of the journey home. By 10:00 P.M. a number of the students were already back at the station, anxious to get on the air-conditioned train and leave. Suddenly, a young girl felt dizzy and collapsed. Within a few minutes, six other girls felt weak, shaky, and were seized by headaches and stomach pain. Before long, police and emergency personnel were swarming. By now, the number of girls affected had risen to thirteen. Sirens blaring, the girls were rushed to the Montreal Children's Hospital. At about this time, rumors began circulating that a "mystery illness" had struck a group of girls at the train station. An army of reporters descended on the scene, and special bulletins were broadcast by local radio stations. Media speculation was rampant. One rumor held that chemicals were leaking from the train's air-conditioning system; others blamed food poisoning. All of the commotion served to heighten the tension. Amid questions by teachers and chaperones who began to ask their students if they felt ill, more and more students succumbed. By midnight, seventeen more pupils said they weren't feeling well and were also taken to the hospital for evaluation.[37]

At the hospital, doctors noticed that the first group of thirteen girls were anxious and overbreathing. Many of those receiving medical attention said that they had felt fine until they saw the other children becoming "sick." By 11:00 P.M. all but two of the original thirteen were cleared for discharge. Confident that the cause was a collective panic attack, doctors calmly explained that while some may have had "a mild intestinal ailment," poisoning was unlikely, and they seemed fine now and were well enough to board the train. Hospital pediatrician Dr. M.E. Moffatt described what happened next: "Upon hearing this, the two remaining girls got up off their stretchers and rejoined the others. One of these girls had had severe vertigo only minutes before, and the other had had severe pseudoparalysis which immediately disappeared."[38]

In addition to fatigue, excitement, the warm weather, and being away from home, Moffatt believes another factor in the outbreak was isolation. Over the previous four days, group members had developed an unusually close-knit bond after being surrounded by French speakers.[39] The final straw was the hot weather, which must have seemed even hotter after traveling in the comfort of the air-conditioned train before the doors opened and the smothering blanket of warm air hit them at the Montreal train station.

The Power of Culture: Close Encounters of the Schoolyard Kind in Asia

Children everywhere have vivid imaginations. Sometimes they exaggerate real events; other times the events they recount are pure fiction. Kids do so because of their limited knowledge of the world, their rich imaginations, and their need to fit in and be liked. This combination of culture, naiveté, and the propensity for weaving a colorful tale can produce some interesting, if not incredible, results. What is believable in one culture and time is often unbelievable in another. You will recall from chapter 4 that Malaysia has been the scene of many strange classroom tales over the years. Yet these accounts cannot match the reports of space aliens in schoolyards. Malay children grow up learning traditional stories about the reality of an array of tiny supernatural creatures that are widely believed to inhabit the lush, tropical Malay Peninsula. Among the most prominent are *toyls* and *pari-pari*, thought to be races of diminutive, mischievous fairies that stand just a few inches high. These same children are also exposed to Western books, films, and TV shows. The result is a strange hybrid of "close encounter" reports blending elements of East and West. Since the late 1960s there have been numerous reports in major Malaysian newspapers describing schoolyard encounters with thumb-sized extraterrestrials. Before reading these accounts, it is important to realize that while the reality of the encounters is questionable, the accounts of the incidents themselves are not, and all were reported by professional journalists from mainstream newspapers, who traveled to the schools, spoke with the principals and interviewed students.

Beginning in the 1950s, children the world over were inundated with science-fiction movies, TV shows, and playthings. Not coincidentally, this was also the era in which UFO reports flourished. Many of these new cultural touchstones stemmed from a confluence of the American and Japanese fascination with all things futuristic. Japanese manufacturers cranked out mechanical toy robots, spaceships, aliens, and spacemen, all bristling with the promise of advanced technologies and eagerly snapped up by kids in both countries. The big screens at theaters and drive-ins were awash with American and Asian films boasting titles such as *Destination Moon*, *Invaders from Mars*, *Battle in Space*, and *The Mysterians*, many of which featured adolescents and teens as hero figures.[40]

Then, on July 20, 1969, humans first set foot on the moon, and almost overnight, science fiction became science fact, creating intense worldwide interest in anything having to do with space travel and the possibility of life on other planets. It was in this same month, in the city of Johor Baru on the southern tip of the Malay Peninsula, that the "visitors" arrived. At 10:25 A.M. students at the Temenggong Abdul Rahman Primary School were on the playground for morning recess when, they said, a tiny silver craft, about the size of a cooking pot, landed in a corner of the schoolyard. Skeptical teachers were told of five entities standing seven inches tall, who scrambled from the saucer, wearing tiny red suits and, in Wild West style, tiny ray guns strapped to their waists. The children said they didn't feel threatened and rushed the creatures, hoping to capture them, but they dove into a tiny hole in the ground. The craft then vanished before their eyes.[41] Perhaps not coincidentally, *toyls* and *pari-pari* are commonly thought to reside in holes and can magically appear and disappear at will.

During 1970, with continuing interest in the Apollo missions, there was a remarkable spate of close encounter reports in schoolyards across the country. The most spectacular incident took place in broad daylight near the Stowell English Primary School in Bukit Mertajam on Penang island. It was August 19. Ten-year-old K. Wigneswaran said that several UFOs had alighted in the bushes near the school grounds. From each object emerged a three-inch-tall entity. He told teachers that just as he was closing in for a better look, the school bell rang and he returned to class.[42]

That evening, six schoolmates reported seeing a tiny, blue UFO resting on the ground in the bushes near the school. The boys said that five little men got out. One was dressed in a yellow suit; the other four, presumably of lesser rank, wore blue uniforms. The boys said they watched as the beings installed what seemed to be an antenna on a tree branch, frightening the boys, who ran away.[43] No one produced the antenna. The next day, Wigneswaran was found unconscious in the schoolyard. He later gave a vivid account of having been shot by aliens. He told of visiting the site of his previous encounter when he spotted a small spacecraft from which five tiny entities emerged. As with the reports of the evening before, one of them wore a yellow uniform and had two horn-like appendages protruding from his head, resembling the alien on the popular TV show *My Favorite Martian*. He seemed to be the leader. The other four wore blue suits.

Wigneswaran said that he tried to catch the leader, who then shot him. He was later found lying in the bushes, and was carried to his classroom where he recovered. Wigneswaran said he had proof of his encounter, pointing to a small red spot on his right leg where the alien had supposedly shot him. The entire incident occurred in broad daylight on the school playground, yet no one saw a thing. After school, two boys went to the spot of Wigneswaran's encounter. There, they reportedly met two tiny entities in the bushes, wearing yellow suits. One was on a rock; the other was perched on a tree branch about three feet off the ground and had only one arm — the left. The boys said the creature was sitting on the branch shaking its head from side to side, grasping what looked like a weapon. Another classmate confirmed the story: Mohamed Ariffin bin Mokhtar, the son of a police corporal. His father told reporters: "When he returned home at 6:30 last night, he told my wife and me he had seen two tiny spacemen in the *belukar* [small woods] outside the school fence. When he tried to catch them, one shot him. He had a small cut on his left hand and my wife treated the wound." His statement seemed to imply that the boy's story should be given credence because his father was a police officer.[44]

At 6:30 that evening, a few of the boys who had encountered the blue UFO on the previous evening returned to the site. One of them, eleven-year-old Mohamed Zulkifli, reported spotting a UFO on the ground surrounded by creatures three inches tall. One of his friends, Mohamed Ali, age 8, told the school's principal, Ooi Keat Guan, that one of the beings had zapped him with a tiny gun.[45] With this incident, the remarkable series of reports at the Stowell School came to a close.

Perhaps fueled by the publicity in Penang, days later, Rawang in the state of Selangor was the site of another encounter report. At 10:00 A.M. several primary students told their teachers that a tiny saucer the size of a car tire had landed in front of their school; five thumb-sized creatures got out. Four had two horn-like appendages protruding from their heads. When several children and teachers moved in for a better look, they said, the creatures scurried back into the object and flew off. Shortly after, police rushed to the school and searched the grounds, but found nothing to support the claims.[46]

In 1979, nearly a decade later, the island of Penang was the site of more bizarre reports. At about 3:00 P.M. on May 20, six children from the Jit Sin Primary School were playing under a tree when they spotted a tiny craft on the ground, they later said. Exploring the nearby terrain were four three-inch-tall creatures. One of the boys, Khor Boon Chew, said that as he tried to catch one, it fired a weapon, causing a "stinging pain" in his right palm. Chew then said the creature fired another shot, striking a stray brick and breaking it in two. Another boy said that as the creatures ran into the saucer, he grabbed onto the craft with both hands but was forced to let go after an electric current jolted him. As the object flew off, they said, it caused leaves from a nearby tree to shower down.

A 21-year-old man playing basketball nearby, Raymond Liang, said he ran toward the school after hearing the commotion and witnessed the students gathered around something. "I rushed to the scene and saw a tiny flying saucer under a tree with four aliens ... three inches tall standing outside," he said. Liang confirmed Khor's claim of having been shot by one of the tiny creatures, saying it used a pistol-like device; after the shooting they all ran back to the saucer. Liang said the creatures wore green uniforms with white helmets or caps. Police eventually came to the school and took statements from the six students. Mr. R. Veerasamy, a senior English instructor at the school, considered the boys' accounts believable: "Can the mind of six children and an adult run wild at the same time? ...

I believe there is some truth in the story and it merits further investigation."⁴⁷

Yet another encounter claim by Malaysian schoolchildren took place during the weekend of August 21 and 22, 1982, when a spacecraft reportedly landed in a durian plantation near Sarikei, on the island of Borneo in East Malaysia. Durians are a spiny, smelly tropical fruit, about the size of an American football. They are loved by Malaysians. Police interviewed several 9-year-old schoolboys who claimed to have seen "little people" with large heads out of proportion to their bodies. Two days later, more creatures were spotted near a UFO on the same plantation. Police surmised that the story was either a lie or due to overactive imaginations, suspicious that the students may have been hunting for durians and used the space creature story to avoid being disciplined by their principal, who had previously forbidden them from the plantation. However, two of the boys steadfastly stuck to their story. The previous week, residents had reported spotting a fireball in broad daylight. The UFO incident followed shortly thereafter. It was later suggested that the "fireball" had been a round from a signal flare gun, apparently fired as a prank. The incident may have sparked the children's imaginations, possibly as a cover for their penchant for durians—which, incidentally, can easily be sold for a handsome profit.⁴⁸

Fairies in the Schoolyard

The Malaysians' belief in fairies is nearly as strong as their belief in space aliens. Encounters with little folk are common in schoolyards across the country. One flurry of reports took place during October 1974 in the state of Pahang, near the center of the Malay Peninsula. The episode began on October 8 in Padang Geroda, as two schoolboys at the Royal Malaysian Air Force Primary School sat behind the school. Suddenly, near a clump of bush, they saw a thumb-sized, brown-skinned creature. "It had two feelers on the head and held a steel-like rod in its hand. A pistol was hanging from its waist," said nine-year-old Paul Lazario. The boy said he spotted the creature as it was stooping down to drink water and captured the being but "it escaped from [his] grip and ran into some undergrowth." The incident took place during school hours. On the same day, three students heading home from school reported spotting a tiny UFO with three-inch-tall creatures near the RMAF base. One boy said he passed out for several minutes after the entity "shot" him.⁴⁹

That evening, after Lazario told his friends of the initial incident, three schoolmates visited the site and claimed to have spotted a three-inch-tall creature. Neo Lee Ann, age twelve, said, "When it saw us, it ran into the undergrowth and disappeared." After hearing the story, teacher Yew Kim Guan went to the site and, while he did not see any creatures, reported finding "a Red Indian-like wigwam beautifully weaved out of grass and *lallang* (tall weeds)."

It was not long before the students had the entire community of Kuantan in an uproar. As news of the encounter spread, residents went on the lookout for the creature. By the end of the next day, there had been three more sightings of tiny entities in the vicinity. One incident was related by Nor Akmar Mahmud, age twenty-two, a passenger on a bus trip from Kampung Melayu in Gambang. Stepping off the bus at the end of her journey, she accidentally kicked what she thought to be a puppet belonging to a fellow passenger. She said that she stared at it for a moment when, to her surprise, the object moved. She soon became aware of three little entities. One was five inches tall and the other two stood about three inches high. She claims to have picked one up and was shocked when it laughed. She then let it go and the three beings held hands and scurried off, disappearing into the crowd waiting for the bus. She described the beings as looking like tiny men, but with slightly larger, chocolate-brown heads and hairy legs. In a second incident on the same day, a woman said she was startled by a tiny creature clinging to her leg as she waited for a bus. She said the entity grinned at her, revealing shiny teeth. She panicked and screamed, accidentally kicking the entity under a moving bus. She added that the creature mysteriously vanished. The final incident of October 8 involved another bus passenger, Maimunah Ahmad, age twenty-two, who reported hearing a strange voice from the empty space beside her for the entire duration of a bus trip from Gambang to Kuantan. She said that she could not understand what the voice was saying.[50]

On October 16, 1985, a group of Islamic children at the Paka Primary School in the state of Terengganu told of encountering seven tiny dark-skinned creatures wearing only shorts. One child said he tried to grab one of the creatures but had to release it when his hand felt itchy. The witnesses pinpointed a woodpile as the creatures' hiding place, so residents rushed to the site and spent hours removing the wood. They found nothing. Earlier reports had occurred on Friday, October 11, followed by another the next day, and yet another on October 15. Different witnesses reported each incident. Thirteen-year-old Mohmed Sabri Zubit said the creatures spoke a language similar to Indonesian and were wearing male Islamic headgear known as a *songkok*. One was wearing a *hijab* (female Islamic cloth used to cover the head) "and the rest were wearing nothing but long pants." Schoolteacher Baharuddin bin Omar initially refused to believe the reports but later conceded, "I had to believe because many people saw them at different times."[51]

In February 1989, several students at the Selayang Baru Primary School in Selangor reportedly spotted six "gnomes." Three nine-year-old students said they saw gnomes that stood six inches tall. The male creatures were described as bald except for tufts of hair near their ears. They weren't dressed for the weather, wearing chocolate-colored, short-sleeved fur coats with matching shorts. The females had flowing hair down to their waists, and also wore waist-length fur coats and shirts. All had pointed ears. The students said the gnomes snapped at their hands when they tried to catch them. On one occasion, they said, when a student grabbed at a creature it wielded an axe, so he quickly let go. The beings appeared in the evenings, during school holidays, and at other quiet times. They were often seen frolicking on school fields and in the parking lot, or having a bath in the drain. Faizul Afendi said the gnomes had sharp teeth and claws, and that he was scratched while trying to catch one. The school's principal, Haji Abdul Aziz Haji Abu, said, "I dared them to catch the gnomes in a bottle or a plastic bag. But till now there is no evidence." He also noted, "The picture given by them and drawn by the art teacher, clearly show the similarity with the toyol," tiny creatures from traditional Malay folklore.[52]

During late June of 1990, four teachers and students of the Tapah Secondary School in Perak reported seeing tiny human-like creatures, about six inches high. They had hairy brown legs, shiny red eyes, oval-shaped ears, and their bodies were whitish gray. Two students, Kuzilan and Murali, both fourteen, said they saw the tiny men exit a cave near the school on June 26 at about 6:00 P.M. They said the men appeared to be looking for food, as, after they spotted a piece of cake, they immediately took it and returned to the cave, reported the *Nanyang Siang Pau* of June 30th.

Pandemonium broke out at the Sultan Sulaiman Primary School in Kuala Terengganu in northeastern Malaysia over two days in 1991 as scores of tiny entities were spotted on school grounds. The incidents occurred on May 12 and 13 during afternoon recess. Eight-year-old Mohamed Izainurie Nor Zaidi said he was stabbed in the left hand by one of the creatures as he tried to catch it. When school officials examined his hand, it appeared bruised. At the time, the boy's father, Norzidi Mohamad, was captain of the Terengganu State soccer team. The boy said he approached an outer fence around the recess area where he saw "hundreds of tiny people coming out of a hole near the drain of a housing estate." Zaidi said he could clearly see the faces of the creatures, who were dressed in red and stood about two and a half inches tall. Another eight-year-old, Hafiza Zakaria, claimed that she and another schoolgirl had seen the tiny folk near a drain. Other students, including ten-year-old Yasmin Hadyah Yyuri, were adamant that they too had seen the tiny people. The sightings were confined to students. Not one of the forty-one teachers at the school reported seeing anything.[53]

In July 1991, two 11-year-old boys said that a tiny man had appeared at the sixteenth mile of Kampung Buluhan near Kota Baru, Kelantan, and that they had played with the creature as it pranced about on their hands. They said they first saw the little man at 6:00 P.M., on Friday, hidden among some stones in the school compound where they had gone to water a vegetable plot. As they were about to pick up a hoe near some stones, a plastic bag moving along the ground startled them. Hiding under the bag was a tiny man about two and a half inches high. Yusof caught the little man, but his friend pleaded with him to release the creature. The boys say the tiny being enjoyed eating chili and other foods that were left near a hole. They described the being as resembling a human male, except that it had white stripes. They weren't sure whether the stripes were part of its clothes or its body. A teacher who heard the tale noted that bananas from the nearby trees were frequently missing and may have been gobbled down by the little fellow.[54]

During the last week of September 1992, a group of students and a few residents in Bandar Baru Sentul, Kuala Lumpur, saw a creature that stood six inches high. Witnesses said it had glittering green skin, with three long fingers on each hand and long nails on each finger. Thirteen-year-old Law Wai Chow of Kuala Lumpur's Maxwell High School said that he had previously encountered the creature and that its eyes were like a human's except that they were red. Another student, Suriakumar Wickramasena, twelve, described the being as human-like but bald. Three days after the initial sighting he "saw the creature sitting near a hole. The creature was frightened and ran very fast into the hole."[55]

Tiny beings in space suits with ray guns strapped to their sides? Fairy-like creatures in schoolyards wearing shorts and T-shirts? These reports are laughable to most of the world. But not to many Malaysians who consider the reality of such beings as plausible. To many Malaysians, the world is filled with an array of tiny magical creatures. Indeed, if one were keeping score, when it comes to school scares and hysterias, Malaysia would likely be declared the world's epicenter of these tales.

Look! Up in the Sky!

It was the night of July 29, 1992. The story begins at the Hishamuddin Secondary Islamic School in Klang, about an hour's drive northwest of the capital city of Kuala Lumpur. It was there that two hundred students and their instructor reported seeing miraculous sights in the sky over a five-hour period. Some said they could plainly see the word Allah (God) in Jawi script. Jawi is Arabic writing that has a special place in Islamic Asia as it is the script in which the Koran was written and is central to religious writings. Soon, someone saw a cloud that looked like a women with her *aurat* exposed, and two dead bodies. One's *aurat* are body parts that must be covered according to Islamic custom such as the hair on a woman's head. In all, twenty-six images were reported.

The next evening at about 6:50, the words "Allah" and "Muhammad" reportedly appeared in Jawi script while all of the students were praying in a school field. This time the script was said to be much larger. All of the images were reportedly formed in clouds. Dr. Jariah Abdullah of the Chemistry Department at the University of Kebangsaan Malaysia heard about the incidents and talked with the students.[56]

The "miracle" near the Hishamuddin School coincided with a flurry of reports beginning in about 1990, involving mostly Muslims, of the appearance of Islamic symbols, most typically Arabic Jawi script, in many different countries. For example, on June 12, 1990, in Algeria, the Islamic Salvation Front Party won an upset election victory. While the party leader was speaking to a crowd of supporters who were standing and shouting, "Allah Akhbar" ("God is great!") in the direction of Mecca (the Muslim Holy Land), a cloud reportedly formed the shape of the word "Allah" in Jawi. There was great excitement, and many people wept and fainted.[57] In 1990 there were many reports of Arabic script appearing in eggplants (referred to in some countries as egg fruits or aubergines). For instance, in Nottingham, England, in March, Islamic accountant Hussain Bhatti cut open an eggplant and became convinced that it contained Jawi script. In another case, Farida Kassam of Leicester, England, reported that the seeds had formed a pattern that was similar to "Yah-Allah" ("God is everywhere") or "Ya-Allah" ("God exists").[58]

During times of crisis and uncertainty, people often see what they want to see in order to make sense of an uncertain world. During the 1980s, two Islamic countries, Iran and Iraq, fought a bitter war that pitted Muslim against Muslim. Further divisions were soon created with the formation of a military coalition of Muslim and Western countries in 1991 to reestablish the sovereignty of Kuwait after its occupation by Iraq. The early 1990s also saw adversities faced by Muslims in Bosnia-Herzegovina and other parts of the former Soviet Union. Under such circumstances, Islamic sympathizers may have been susceptible to misperceiving mundane events and circumstances relative to the those specific beliefs. The

Klang "miracle" seems explainable in a more straightforward fashion: religious devoutness—or fanaticism, depending on how one looks at it. A group of Islamic students attending an Islamic boarding school drill for hours a day on the teachings of Islam. It's late at night when they return from instruction, and there are clouds in the distance. It would seem that during the Klang "miracle," clouds in the sky became a Rorschach ink blot test, reflecting the state of the students' minds and their dedication to Islam. Under similar circumstances, a class of Christian students might have seen Jesus, and Hindus might have glimpsed Ganesh. In this instance, it would seem that believing was seeing.

Schoolchildren Trigger a Moving Statue "Epidemic" in Ireland

In February 1985, a group of schoolchildren triggered a series of extraordinary events across Ireland involving claims that religious statues were moving. On the 14th, around noon, 30 children from the school in Asdee, County Kerry, went next door to the church of St. Mary to pray, as was their daily custom. Five of the students (three from one family) were the first to see the two near life-sized statues of Jesus and Mary move. Seven-year-old Elizabeth Flynn said: "I saw Jesus moving. His hand moved and he called me. Then I saw the eyes of the Blessed Virgin move." Her sister Mary, twelve, brother Connie, nine, and his nine-year-old friend Michael Scully also said they saw the beckoning hand and moving eyes. They rushed back to school and told their friends in the playground, unwittingly triggering an epidemic of moving masonry. For the next seven months, tens of thousands of the faithful and the curious flocked to local Marian shrines, and there were reports of moving statues from more than 40 locations in 13 Irish counties.

By July 17, there was a major incident at Ballinspittal in County Cork, when a girl was convinced she saw the Virgin's statue rocking back and forth. Upon returning with some 40 friends and family, many saw further movements. At its peak, 20,000 pilgrims stood and watched in nonstop vigils at the shrine. In Cork City, three children said a statue rocked so much they were afraid it would fall on them. At Mitchelstown, four teenage girls reportedly entered a trance during which the statue spoke to them, "calling for peace." In Dublin, a crowd of children, who claimed they saw a statue move, were dismissed by a priest. At Mountcollins, several women and children said that a statue swayed and blood poured from its hands. At Carns, four girls had a vision of Mary, then others claimed to see St.

Bernadette and a crucifix in the sky. In Mooncoin, children claimed to see the Virgin's eyes open and close and shed tears. At Mount Melfry, three children claimed that the Virgin Mary got down from her pedestal to tell them "God was angry with the world." Some blamed the incident on the children's hunger at the end of the day; and at least one theory attributed the cause to collective guilt over the large numbers of teenage pregnancies and unwanted babies.

Psychologist Jurek Kirakowski of Cork University and colleague Tim Ryan explained the reports as optical illusions, noting that most people do not spend their time in fields staring at illuminated statues at night that are hundreds of yards away. If your body begins to sway or your neck muscles start to tremble, as often happens under such circumstances, "the image in your eye of the statue will move. If you have no idea you are moving you are likely to attribute the movement to the lighted portion of the statue rather than to yourself.... Since it is yourself that's really moving, you will tend to see the entire lighted portion of the status moving as a solid mass, rosary and all."[59] Ironically, when the TV crews began to appear and turned on their bright camera lights to illuminate the faithful, far fewer people reported the perceived movement. The strong lights seem to have created a greater visual connection with the surrounding environment and the perception of movement diminished. Others claimed these were psychic phenomena. Once "mass hysteria" was suggested, many of the faithful got angry. But the famous Irish wit was in evidence too, as jokes sprung up, such as "how church lights are now being left on so the statues don't bump into each other at night." After a meeting of bishops to discuss the phenomenon, a spokesman said: "Without wishing to poke fun at anyone ... I can say that the Church moves much more slowly in these matters than do the statues."[60]

At Mitchelstown, in County Cork, the reports took a darker tone on the 5th of September when an expectant crowd began to panic. Teenagers and children began screaming and crying that they had seen a devil. An unnamed 16-year-old boy went home, trembling, to tell his mother he had seen "shocking things." His mother told the *Sunday World* of September 15, 1985: "While looking at the statue of the Blessed Virgin he saw it changing into various forms. He saw the face of the Devil. The thing he saw had horns and was a dark figure. He was terrified. Then he saw the face of Jesus and a Pope with glasses." The panic seems to have started with this boy and was picked up by a group of three girls before spreading through the crowd with some fainting. Mrs. Eileen Graham, who had been present, told the paper, "It was as if the children were tuned in to something. They began shouting 'He's here! He's here!'" The local priest, Dennis

O'Connor, said that several of his altar boys also claimed to have seen the demonic face. He urged them to pray in the church, not at the shrine.

As an indication of the mounting, and perhaps confused, expectations among the crowds as incident after incident was prominently reported, mention was made by pilgrims, who had been to Ballinspittal first, that the atmosphere at Mitchelstown "was not as comforting but cold and frightening." Also, Mrs. Graham revealed that a woman had seen a vision of the devil at the shrine *some six weeks previously*. Of her own experience, she said, she saw the face of an old woman in a nun's habit. "Another woman saw the same thing. Then I saw Our Lady's face and half of it growing old. I cried."[61]

Chapter 9

Global Lessons

> Confusion is a word we have invented for an order which is not understood. — Henry Miller[1]

When viewed through the lens of twenty-first century Western eyes, these tales from classrooms and schoolyards around the world may appear to be strange, irrational reactions. As isolated press reports, they seem to have no rhyme or reason. They appear less strange when understood within their local contexts. It is only by placing ourselves in the participants' shoes, understanding *their* circumstances, unraveling *their* conduct codes, and seeing the world through *their* eyes, that we are able to comprehend these accounts. We are able to see ourselves in them, for if we had been in their shoes, we would have acted the same way. Anthropologist David Mayberry-Louis puts it this way: "In learning about the other, about many 'others,' our conception of humanity is enlarged and enriched. We gain insight into the plasticity of human culture. We begin to see that our way of life is determined not so much by nature but by culture and history. Only then can we see that our way of life is just one of many possible ones."[2]

It is tempting for those from the developed world to pity the "ignorant" native who sacrifices a chicken to appease spirits in a bid to stop an outbreak of hysteria in Ghana. We may laugh at attempts to bring in a native healer to drive out "evil spirits" from a school in Malaysia or to exorcise ghosts from a classroom in India. Yet to those attending these schools, Western students likewise may seem equally out of touch with reality as most go about their daily routines oblivious to the throngs of supernatural beings that they take for granted. To many Malays, the world *is* inhabited by jinn creatures. Many Africans *know* that the spirits of their dead ancestors follow them everywhere. To many of these Asian and African students, their American and European counterparts are a strange lot.

In the West, fear of ghosts, witches and demons has been superseded by anxieties involving terrorists and toxins. These threats have a greater grounding in reality than their shadowy predecessors from the spirit world, but are nonetheless exaggerated. Today Western school children are suspicious that anyone or anything out of the ordinary might be evidence of a terror attack. From the late 1940s to 1990, Western school children lived under the constant threat of a Soviet nuclear attack. During mock drills in American schools, students hid under their desks until given the all-clear. With each announcement that it was only a drill came a collective sigh of relief. But as the threat subsided with the breakup of the Soviet Union and the collapse of communism worldwide, other threats took its place. Expect pollution and terror fears to dominate Western school outbreaks for the foreseeable future.

History Lessons from Europe

These strange tales offer lessons about the psychological dangers of treating students as robots to be programmed. Mental discipline as formulated by Christian von Wolff in the early 1700s was a simplistic solution to education. The brain was one big muscle in need of daily exercise. Teachers across North America and Europe were soon using this strategy. How much information was transferred into one's ability to learn other subjects depended on the effort in their practice drills. In certain European schools, teachers drilled hard, especially in such tedious areas as Latin, though nothing was deemed better for building reasoning than math. But by the late 1800s it was clear that this approach was the cause of countless outbreaks of twitching, shaking, and other strange behaviors in the European schools where this method was applied in the extreme. American schools were spared these hysteria episodes because their approach to teaching was more relaxed.

As we enter the twenty-first century, there is a lesson here about the unintended consequences of replacing flesh-and-blood teachers with computer programs. Most studies on the effectiveness of computers give short-term results. What are we doing to our children, and what will be the impact of decreasing levels of human interaction? What is it doing to our social skills? There is no substitute for human interaction.

There is also a lesson about the importance of teaching subjects in a way to which students can relate — not learning for the sake of learning, or giving students busy work and perfunctory assignments, but constructing practical, personally meaningful lessons. This means that instead of lecturing students and dispensing "truth," we must foster an appreciation for the notion that good teaching is often messy. That is, the social sciences are open to interpretation and debate. For instance, the documentation of history is a subjective, value-laden process that often reveals more about those writing it than those being written about. It is important to sharpen our critical thinking skills when approaching this or any other subject. When was it written? What is the writer's motive? What is their background and worldview? What is their hidden agenda? Everyone has a motive for writing. Our agenda is to recall lessons from the past, lest we repeat them, and to learn from experiences around the world.

Learning from Fear: Panic Attacks in America

The September 11, 2001, attacks on the United States were immediately followed by the anthrax scare in which five envelopes containing spores of *Bacillus anthracis* resulted in twenty-two cases of illness and five deaths. These events further traumatized the United States. It was not long before any powdery substance found on school grounds was cause for alarm, forcing full-scale evacuations. Decontamination teams would rush to the scene as people in "haz-mat suits" removed the suspicious substance. Of the hundreds of cases from schools across the United States and the world, not one was anthrax. They were later identified as granulated soap, sugar, flour, foot powder, spilled cake mix — everything *but* anthrax. Strange odors wafting through the hallways also prompted worried looks. Was it a bio-terror attack or just an overdone pot roast in cooking class?

Lessons from Africa

In Africa, the lesson is to celebrate diverse beliefs and customs instead of trying to eradicate them and substitute foreign idols and ideas. It is a story of injustice, of poor people so desperate for a quality education that they send their children to the best schools around — missionary schools. But the higher level of education comes at a price — they must discard their traditional beliefs and embrace Christianity or Islam. For the children caught in this dilemma, the psychological conflict is often more than they can bear.

There is also a lesson for Westerners who cannot resist making light of "bizarre" laughing outbursts. The African laughing mania is the posterchild of the truly bizarre — the epitome of strangeness among "strange" peoples who are seemingly primitive and backward. Yet laughing fits have been happening in America and Europe for two centuries, ever since the Holy Laugh became a common feature of tent revivals. Even today, the Toronto Blessing has helped to spread the Holy Laugh throughout the world. The only difference between the Western Holy Laugh and the African laughing mania may be the location and its occurrence in a more controlled religious setting.

Lessons from Asia

In Asia, outbreaks of spirit possession and hysteria among Malay schoolgirls are warnings of the emotional turmoil that can occur when previously sheltered girls are pushed from the nest too soon and sent to distant boarding schools. Isolated from boys and kept to strict curfews, these schoolgirls endure long days of tedious schoolwork and religious studies, with little time for play. The resulting fits and spirit possession are predictable. The outbreaks of hysteria in Malaysia are nearly identical to those experienced by cloistered nuns in medieval European convents. The episodes serve as cautionary tales about the dangers facing Asian youth when sent away to suffocating boarding schools to be raised by strangers.

Diploma Mills and Rumor Mills

With their hallways filled with insecure students with raging hormones and limited life experience (though they often think they know everything), schools are ideal rumor-breeding grounds. Rumors often trigger strange outbreaks in classrooms around the world. Sometimes they lead to anxiety and panic; other times they evolve into mass hysteria. The sudden blossoming of a rumor, such as toxic gas in a school building or contamination of cafeteria food, usually gives rise to short, intense outbreaks of anxiety hysteria. Headache, nausea, dizziness, and stomach pain are common symptoms. These outbreaks were rare before the twentieth century, but have risen in developed countries and are common today. Most involve contamination fears such as a gas leak or terror attack. With no prior warning, there is usually little or no pre-existing group tension. Most episodes are over in a day or two.

When rumors fester over weeks or months, the ongoing tension may result in motor hysteria: twitching, shaking, fainting, and trance states. Such was the case during the pregnancy scare at the Bethume Negro School in Louisiana during 1960. Rumors that the girls would be given pregnancy tests sent fear through the sexually active students. The result was a wave of seizures, headaches, shaking, and catatonic posturing. Motor hysteria appears gradually and usually takes weeks or months to subside. The fits lasted more than half a year. In parts of Africa and Asia, the Petri dish for rumors is the lack of an outlet for students to express their frustrations. Those boarding schools live under strict rules twenty-four hours a day. The harsh conditions trigger hysteria in one or two students, after which rumors swirl — usually that there are spirits in the school — as fellow classmates fear that they may be the next targets.

A rumor is born when an unverified but plausible story spreads within a group. There is often a kernel of truth to the story, enough to make it seem believable, but no substantiating evidence. Rumors spawn in times of uncertainty and fear and typically last from a few days to several months. Rumors, essential components of most school scares and hysterias, take root in the fertile soil of ambiguous situations of perceived importance. People unconsciously construct these stories in an attempt to regain a sense of certainty and reduce fear and anxiety. In other words, "rumor is most likely to occur when people are intensely interested in a topic and little definite news or official information is available."[3] Conversely, if there is little interest and authoritative information is abundant, a rumor is unlikely to sprout. The more unclear the situation and the greater the perceived significance of the story, the greater the likelihood rumors will develop. This is why there are so many rumors about the stock market during periods of war and crisis.

Plausibility is a key in triggering rumors. What is unbelievable to one person or group may be quite believable to another depending on the time and place. Over several weeks in late 1979, a headhunter scare broke out on the island of Borneo in Southeast Asia, where head-taking was once common. Anthropologist Richard Drake was studying the Mualang peoples when rumors paralyzed village life and forced the local school to close for lack of attendance. The scare started with rumors that the Indonesian government was building a nearby bridge and needed a body to place in the foundation to strengthen it. The locals distrusted the government and grew up believing such stories.[4] An American or European might laugh at the rumors, but to the locals, they were possible. Another example of the role of plausibility is the Chinese Zombie Robot Scare of March 1993, when a bizarre scene unfolded in the city of Chongqing, in Sichuan Province. A rumor spread rapidly through this city's primary and middle-school students that an American robot had gone out of control and escaped to their city. Remarkably, many students believed the rumor. A report by *Agence France-Press* described the children's belief that the robot was a "zombie specialized in eating children wearing red clothes" and it was said "to have devoured several kids already." Many of the children refused to go to school unless their parents made crosses out of chopsticks and put garlic in their schoolbags. The children's anxiety was soon picked up by adults who had no way of judging the factuality of their fears. The newspaper noted the sudden local shortage of garlic. This panic appears to have been a hybrid of Western folk motifs and remedies as interpreted through the imagination of children in another culture. It is similar to the story in chapter 3 of the panic among schoolchildren in Houston, Texas, that a gang of Smurfs was about to attack kids wearing blue. In the Smurfs case, the panic began in January 1993 and came to a climax in March, at roughly the same time the kids in Chongqing were worrying about their robot-zombie.[5]

Psychologists Gordon Allport and Leo Postman have tracked the formation of rumors in laboratory experiments and found that they develop in three stages. *Leveling* is the tendency for a story to become shorter and understood more easily. During *sharpening*, some key details become prominent while others lose importance or disappear entirely. Then *assimilation*, the tendency for stories to be sharpened and leveled in ways that reflect a person's culture, biases, and stereotypes, occurs.[6] Rumors are a key part of most school scares, such as the following incident, involving sexually transmitted disease among Pennsylvania schoolgirls in the early 1960s.

Rumor in Action: A Phantom Gonorrhea Outbreak

In 1961, Christmas holidays were anything but cheerful for girls at the Lebanon Elementary School in Fellsburg, Pennsylvania. Many of them were anxious about rumors sweeping through the community that many of them had a venereal disease — possibly gonorrhea. On Friday evening, December 12, the school board ordered the doors closed for a week while doctors tried to solve the mystery of why some of the girls had discharge coming from their vaginas. School physician Dr. Eugene O'Leary told board members that tests appeared to indicate vaginitis — a common bacterial infection — and that the problem was not serious. However, board members decided to close the school upon learning that a local doctor was convinced the illness was gonorrhea. Every schoolgirl was tested before being allowed back in class. The community was besieged with rumors, among them that the disease was spread in the school toilets. The rumors of illness may have masked the parents' greater fears—that their girls were sexually active.[7]

A team of University of Pittsburgh doctors were asked to investigate the "outbreak" and soon found that not a single student had gonorrhea. Further, while a few of the girls showed symptoms of a mild infection, most of the vaginal discharge may have been normal. The initial misdiagnosis of gonorrhea by the local doctor, coupled with worried parents, produced a hotbed of rumor and fear. The school administration added to the worry by issuing no less than seven written statements on the affair. While these reports were factual, they encouraged rumors with such phrases as "mysterious infection" and "strange malady," while the local newspaper referred several times to the school's "mystery infection." When school officials denied the presence of a mysterious illness in the school, some parents interpreted it as a cover-up. Adding to the tension at the time of the episode was the fear of outsiders. At the start of the new school year in September, several poorer children from a nearby community had transferred into the school after their building was condemned. The presence of these newcomers may have heightened tension among "the more prosperous parents and increased their tendency to view the school as a possible source of infection." At the start of the scare, this distrust played a major role.[8]

Major Explanations

The earliest recorded explanation for mass hysteria was that demonic agents were responsible for an outbreak of mysterious convulsions at an orphan school in Holland during the sixteenth and seventeenth centuries. In many countries in Africa, Asia, and the Pacific islands, similar views continue to hold sway to this day. On Papua New Guinea it is often thought that bush spirits are to blame for hysteria outbreaks; many Malaysians point the finger at Islamic *jinn* spirits mentioned in the Koran; and in South Africa the culprit is frequently demons from the Holy Bible. One thing is certain: Intense religious beliefs about the reality of demonic agents often play a role in triggering outbreaks, even today.[9]

In addition to demons, another cause for strange student behavior discussed during the sixteenth century was the possibility that the Dutch orphan students were suffering from a physical ailment. A third view held that they were feigning illness or strange behaviors in order to get some benefit. At Hoorn, the outbreak conveniently stopped when the children were lodged with families around the city. On the other hand, such a remedy likely reduced stress, and any cases of hysteria were likely to have subsided in any event. The "feigning" explanation still prevails in some quarters today. During the Palestinian schoolgirl "poisoning" episode of 1983, several Israeli doctors believed the girls were faking symptoms to make the Israeli government look evil and gain greater sympathy for the Palestinian bid to retake their homeland.[10]

Modern-day explanations for mass hysteria in schools fall into five broad categories: psychoanalytic, sociological, social-psychological, biological, and anthropological. These theories often share overlapping features.

A View from the Couch: The Brain in Conflict

Psychoanalysts believe that many victims of mass hysteria have deep subconscious conflicts that are converted into symptoms, although how it happens on a biological level is a mystery. The affected body parts usually relate to the conflict. The epidemic of leg twitching at an American school in 1939 began in the single student, Helen, who thought she was a poor dancer and feared dance class. The twitching allowed Helen to avoid dance classes and rekindle her boyfriend's affection. Investigators surmise that after seeing Helen's success, over the next few weeks six classmates experienced similar unconscious twitching in order to get attention and emulate Helen, who was a role model for the group.[11]

In chapter 1 we learned that outbreaks of hand tremor were common across Europe during the nineteenth and early twentieth centuries. Episodes struck in the most rigid schools, where students were forced to complete boring, tedious writing drills. What became popularly known as "the trembling disease" seems to be a classic example of conversion disorder. The pupils were socialized into staying in school and achieving a high standard; but they were stifled by the excessive, repetitious workload. Anxiety and frustration rose, and eventually the pent-up emotions were converted into hand tremors, which gave students attention for their plight and often a temporary respite from assignments. Mass hysterical tremor struck at a Swiss girls' school in 1893, then again eleven years later at the same school. In both cases, investigators concluded that the outbreaks were unconscious attempts to avoid schoolwork.[12] The mechanism has parallels to military cases wherein a combat soldier with deep moral opposition to killing is unable to move his hand to fire a weapon.

A Sociologist's View: Blame Society

Sociologist Neil Smelser blames school hysteria outbreaks on society. He believes that societies can become abnormal; for example, some surmise that in Germany before World War II, something went wrong in the structure of the society that gave rise to Nazism. Smelser believes that rapid changes produce an imbalance in the "normal" state of society. Another key ingredient is strain or conflict, such as a strange odor or an ongoing rift between students and teachers. Eventually pupils redefine a strange smell from a situation that is vague and harmless to one that is toxic and threatening. In June 1980, students at several schools near an industrial complex in Hong Kong reported a strange odor and began keeling over in droves with stomach pain, nausea, headache, and dizziness. Before the incident, rumors of a recent gas scare at a nearby school were already circulating, and several teachers were advising students on what action to take if toxic gas got into the school. Smelser says that one look of indecision, confusion or panic on the face of a teacher can quickly spark an episode or, just as quickly, quell it.[13]

Social Psychology: The Power of Belief

Some social psychologists theorize that students stricken during outbreaks tend to be the ones that have personality problems. They have tried to confirm this by answering the question: Why do some students in the same classroom feel ill or act strangely, while others don't? More recently, researchers have tried to answer this question by giving the students personality tests. Is there a mass-hysteria-prone personality? There have been no consistent findings in this area. Some stricken students have scored higher on scales for paranoia, neuroticism, and hysterical traits, while others have not. In the United States, Dr. Gary Small found a link between students' grades and their likelihood of being stricken. In Singapore, Dr. K.T. Goh found no association. Some researchers note that affected pupils had low IQs, while others found the opposite to be true.[14]

Other psychologists focus on the context of outbreaks.[15] Instead of emphasizing the role of stress or disturbed students, they focus on how the students view a given situation. To a Hindu, eating a hamburger can be a threatening event; they may think they are eating their dead grandmother, as it is widely believed that the deceased are reincarnated as animals. For Muslims, eating pork is a sin; it says so in the Koran. To students from these backgrounds, the simple act of eating can be fraught with fear.

Many things determine whether a student becomes affected: their cultural beliefs, their education level, how close they were to the stressful agent such as a strange smell, or whether they had heard rumors or seen others being stricken.

British psychiatrist David Taylor thinks that mass hysteria is a drama that gains a foothold in the imagination of students. In a similar vein, when we watch a film or TV show, we often get caught up in the drama as if it were really happening. Belief is a powerful force that is often supported by relatives of victims. Students who think they are sick may start feeling sick: "In these dramas the actors and the audience are equal partners. When the sick are presented to doctors the doctors are compelled to act from their perspective just as the parents or the crowd acted from theirs. In this way, the medical procedures tend to validate the sickness to the relatives in the same process which invalidates it to the doctors."[16] Taylor emphasizes the importance of understanding the victim's context: "Epidemic hysterias arise couched in social settings that enhance emotionality and promote the rapid 'mental acceptance of propositions as true even if beyond observations.' The sorts of events that produce these responses are unavoidable apparent threats that have emerged through some form of ultra-rapid group consensus."[17]

How strong is the power of suggestion? Consider the strange case of psychogenic hallucinations at a California middle school in 1998. On September 23, three fourth-graders unintentionally swallowed a substance that turned out to be the powerful hallucinogenic drug LSD. The students were taken to a nearby hospital for treatment amid a flurry of media publicity. That day, eleven other students at the same school recalled that they had sampled a white powder from a vial, and believing that they too had ingested LSD, were rushed to the hospital with symptoms ranging from violent outbursts to hallucinations. In reality, the powder was harmless. After drug tests proved negative, they quickly felt better and were released a few hours later.[18]

The Biologist: Nature

It is easy to see why some people think that biological factors are at work, as it is undeniable that most school hysteria episodes involve girls. I have collected nearly five hundred articles on mass hysteria in schools, factories, prisons, convents, and communities dating back to the fifteenth century, in languages including Polish, Indonesian, Russian, German, Malay, Spanish, Italian, and French. The proportion of victims who are female is overwhelming and well over 90 percent. The question is why. Not long ago, it was commonly thought that females were prone to emotional instability, making them prime candidates for hysteria. Some say this view is sexist, arguing that proponents have not taken into account the way that females are raised. For instance, girls are usually encouraged from childhood to express their feelings.[19] During an outbreak they may be more likely to report symptoms, while boys might try to act macho. In many cultures around the world, females are dominated by males, increasing the likelihood of their experiencing emotional frustration.

But what of the role of biology? In most developed countries, classroom social conditions are fairly uniform for both male and female students, yet hysteria continues to be reported mostly in girls. One explanation is the finding that women of menstruating age are susceptible to panic disorder and hyperventilation. Menstruation and the chemical changes it brings may account for the large proportion of schoolgirls stricken. Hysterical disorders, in which a person experiences various aches and pains for which there is no pathological basis, are also more common in females. One such disorder is *globus hystericus*—a feeling of a lump in the throat that gives a feeling of choking. Another is psychogenic pain disorder. Conversion disorder, in which emotional trauma is converted into physical symptoms, is more common in females, with studies finding ratios varying from 2 to 1 to as high as 10 to 1, paralleling the range in prevalence ratios in school hysteria outbreaks.[20]

The Anthropologist: Nurture

British anthropologist Ioan Lewis observes that in some "primitive" societies, groups of stressed people often enter trances and act as if they are possessed by spirits. Most are women. He also notes that most people who enter trances during emotionally charged religious meetings are women. Lewis thinks this is because in most societies women have low status and are often oppressed by men, especially in less developed countries. In women who enter trance and possession states—sometimes alone, other times in groups—twitching, shaking and anxiety-related aches and pains are common. Curiously, these are the same conditions that crop up in many Asian and African schools where mass hysteria is common. In these places, outbreaks most often strike female pupils, who may insult authorities and criticize administration policies. They may even hit males. Yet students are able to escape punishment because the behavior is blamed on the possessing demon, who was talking *through* them. As a result, mass hysteria in Africa and Asia may have developed as a means of subconscious negotiation. Most anthropologists assume that females are not susceptible just because of their genes, but are rendered so through the way they are socialized. For instance, in Malaysia girls are raised to be obedient and submissive, and to avoid direct confrontation with authority. Malaysian researchers Raymond Lee and Susan Ackerman suggest that mass hysteria and spirit possession in Asia are simply culturally appropriate ways of indirectly negotiating problems—a kind of collective bargaining.[21]

A Neurologist's View

Many school outbreaks of psychogenic illness are triggered by strange odors. British neuroscientist David Ray says that contamination fear coupled with a strong odor can trigger mass hysteria: "Smell can precipitate a strong emotional reaction that can make people ill in a subjective way ... [even] where the children could be shown not to have had any measurable exposure."[22] Why? Because the olfactory nerves that deal with smell are closely connected to the so-called nausea center. Humans may have developed such a connection in part as a biological defense mechanism to stop us from eating rotten food, especially decaying animals, that could be harmful for us.

Hypnosis and Chemicals

During the nineteenth century, some scientists thought that all sorts of mass behavior—from hysterical school children to soccer riots—were the result of group hypnosis. Psychoanalyst Casper Schmidt holds a group trance interpretation of mass hysteria in school children. Physician Gary Elkins thinks that trances play a role in school outbreaks and compares mass hysteria to the active-alert hypnotic state. Elkins surmises that when the first student falls ill and receives medical attention, classmates focus on the crisis, fostering a natural trance. He writes: "Alarmed and uncertain of their own feelings, the group members become susceptible to suggestions of illness. These suggestions were received with very little critical or reflexive thought." It is well known that a person can enter a hypnotic trance without a formal induction and that those under hypnosis are prone to suggestion. Sometimes tests reveal minute amounts of harmful agents, but at such low levels that they should pose no threat. Public health experts Halley Faust and Lawrence Brilliant speculate that chemicals or organic mixtures may trigger mysterious outbreaks of illness or strange behavior. This could explain why young girls are most vulnerable: they typically weigh less than males their age.[23]

Handling Outbreaks

So what is a principal or headmaster to do when faced with a school full of anxious students who think they may have breathed toxic fumes or be suffering from food poisoning? Err on the side of caution and assume the worst. But when it is evident that mass psychology has taken over, reassurance is vital. Western outbreaks are usually reactions to sudden, extreme fear. Administrators and teachers must stay calm. One worried look or "Oh my God" by a teacher can turn a docile crowd of students into what resembles a herd of stampeding cattle.

And how is the African or Asian administrator to deal with a schoolhouse of students who are seemingly possessed by spirits? Identify, then resolve, the underlying stress or conflict. Native healers are sometimes helpful, but not always. If a witchdoctor promises to rid the school of spirits and the symptoms remain — and remember, motor disturbances don't go away overnight — an even greater panic may occur and last longer. Similarly, if Western medics fail to address the perceived terrors and their symptoms, the outbreak is likely to continue. Teachers should handle new cases by confidently labeling the incident as psychological, removing the student from classmates, and sending him or her home until they feel better. In stopping ghost scares, open communication is essential to counteract misinformation and rumors. As in Western schools, staying calm is essential in quelling the spread of fear, which fuels outbreaks. If school personnel fail to heed this advice, chaos may ensue. In this regard, some teachers have not only fanned the flames of hysteria and fear — they have inadvertently lit them.

In 1987 an outbreak of fainting took place at a primary school in Pretoria, South Africa — an outbreak that was triggered by teachers. One day a teacher began acting strange and seemed to enter a trance. She had a horrific vision of her classroom being filled with buckets of blood and the walls smeared with blood and human waste. She then collapsed on the floor and later regained her senses. Soon other teachers had similar visions, then collapsed. Before long, several pupils were collapsing onto the school floor and having visions. By early 1989 the situation at the school spiraled out of control when as many as 60 students fainted or fell at the same time. Many parents in the community thought witches were at work. It was rumored that the school had been bewitched by someone wanting to take over the principal's job. Many teachers even believed the witchcraft rumors.

When the psychiatric team arrived, the school was in chaos. Children were running about aimlessly, screaming and falling to the floor. Some were passed out, others twitching or convulsing. Many were hallucinating. Psychologist Bernadette Wittstock said that the students "described visions of small, dark people; of women dressed in tattered clothes threatening to hit them with sticks or knives; of frightening animals." Some of the animals were strange, such as a creature with a monkey's head and a dog's body. Wittstock said the visions had a profound impact on the kids: "The figures in the visions called the children to leave the classroom and told them that they would be killed if they discussed their visions with others." Many students steadfastly believed a witch was casting spells on the school. Some investigators were so unnerved by these events that shortly after arriving, they wanted to leave and not come back. The falling and visions gradually subsided over the next several months.[24]

The Most Important Lesson of All

These seemingly strange classroom accounts are not tales of sickness but of distress; they are not tales of chaos and disarray but of rebellion; they are not tales of irrationality but logical responses to unique circumstances and worldviews. When we look only at the behaviors and forget about their context and meaning, we grow vulnerable to mistaking the exotic as strange, the unfamiliar as bizarre, and folk beliefs as superstitions. We must remember that there *are* ghosts, students *do* become possessed by spirits, and terrorists *have* attacked American schools. That is to say, for the students, teachers and parents in these community soap operas, the events *were* real. Events happen in specific social and cultural contexts that those involved cannot see. As anthropologist Clyde Kluckhohn once observed: "Culture is like the water fish swim in; it is everywhere around the fish, yet impossible for the fish to see."[25] Far from being abnormal or dysfunctional, school scares, panics, and hysterias are collective coping mechanisms and ways of making sense of the world. As such, these episodes of distress afford us insights into students and their capacity to adapt to and cope with change. Ultimately, they are tales of the indomitable human spirit; clever and creative in its response to repression, fear, uncertainty and injustice.

Chapter Notes

Introduction

1. William H. Burnham, *The Normal Mind* (New York: D. Appleton, 1924), p. 327.
2. Johannes Schödel, "Über Induzierte Krankheiten [On Induced Illness]," *Jahrbuch für Kinderheilkunde* 14 (1906): 521–28.
3. L. Hirt, "Eine Epidemie von Hysterischen Krämpfen in einer Schleisischen Dorfschule [An Epidemic of Hysterical Cramp in a Village School in Schleisischen]," *Zeitschrift für Schulgesundheitspflege* 6 (1893): 225–29 (summary of an article by L. Hirt in the *Berliner Klinische Wochenschrift*); P. Schutte, "Eine neue form Hysterischer Zustande bei Schulkindern [A New Form of Hysterical Conditions in School Children]," *Münchener Medizinische Wochenschrift* 53 (1906): 1763–64; E. Zollinger, "Über die Pädagogische Behandlung des Nervösen Zitterns der Schulkinder [On the Educational Treatment of Nervous Trembling in School Children]," *Jahrbuch der Schweiz Gesellschaft für Schulgesundheitspflege* 7 (1906): 20–47.
4. Gary Small and Jonathan Borus, "Outbreak of Illness in a School Chorus: Toxic Poisoning or Mass Hysteria?" *New England Journal of Medicine* 308 (1983): 632–35; H. C. T. Smith and E. J. Eastham, "Outbreak of Abdominal Pain," *The Lancet* 2 (1973): 956–59.
5. S. Krug, "Mass Illness at an Intermediate School: Toxic Fumes or Epidemic Hysteria?" *Pediatric Emergency Care* 8 (1992): 280–82.
6. American Psychiatric Association, *Diagnostic and Statistical Manual of Mental Disorders*, 3rd edition (Washington, DC: APA, 1994).
7. Hysteria became officially passé in 1994 when the American Psychiatric Association voted it out of existence, yet the term stubbornly persists, most notably in the fields of medicine and psychiatry. See Francois Sirois, "Epidemic Hysteria: School Outbreaks 1973–1993," *Medical Principles and Practice* 8 (1999): 12–25; M. S. Micale, *Approaching Hysteria: Disease and Its Interpretations* (Princeton, NJ: Princeton University Press, 1995).
8. Robert E. Bartholomew, "Dancing with Myths: The Misogynist Construction of Dancing Mania," *Feminism and Psychology* 8.2 (1998): 173–183.
9. Richard L. Sjoberg, "The Catechism Effect: Child Testimonies during a 17th-Century Witch Panic as Related to Educational Achievement," *Memory* 8.2 (2000): 65–69; Richard L. Sjoberg, "False Allegations of Satanic Abuse: Case Studies from the Witch Panic in Rattvik 1670–71," *European Child and Adolescent Psychiatry* 6 (1997): 219–226; Rossell Hope Robbins, *The Encyclopedia of Witchcraft and Demonology* (New York: Crown, 1966), pp. 348–350; George S. Rosen, "Psychopathology in the Social Process: Dance Frenzies, Demonic Possession, Revival Movements and Similar So-Called Psychic Epidemics: An Interpretation," *Bulletin of the History of Medicine* 36 (1962): 13–44; Oliver Maddox Hueffer, *The Book of Witches* (East Ardsley, United Kingdom: EP, 1908 [1973]).
10. Balthasar Bekker, *Le Monde Enchanté*, vol. 4 (Amsterdam: Pierre Rotterdam, 1694), p. 517; Jean Wier (Johann Weyer), *Histoires, Disputes et Discours Des Illusions et Impostures des Diables, des Magiciens Infames, Sorcières et Empoisonneurs*, translated from the Latin original, published 1563, vol. 1 (Paris: Bureaux du Progrès Médical, 1885), p. 521; Johann Joseph von Görres, *La Mystique Divine, Naturelle et Diabolique*, vol. 5 (Paris: Poussielgue-Rusand, 1855, translated

from the German *Christliche Mystik* 1845), p. 231.

11. Charles Mackay, *Memoirs of Extraordinary Popular Delusions and the Madness of Crowds*, vol. 2 (London: Office of the National Illustrated Library, 1852), pp. 539–540.

12. Elaine Showalter, "Scratching the Bin Laden Itch," *New Statesman* 131 (July 29, 2002): 12; Robert E. Bartholomew and Benjamin Radford, "Rash of Mysterious Rashes May Be Linked to Mass Hysteria," *Skeptical Inquirer* 26.3 (2002): 8; "Update: Rashes Among Schoolchildren — 27 States, October 4, 2001–June 3, 2002," *Morbidity and Mortality Weekly Report* (Center for Disease Control, Atlanta) 51.24 (June 21, 2002): 524–52.

13. M. F. Goldsmith, "Physicians with Georgia on Their Minds," *Journal of the American Medical Association* 262 (1989): 603–604; Zoran Radovanovic, "On the origin of mass casualty incidents in Kosovo, Yugoslavia, in 1990," *European Journal of Epidemiology* 11 (1995): 1–13; Alastair Hay and John Foran, "Yugoslavia: Poisoning or Epidemic Hysteria in Kosovo?" *The Lancet* 338.8776 (November 9, 1991): 1196; Baruch Modan, Moshe Tirosh, Emil Weissenberg, Cilla Acker, T. A. Swartz, Corina Coston, Alexander Donagi, Moshe Revach and Gaston Vettorazzi, "The Arjenyattah Epidemic," *The Lancet* 2 (1983): 1472–74; Philip J. Landrigan and Bess Miller, "The Arjenyattah Epidemic: Home Interview Data and Toxicological Aspects," *The Lancet* 2 (1983): 1474–76.

14. See, for example: Aphaluck Bhatiasevi, "Belief in Ghosts Sparks Hysteria: Students Freak Out at School Camp," *Bangkok Post*, February 4, 2001.

15. Sivagnanachelvi Selvadurai, "Problems of Residential Students in a Secondary Technical School" (Master's thesis, University of Malaya, Kuala Lumpur, 1985).

16. Teoh Jin-Inn, Saesmalijah Soewondo, and Sidharta Myra, "Epidemic Hysteria in Malaysia: An Illustrative Episode," *Psychiatry* 8.3 (1975): 260.

17. Manohar Dhadphale and S. P. Shaikh, "Epidemic Hysteria in a Zambian School: 'The Mysterious Madness of Mwinilunga,'" *British Journal of Psychiatry* 142 (1983): 85–88.

18. Robert Conley, "Laughing Malady a Puzzle in Africa. 1000 Along Lake Victoria Afflicted in 18 Months—Most Are Youngsters. Schools Close Down," *New York Times*, August 8, 1963, p. 29; *New York Times*, August 9, 1963, p. 4; A. M. Rankin and P. J. Philip, "An Epidemic of Laughing in the Buboka District of Tanganyika," *Central African Journal of Medicine* 9 (1963): 167–170; Benjamin H. Kagwa, "The Problem of Mass Hysteria in East Africa," *East African Medical Journal* 41 (1964): 560–66; Anonymous, "Two Schools Close in Tanzania Till Siege of Hysteria Ends," *New York Times*, May 25, 1966, p. 36; J. R. Muhangi, "Mass Hysteria in an Ankole School," *East African Medical Journal* 50 (1973): 304–09; Gideon Nkala, "Mass Hysteria Forces School Closure," *Middle East Intelligence Wire*, March 13, 2000; Wene Owino, "Mass Hysteria Causes School's Temporary Closure," Pan African News Agency, March 8, 2000.

19. G. J. Ebrahim, "Mass Hysteria in School Children, Notes on Three Outbreaks in East Africa," *Clinical Pediatrics* 7 (1968): 438.

20. Stephen Frankel, "Mass Hysteria in the New Guinea Highlands: A Telefomin Outbreak and Its Relationship to Other New Guinea Hysterical Reactions," *Oceania* 47 (1976): 105–33.

21. Smith and Eastham (1973), op. cit.; *Daily Mirror*, July 10, 1972.

22. R. Levine, "Epidemic Faintness and Syncope in a School Marching Band," *Journal of the American Medical Association* 238.22 (1977): 2373–74; E. Bebbington, C. Hopton, H. I. Lockett, and R. J. Madeley, "From Experience: Epidemic Syncope in Jazz Bands," *Community Medicine* 2 (1980): 302–07.

23. M. Smothers, "Mysterious Malady Strikes Kids on Bus," *Journal Star* (Peoria, Illinois), May 19, 2000.

24. Robert E. Bartholomew and Simon Wessely, "Protean Nature of Mass Sociogenic Illness: From Possessed Nuns to Chemical and Biological Terrorism Fears," *The British Journal of Psychiatry* 180 (2002): 300–06; Robert E. Bartholomew and Simon Wessely, "Epidemic Hysteria in Virginia: The Case of the Phantom Gasser of 1933–34," *The Southern Medical Journal* 92.8 (1999): 762–69; Simon Wessely, "Mass Hysteria: Two Syndromes? *Psychological Medicine* 17 (1987): 109–20.

25. J. S. Victor, *Satanic Panic: The Creation of a Contemporary Legend* (Chicago, IL: Open Court, 1993); J. S. Victor, "The Dynamics of Rumor-panics about Satanic

Cults," in *The Satanism Scare*, ed. James Richardson, Joel Best and D. Bromley, pp. 221–236 (New York: Aldine de Gruyter, 1991); R. Hicks, "Police Pursuit of Satanic Crime Part II: The Satanic Conspiracy and Urban Legends," *The Skeptical Inquirer* 14 (1990): 378–89; J. S. Victor, "A Rumor-Panic About a Dangerous Satanic Cult in Western New York," *New York Folklore* 15 (1989): 23–49.

Chapter 1

1. The *Malleus* was published the following year, 1487, and saw many reprints over the centuries, even into the present era. It was written chiefly to refute the belief that witchcraft did not exist. By setting out the types of acts for which witches can be held responsible, how to identify witches, prosecute and suitably punish them, the *Malleus* was widely used as a practical handbook by witch-hunters. It gained additional authority from the inclusion of the bull of 1484 issued by Pope Innocent VIII. Closer examination of this document, which was addressed to Kramer in his capacity as an inquisitor, shows it bluntly orders local authorities to cooperate with inquisitors in their pursuit of heretics, and does not, as parlayed by Kramer, give full papal approval for his enthusiastic and systematic torture and execution of confessed witches. Because of this subterfuge, the book itself played a significant part in driving the fatal pogroms against local witches that lasted in Europe from the middle of the fifteenth century until at least the seventeenth century.

2. Eric Maple, *Witchcraft: The Story of Man's Search for Supernatural Power* (London: Octopus, 1973), p. 45.

3. Rossell Hope Robbins, *The Encyclopedia of Witchcraft and Demonology* (New York: Crown, 1966), p. 180.

4. Erich Goode, *Deviant Behavior*, 6th ed. (Upper Saddle River, NJ: Prentice-Hall, 2001), pp. 344–45.

5. See, for example, Jenny Gibbons, "Recent Developments in the Study of the Great European Witch Hunt," in *Pomegranate*, issue 5 (Lammas, 1998). Gibbons writes: "To date, less than 15,000 definite executions have been discovered in all of Europe and America combined. Even though many records are missing, it is now clear that death tolls higher than 100,000 are not believable."

6. M. Wolf, "Witchcraft and Mass Hysteria in Terms of Current Psychological Theories," *Journal of Practical Nursing and Mental Health Services*, March 1976, p. 24.

7. Wolf (1976), op. cit., p. 24.

8. Jean Wier (Johann Weyer), *Histoires, Disputes et Discours des Illusions et Impostures des Diables, des Magiciens Infames, Sorcières et Empoisonneurs*, translated from the 1653 Latin original (Paris: Bureaux du Progrès Médical, 1885), vol. 1, p. 521.

9. Johann Joseph von Görres, *La Mystique Divine, Naturelle et Diabolique*, translated from the German *Christliche Mystik* (Paris: Poussielgue-Rusand, 1855), vol. 5, p. 231.

10. Balthasar Bekker, *Le Monde Enchanté* (Amsterdam: Pierre Rotterdam, 1694), vol. 4, p. 517. All other authorities, explicitly or otherwise, use him as their source. "Strange, unintelligible language" is an apparent reference to *glossolalia* or "speaking in tongues," which occurs in a variety of cultural settings. Theologian Anthony Hoekema defines it as "a spontaneous utterance of sounds in a language the speaker has never learned and does not even understand. This tongue-speaking is usually done only in certain types of religious groups" (*What About Tongue-Speaking?* [Grand Rapids, MI: William B. Eerdmans, 1966] p. 9). Glossolalia comes from the Greek *glossa* (tongue) and *lalia* (speaking). The literal translation is "tongue speaking." Psychologist Nicholas Spanos studied whether tongue speaking is an altered state of consciousness or learned behavior. His conclusion: it can be learned by anyone with a proper model to imitate and practice. Nicholas P. Spanos, Wendy Cross, Mark Lepage and Marjorie Coristine, "Glossolalia as Learned Behavior: An Experimental Demonstration," *Journal of Abnormal Psychology* 95.1 (1987): 23.

11. Robert Darnton, *The Great Cat Massacre and Other Episodes in French Cultural History* (New York: Basic Books, 1984), p. 83.

12. Darnton, op. cit., pp. 83–84. During the carnival of Burgundy, youths would pass around cats as each person would tear out a chunk of fur and relish its howls of agony (p. 83). At the St. John the Baptist festival, crowds often lit bonfires, tossing into them "cats tied up in bags, cats suspended from ropes, or cats burned at the stake. Parisians liked to incinerate cats by the sackful ... [others] preferred to chase a flaming cat through the streets" (pp. 83–84).

13. Perhaps the best known is the case of the meowing nuns. Hecker writes: "I have read in a good medical work that a nun, in a very large convent in France, began to meow like a cat; shortly afterwards other nuns also meowed. At last all the nuns meowed together every day at a certain time for several hours. The whole surrounding Christian neighborhood heard, with equal chagrin and astonishment, this daily cat-concert, which did not cease until all the nuns were informed that a company of soldiers were placed by the police before the entrance of the convent, and that they were provided with rods, and would continue whipping them until they promised not to meow any more" (Justus Friedrich Hecker, *Epidemics of the Middle Ages*, translated from German by B. Babington [London: The Sydenham Society, 1844], p. 127).

14. Robb Wellert and Gary H. Grossman, producers, *History's Mysteries: Legends of the Werewolves* (Weller/Grossman Productions for the History Channel, 1998); H. Sidky, *Witchcraft, Lycanthropy, Drugs, and Disease: An Anthropological Study of the European Witch-Hunts* (New York: Peter Lang, 1997); Sabine Baring-Gould, *The Book of Werewolves: Being an Account of a Terrible Superstition* (London: Smith, Elder, 1865).

15. John Howells, ed., *World History of Psychiatry* (New York: Brunner/Mazel, 1975), p. 153; Rossell Hope Robbins, *The Encyclopedia of Witchcraft and Demonology* (New York: Crown, 1966), p. 393; Richard Robert Madden, *Phantasmata or Illusions and Fanaticisms of Protean Forms Productive of Great Evils* (London: T. C. Newby, 1857), p. 253; personal communication from historian Hilary Evans in London, February 2004.

16. Personal communication, February 2004, from British historian Hilary Evans, 2003. Mr. Evans was director of the Mary Evans Picture Library, 59 Tranquil Vale, London, England.

17. Samuel Garnier, *Barbe Buvée, en Religion, Sœur Sainte-Colombe et la Prétendue Possession des Ursulines d'Auxonne [Barbara Buvée, and Religion, Sister Columbe and the Feigned Possession of the Ursulines at Auxonne]* (Paris: Felix Alcan, 1895); Vladimir Mikhailovich Bekhterev, *Suggestion and Its Role in Social Life*, 3rd ed., translated from the Russian by Tzvetanka Dobreva-Martinova (New Brunswick, NJ: Transaction, 1998 [1908]), p. 78; Rossell Hope Robbins, *The Encyclopedia of Witchcraft and Demonology* (New York: Crown, 1966), p. 393; Justus Friedrich Hecker, *Epidemics of the Middle Ages*, translated from the German by B. Babington (London: The Sydenham Society, 1844), p. 127.

18. Charles Mackay, *Memoirs of Extraordinary Popular Delusions and the Madness of Crowds*, vol. 2 (London: Office of the National Illustrated Library, 1852), pp. 539–40.

19. Charles Mackay (1852), op. cit.

20. Robbins (1959, p. 307f) and some archival authorities (e.g., the Christian Classics Ethereal Library [CCEL], an online project of Calvin College, Grand Rapids, Michigan), who cite writings by and about Antoinette Bourignon — http://www.ccel.org/s/schaff/encyc/encyc02/htm/iv.v.ccl.htm — suggest a very different account to Mackay's, but one that still illustrates our thesis. First, she is described as a "fanatical enthusiast" who developed a very controversial theology that was condemned by clergy wherever she settled, and yet it survived into the early eighteenth century in Scotland. She was more a mystic leaning towards asceticism than a schoolmistress. Second, her school, variously described as a "correctional institution," "orphanage" or "convent," was founded in 1653 and established as a cloistered convent under Augustinian rules in 1658. Third, although she began with fifty girls of various ages, by the time of the outbreak — most likely between 1658 and 1662 (not 1639 as in Mackay) — only 32 were involved. Fourth, being devout herself, she was strict with the girls, or attempted to be, and their confined, repressed little world inevitably fomented rebellion and resentment. Her wilful charges soon found ways to manipulate Bourignon's credulity and avoid her disciplines (reminding us of the Amsterdam "cat" children). Robbins gives the example of one twelve-year-old's apparently innocent daydream: while playing with other children, they asked her if she would come with them to the sabbat. As soon as she consented, her lover arrived on a little horse "which catched up into the air with him and the other girls and they flew together to a great castle, where they played upon instruments, danced, feasted and drank wine." Another girl escaped being whipped for stealing by claiming to have been tempted by a "handsome young devil," an example other girls readily employed. By the time of the official investigation their

imaginations were rampant. All 32 girls, aged between 8 and 22, concurred in telling an examiner "that they had daily carnal cohabitation with the devil, that they went to the sabbat or meetings, where they ate, drank, danced, and committed other whoredom and sensualities"; in other words, all the things they were forbidden under Bourignon's harsh regime. Fifth, the CCEL source (http://www.ccel.org/s/schaff/encyc/encyc02/htm/iv.v.ccl.htm) notes that Bourignon only fled, in 1662, "under serious accusations of cruelty" (no mention of being accused of witchcraft); and another says she fled the row over the death of a child. David Pickering's *Dictionary of Witchcraft* (1996, "Lille Novices") comments: "Remarkably, no one thought of accusing Bourignon herself of bewitching the children.... Instead, news of the case spread far and wide and she became a recognized authority on similar cases of demonic possession." Sixth, her flight "in disguise" was from the prospect of an arranged marriage in 1636. She had a habit of running from trouble in several other places too, until (finally, and again in disguise) 1679, when she was formally accused of sorcery by a former disciple in Hamburg. She died the following year, in Freisland, Holland (not Freidland, Prussia, as in Mackay), where she had established a hospital. (Wikipedia, http://en.wikipedia.org/wiki/Antoinette_Bourignon).

21. Paul Devereux, *Haunted Land: Investigations into Ancient Mysteries and Modern Day Phenomena* (London: Piatkus, 2001). It is worth noticing, as a possible vector of the witchcraft fear in this case, that both the town's name, Älvdalen (Elf Valley), and that of its region, Mora, are rich with supernatural associations in the countries adjacent to Sweden. In Polish, Slovak and Czech lore, *mora* (and variants) were the exorcised souls of the living, perceived as moths or wind-blown straws; in Slavic lore generally, *mora* could refer to a nightmare or a seductive night-visitor (a succubus).

22. The city of Mora sits at the north end of Lake Siljan, and its municipality includes Älvdalen (about 20 miles to its north) and Rättvik (about 20 miles southeast of Mora) at the other end of Lake Siljan.

23. It has been suggested that a woodcut that was made in 1670 to illustrate the Royal Commission on the terror at Mora, and that circulated widely throughout Europe and was re-used in some influential anti-witch tracts, may have had significant influence in shaping descriptions of what went on at a witches' sabbat in subsequent cases, including that of Salem just 24 years later.

24. Oliver Maddox Hueffer, *The Book of Witches* (East Ardsley, UK: EP, 1908 [1973]; Rossell Hope Robbins, *The Encyclopedia of Witchcraft and Demonology* (New York: Crown, 1966), pp. 348–50; personal communication from British historian Hilary Evans, 2003.

25. Richard L. Sjoberg, "The Catechism Effect: Child Testimonies during a 17th-Century Witch Panic as Related to Educational Achievement," *Memory* 8.2 (2000): 65. The legendary Blåkulla (Blue Hill) is actually a small, rocky island off southern Sweden's Baltic coast, about 360 miles almost due south of Mora. Its association with witches and other superstitions was recorded more than a century before the Mora incidents in Olaus Magnus' *Historia de Gentibus Septentrionalibus* (1555), and is probably much older still.

26. Paul Eberle and Shirley Eberle, *The Abuse of Innocence* (Buffalo, NY: Prometheus, 1993).

27. Hueffer (1908 [1973]), op. cit.; Robbins (1966), op. cit., pp. 348–50. The Älvdalen and Rättvik outbreaks were not isolated incidents but parts of "the Great Swedish Witch Panic"; one continuous phenomenon, the first (1668) feeding the latter (1669), and subsequently inspiring similar panics as far north as Finland and as far south as Stockholm in 1675.

28. Richard L. Sjoberg, "False Allegations of Satanic Abuse: Case Studies from the Witch Panic in Rättvik 1670-71," *European Child and Adolescent Psychiatry* 6 (1997): 219–26.

29. Pierre De Lancre, *Tableau de l'inconstance des Mauvais anges et Démons* (Paris: Buon, 1613), p. 357; L. F. Calmeil, *De la Folie, Considérée Sous le Point de vue Pathologique, Philosophique, Historique et Judiciaire [On the Crowd, Considerations on the Point of Pathology, Philosophy, History and Justice]* (Paris: Baillere, 1845), vol. 1, p. 503; Jean Wier (Johann Weyer), *Histoires, Disputes et Discours des Illusions et Impostures des Diables, des Magiciens Infames, Sorcières et Empoisonneurs*, vol. 1, translated from the Latin original published 1563 (Paris: Bureaux du Progrès Médical, 1885), p. 532; George S. Rosen, "Psychopathology in the Social Process: Dance Frenzies, Demonic

Possession, Revival Movements and Similar So-Called Psychic Epidemics: An Interpretation," *Bulletin of the History of Medicine* 36 (1962): 35; Ronald A. Knox, *Enthusiasm* (Oxford, UK: Clarendon Press, 1950), pp. 560–61.

30. Bekker (1694), op. cit.
31. Bekker (1694), op. cit.
32. Bekker (1694), op. cit.
33. For a comprehensive overview, see Jeffrey S. Victor, "Social Construction of Satanic Ritual Abuse and the Creation of False Memories," in *Believed-In Imaginings: The Narrative Construction of Reality*, ed. by Joseph de Rivera and Theodore R. Sarbin (Washington, DC: American Psychological Association, 1998), p. 200; J. S. Victor, *Satanic Panic: The Creation of a Contemporary Legend* (Chicago, IL: Open Court, 1993); J.S. Victor, "The Dynamics of Rumor-Panics about Satanic Cults," in *The Satanism Scare*, J. T. Richardson, J. Best and D. G. Bromely, eds. (New York A. DeGruyter, 1991), pp. 221–236.
34. Douglas Besharav, "Unfounded Allegations—A New Child Abuse Problem," *The Public Interest* 83 (1986): 22–24.
35. Margaret Talbot, "The Devil in the Nursery," *New York Times Magazine*, January 7, 2001. Other accusations included "teachers who took children on airplane rides to Palm Springs and lured them into a labyrinth of underground tunnels where the accused 'flew in the air' and others were 'all dressed up as witches.'"
36. Paul Eberle and Shirley Eberle, *The Abuse of Innocence: The McMartin Preschool Trial* (Buffalo, NY: Prometheus, 1993), p. 21.
37. Edgar W. Butler, Hiroshi Fukurai, Jo-Ellen Dimitrius, and Richard Krooth, *Anatomy of the McMartin Child Molestation Case* (Lanham, MD: University Press of America, 2001), pp. 28–34.
38. Butler et al. (2001), op. cit., pp. 14–15.
39. Butler et al. (2001), op. cit., pp. 13–14.
40. Butler et al. (2001), op. cit., pp. 13–14.
41. Stephen J. Ceci and Maggie Bruck, "Child Witnesses: Translating Research into Policy," *Social Policy Report* 7.3 (1993): 2–32.
42. News reports appearing on WRGB, Schenectady, New York (Channel 6) and WAST, Menands, New York (Channel 13), airing on the day the Buckeys were acquitted.

43. Butler et al. (2001), op. cit., p. 5.
44. Eberle and Eberle (1993), op. cit., pp. 149–50.
45. Eberle and Eberle (1993), op. cit., pp. 150–151.
46. Eberle and Eberle (1993), op. cit., p. 151.
47. "Sample Interviews by Investigators with Former Students of the McMartin Preschool," http://www.law.umkc.edu/faculty/projects/ftrials/mcmartin/victiminterviews.html.
48. Eberle and Eberle (1993), op. cit., pp. 380–81.
49. Eberle and Eberle (1993), op. cit., p. 202.
50. Talbot (2001), op. cit. "[Peggy McMartin Buckey] served two years in jail, and her son, Raymond, served five. They spent their life's savings on lawyers' fees and in the end went 'through hell' and 'lost everything,' as she put it after her 1990 acquittal."
51. Talbot (2001), op. cit. "'Believe the children' was the sanctified slogan of the moment — but what it came to mean, all too often, was believe them unless they say they were not abused. It didn't matter that no trace of the secret tunnels was ever found, that no physical evidence corroborated the charges (a black robe seized by the police as a Satanic get-up turned out to be Peggy's graduation gown), that none of the kiddie porn the abusers were supposedly manufacturing ever turned up, despite an extensive investigation by the F.B.I. and Interpol, that no parents who stopped by during the day had ever noticed, say, the killing of a horse. ... The prosecution charged forward nonetheless, with a seven-year trial that became the longest and, at a cost of $15 million, the most expensive criminal trial in American history. It resulted in not a single conviction, though seven people were charged in the McMartin case, on a total of 135 counts — just a series of deadlocks, acquittals and mistrials."
52. Jeffrey S. Victor, "The Search for Scapegoat Deviants," *The Humanist*, September/October 1992, pp. 10–13.
53. Victor (1992), op. cit., p. 13.
54. Dorothy Rabinowitz, "From the Mouths of Babes to a Jail Cell: Child Abuse and the Abuse of Justice: A Case Study," *Harper's Magazine*, May 1990, pp. 52–63, quoted in "Evil in the American Justice System," http://www.law.umkc.edu/faculty/projects/ftrials/evil/evilP18.html.

Chapter 2

1. Lewis A. Coser, Steven Nock, Patricia Steffan, and Daphne Spain, *Introduction to Sociology*, 2nd ed. (San Diego, CA: Harcourt-Brace Jovanovich, 1987), p. 2.
2. "Faculty Psychology and Mental Discipline: A Brief Overview," http://employees.csbsju.edu/esass/facultypsychology.htm, accessed July 26, 2004.
3. E. L. Thorndike and R. S. Woodworth, "The Influence of Improvement on One Mental Function upon the Efficiency of Other Functions," *Psychological Review* 8 (1901): 247–61.
4. "Transfer of Training," *Encyclopedia Britannica*, 2004, http://www.britannica.com/eb/article?eu=114763, accessed July 25, 2004.
5. Wessely Simon, "Mass Hysteria: Two Syndromes?" *Psychological Medicine* 17 (1987): 109–20.
6. M. Armainguad, "Recherches Cliniques sur L'hystérie; Relation d'une Petite Épidémie d'hystérie Observée à Bordeaux [Clinical Research on Hysteria and Its Relation to a Small Epidemic of Hysteria Observed in Bordeaux]," *Mémoire et Bulletin de la Société de Médecine et Chirurgie de Bordeaux*, 1879, pp. 551–79; E. Hagenbach, "Chorea-epidemie [Epidemic Chorea]," *Kor-Blatt f Schweit Arzte* (Basel) 23 (1893): 631–32.
7. M. Regnard and J. Simon, "Sur une Epidémie de Contracture des Êxtrêmités Observée à Gentilly [On an Epidemic of Limb Contracture Observed in Gentilly]," *Comptes Rendus des Séances de la Société de Biologie* (Paris) 3 (1887): 344–47, 350–53.
8. L. Laquer, "Über eine Chorea-Epidemie [An Epidemic of Chorea]," *Deutsche Medizinische Wochenschrift* (Leipzig) 14 (1888): 1045–46; R. Wichmann, "Eine Sogenannte Veitstanzepidemie in Wildbad [A So-called Epidemic of St. Vitus Dance in Wildbad]," *Deutsche Medizinische Wochenschrift* (Leipzig) 16 (1890): 632–36, 659–63.
9. S. Rembold, "Acute Psychiche Contagion in Einer Mädchenschule [Acute Psychic Contagion in a Girls' School]," *Berliner Klinische Wochenschrift* 30 (1893): 662–63.
10. H. Johnson, "Moral Instruction and Training in France," in *Moral Instruction and Training in Schools: Report of an International Inquiry*, ed. Sir Michael Sadler, vol. 2, pp. 1–50 (London: Longmans, Green, 1908), p. 26.
11. Johnson (1908), op. cit., p. 26. This is becoming more widespread as a doctrine in British schools due to the placing of restrictions on play and school trips, etc. But unlike in the latter 19th century European schools experiencing outbreaks, in general modern-day education authorities are steadily lowering standards on exams to qualify pass rates in schools, so there is actually less pressure on kids to perform. At the same time there is pressure on universities to accept these less qualified students. It looks as though this is a pressure relief valve on what could have otherwise been a recipe for hysterical outbreaks. Of course, the general lack of respect and propensity to talk back to school authorities, and even for students to express their displeasure with swear words, is also a major source of stress release in many contemporary Western schools. In the Far East, there is still extreme pressure to perform at school, and failure seems to be internalized more on an individual basis; suicides among failing students having been a serious issue in modern times.
12. Johnson (1908), op. cit., p. 27.
13. B. Dumville, "Should the French System of Moral Instruction be Introduced into England," in *Moral Instruction and Training in Schools: Report of an International Inquiry*, vol. 2, ed. M. E. Sadler (London: Longmans, Green, 1908), pp. 116–17.
14. G. Spiller, "Moral Education in the Boys' Schools of Germany," in *Moral Instruction and Training in Schools: Report of an International Inquiry*, vol. 2, ed. M. E. Sadler, pp. 213–30 (London: Longmans, Green, 1908), p. 215.
15. J. D. Montgomery, "The Education of Girls in Germany: Its Methods of Moral Instruction and Training," in *Moral Instruction and Training in Schools: Report of an International Inquiry*, vol. 2, ed. M. E. Sadler, pp. 231–41 (London: Longmans, Green, 1908), pp. 237–38.
16. Joseph Lukas, *Der Schulmeister von Sadowa* (Maniz: Kirchheim, 1878), p. 475.
17. Steven R. Welch, *Subjects or Citizens? Elementary School Policy and Practice in Bavaria 1800–1918* (Melbourne, Australia: University of Melbourne, Department of History Monograph 26, 1998). The Swiss education system was similar to that of the Germans, with discipline extreme, games infrequent, and creativity stifled. See G. Spiller, "An Educational Democracy: Moral Instruction and Training in the Schools of Switzer-

land," in *Moral Instruction and Training in Schools: Report of an International Inquiry*, vol. 2, ed. M. E. Sadler, pp. 196–206 (London: Longmans, Green, 1908), pp. 196, 199 and 203.

18. William H. Burnham, *The Normal Mind* (New York: D. Appleton, 1924), p. 324. The students were ages 9 to 15.

19. Dr. Palmer, "Psychische seuche in der Sbersten Slasse einer Sadchenschule [A Psychic Epidemic in the First Class of a Girls School]," *Zentralblatt für Nervenheilkunde und Psychiatrie* 3 (1892): 301–08.

20. W. H. Burnham, "Suggestion in School Hygiene," *Pedagogical Seminary* 19 (1912): 229.

21. Rembold (1893), op. cit. The affected girls ranged in age from nine to twelve.

22. Burnham (1912), op. cit., p. 230.

23. Burnham (1912), op. cit., p. 230.

24. Burnham (1912), op. cit., pp. 230–31. The trouble began near the start of classes: "Immediately after the beginning of instruction one child without any cause had fallen unconscious on her seat, and in a short time a considerable number, altogether perhaps one-third of the class, were attacked in the same way."

25. Unusual buzzing noises have been associated with some reports of anomalous phenomena; e.g., during the series of apparitions at Fátima, in Portugal, which began on the 13th day of May, 1917, and on the same day in the following five months. While the three young shepherd children went into rapture with their own visions, the huge crowds gathered on a bleak hillside were in their own heightened state, having waited for hours packed together in cooling air, straining with great expectation to see something inspiring. Those close to the visionary children reported hearing a buzzing sound — like that of a single bee — at the times the Virgin Mary was said to be speaking. In contemporary interviews and records, it is significant that the witnesses expressed puzzlement and no one attempted to impose an interpretation upon it (Dr. Joaquim Fernandes and Fina D'Armada, *Heavenly Lights: The Apparitions of Fatima and the UFO Phenomenon* [Victoria, BC: EccoNova, 2005] pp. 35–40). Parallels on the morphology of UFO cases are also given.

26. Burnham (1912), op. cit., p. 231.

27. Charles Fort, *The Complete Books of Charles Fort* (New York: Dover, 1974), p. 851, citing the *Derby Mercury*, May 15, 1905. Canaries were once used in coal mines to indicate the presence of toxic gasses. They have very sensitive lungs. If a canary keeled over, the mine would immediately be evacuated.

28. L. Hirt, "Eine Epidemie von Hysterischen Krämpfen in einer Schleisischen Dorfschule [An Epidemic of Hysterical Cramp in a Village School in Schleisischen]," *Zeitschrift für Schulgesundheitspflege* 6 (1893): 225–29 (summary of an article by L. Hirt in the *Berliner Klinische Wochenschrift*).

29. Burnham (1912), op. cit., p. 233.

30. Burnham (1912), op. cit., p. 229.

31. Burnham (1912), op. cit., p. 229. The similarities between the states induced by both hypnotism and hysteria were formally recognized by Jean-Martin Charcot (1825–1893), the pioneer of neurology and psychiatry at the Salpêtrière Hospital, Paris, who discovered how some neurological and psychological conditions can be replicated using hypnosis under clinical conditions (J.M. Charcot, *Lectures on the Diseases of the Nervous System* [London: New Sydenham Society, 1877], 3 vols.). One of the conditions that fascinated Charcot was the sensitivity of the subjects to suggestion and the degree to which they would mimic what they saw or heard. Imitation may well be one of the characteristics of the curious psychological conditions pertaining to stressed groups of youngsters; it is certainly something we see repeated in many of these cases.

32. Fritz Aemmer, *Eine Schulepidemie von Tremor Hystericus* [A School Epidemic of Hysterical Tremor], Inaugural dissertation Basel, 1893; Burnham, 1924, op cit., p. 329.

33. E. Zollinger, "Über die Pädagogische Behandlung des Nervösen Zitterns der Schulkinder [On the Educational Treatment of Nervous Trembling in School Children]," *Jahrbuch der Schweiz Gesellschaft für Schulgesundheitspflege* 7 (1906): 20–47; Brunham (1924), op. cit., pp. 329–31.

34. "Ellie" is a pseudonym; Burnham (1924), op. cit., p. 331.

35. Burnham (1912), op. cit., p. 229. It is possible that a few cases may have persisted. P. Schutte, "Eine neue form Hysterischer Zustande bei Schulkindern [A New Form of Hysterical Conditions in School Children]," *Münchener Medizinsche Wochenschrift* 53 (1906): 1763–64, translated from German by Edgar Schuler and Vincent Parenton and cited in E. A. Schuler and V. J. Parenton, "A Recent Epidemic of Hysteria in a Louisiana

High School," *Journal of Social Psychology* 17 (1943): 222. According to a report on the outbreak, most victims were nine- to thirteen-year-old girls from the elementary and middle schools, and the tremor started in their right hands. "The trembling often extends to the forearm and sometimes it also seizes the left side.... The trembling ... occur[s] with varying frequencies, sometimes also at night, and they last from a few minutes to half an hour. During the intervals the children usually feel entirely well, except for a certain nervous excitement, until the attack again sets in with more or less renewed vigor. This condition can last for weeks or months."

36. Burnham (1924), op. cit., p. 327; Johannes Schödel, "Über Induzierte Krankheiten [On Induced Illness]," *Jahrbuch für Kinderheilkunde* 14 (1906): 521–28; Burnham (1912), op. cit., p. 234.

37. Based on a search of Newspaper Archives.com conducted during December 2013.

38. Arthur Pinsent, *The Principles of Teaching-Method with Special Reference to Secondary Education*, 3rd ed. rev. (London: George G. Harrap, 1969), p. 264. Italics in original.

39. Pinsent (1969), op. cit., p. 264.

40. "Brevities," *Nevada State Journal* [Reno], May 29, 1894.

41. "Just a Curtain Fire," *The North Adams Evening Transcript*, February 2, 1899, citing *The New York Sun*.

42. "...Seven Hundred School Children Panic-Stricken by Fire," *The Daily Gazette* (Colorado Springs, Colorado), February 21, 1883, p. 1; "To Reward Heroine. Costly Present for Girl Scholar Who Stopped Fire Panic," *The Daily Northwestern* (Oshkosh, Wisconsin), October 20, 1900; "Denver Deluged. Storm of Rain, Hail and Wind causes Excitement," *The Democratic Standard* (Coshocton, Ohio), June 4, 1897; "Four Girls Fainted," *Brooklyn Daily Eagle*, June 16, 1897, p. 16.

43. Silvio Benaim, John Horder, and Jennifer Anderson, "Hysterical Epidemic in a Classroom," *Psychological Medicine* 3 (1973): 366–73.

44. Benaim et al., op. cit., p. 369.

45. Benaim et al., op. cit., p. 369.

46. E. A. Schuler and V. J. Parenton, "A Recent Epidemic of Hysteria in a Louisiana High School," *Journal of Social Psychology* 17 (1943): 228, 229, 230. About 60 years before the twitchers of Bellevue, the phenomenon that was Lulu Hearst was big news across America. Lulu claimed her "ability" first arrived during a thunderstorm. Afterwards she seemed able to "charge" furniture such that a chair simply could not be sat upon after she touched it; either the sitter or the chair flying away from the other when they tried. A slight girl, she reportedly resisted the efforts of 240-pound men to move her; and conversely they could not stop her from moving herself or objects. Chairs could not be wrested from her grasp without breaking the chair. She could lift a 200-pound man on a chair and hold him up for two minutes while measurements were taken. More pertinently, no amount of pushing or pulling could move her from a spot when she decided to "stay put," if the reports are to be believed. Between 1883 and 1885 she toured as "The Georgia Wonder" before she quit to marry her manager (Barry H. Wiley, *The Georgia Wonder: Lulu Hurst and the Secret that Shook America* [Seattle: Hermetic Press, 2004]). In her biography of 1897, she confessed to some showmanship, raising the question as to whether her feats were achieved entirely via illusion, magic and technique. Nevertheless, where Lulu could demonstrate immovability on the stage, other so-called "electric girls"—such as Angelique Cottin, of La Perrière, France, aged fourteen, who also could not be restrained by strong men—have endured it in a domestic environment. Other claims included her ability to exhibit extraordinary variations in weight, strength and physical resistance (Charles Fort [1974], op. cit.), p. 1032.

47. Schuler and Parenton (1943), op. cit., p. 231.

48. Schuler and Parenton (1943), op. cit., p. 231.

49. Schuler and Parenton (1943), op. cit., pp. 233.

50. Cal Harrison, "Mysterious Ailment Strikes Students at Welsh," *Lake Charles American Press*, March 28, 1962, p. 1.

51. James A. Knight, Theodore I. Friedman, and Julie Sulianti, "Epidemic Hysteria: A Field Study," *American Journal of Public Health* 55 (1965): 858–65.

52. Knight et al. (1965), op. cit., pp. 858–60.

53. Knight et al. (1965), op. cit.

54. Cal Harrison, "Mysterious Ailment Strikes Students at Welsh," *Lake Charles American Press*, March 28, 1962, p. 1.

55. Jerry is a pseudonym; Knight et al. (1965), op. cit., p. 861.

56. Knight et al. (1965), op. cit., p. 861.
57. "Fainting Spells Making School Nervous," *Oshkosh Daily Northwestern*, April 10, 1976, p. 1.
58. "Explanation Sought for Teen-Age Fainting Spells," *Stevens Point Daily Journal* (Wisconsin), April 10, 1976, p. 11.
59. Steven E. Roach and Ricky L. Langley, "Episodic Neurological Dysfunction Due to Mass Hysteria," *Archives of Neurology* 61.8 (August 2004): 1270.
60. Roach and Langley (2004), op. cit.
61. David Harrison, "Expert: Mystery Illness Is Stress," *The Roanoke Times*, November 18, 2007.
62. "Dr. Predicts PANDAS Syndrome in New York State Mystery Illness," http://www.youtube.com/watch?v=eOSJs3aOTlE&feature=related. A radio commentator suggested that Gardasil was the cause: http://www.youtube.com/watch?v=T76zHRbB-Zg&feature=related. Both links accessed January 23, 2012.
63. E. Drantch, "Dr: Leroy girls have PANDAS-like Illness," report filed by WIVB–TV, Buffalo, New York (Channel 4) on February 7, 2012.
64. "Dr. Speaks on NBC's Today Show," http://www.wgrz.com/news/article/151637/13/Parent-Disagrees-With-LeRoy-Illness-Diagnosis, accessed January 23, 2012.
65. "12 Girls at NY High School Develop Involuntary Tics; Doc Says It's 'Mass Psychogenic Illness,'" *Washington Post*, January 20, 2012.
66. Paul Cropper, letter to Robert Bartholomew dated January 24, 2012.
67. Paul Cropper, op. cit.
68. http://www.huffingtonpost.com/2012/01/17/thera-sanchez-tourettes-like-illness-tics-leroy-high-school_n_1210681.html, accessed January 26, 2012.
69. Jim Dupont, telephone conversation with Robert Bartholomew, circa January 20, 2012.
70. Bates, Daniel (2012). "Facebook to Blame for the Panic..." *Daily Mail* (London); February 5.
71. J. McVige and L. Mechtler, Dent Neurological Institute, Amherst, New York, personal communication, June 11, 2012.

Chapter 3

1. Quoted in R. T. Tripp, compiler, *The International Thesaurus of Quotations* (New York: Thomas Y. Crowell, 1970), p. 217.
2. Aaron Wildavsky, *But Is It True? A Citizen's Guide to Environmental Health and Safety Issues* (Boston: Harvard University Press, 1997), p. 442; David S. Wilson and Angus Gillespie, *Rooted in America: Foodlore of Popular Fruits and Vegetables* (Knoxville: University of Tennessee Press, 2000), p. 81.
3. Joel L. Nitzkin, "Epidemic Transient Situational Disturbance in an Elementary School," *Journal of the Florida Medical Association* 63 (1976): 357.
4. Berton Roueche, "Annals of Medicine. Sandy" (Interview with Dr. Joel Nitzkin), *The New Yorker* 21 (1978): 63, italics in original.
5. Nitzkin (1976), op. cit., pp. 357, 358.
6. Nitzkin (1976), op. cit., p. 358.
7. Nitzkin (1976), op. cit., p. 358.
8. Nitzkin (1976), op. cit., p. 358.
9. B. Roueche (1978), op. cit., p. 68.
10. Nitzkin (1976), op. cit., p. 359.
11. B. Roueche (1978), op. cit., p. 70.
12. P. Baker and D. Selvey, "Malathion-induced Epidemic Hysteria in an Elementary School," *Veterinary and Human Toxicology* 34 (1992): 157. The secretary's actions are certainly understandable, choosing to err on the side of caution.
13. Baker and Selvey (1992), op. cit., p. 157.
14. Baker and Selvey (1992), op. cit., pp. 159–60.
15. Baker and Selvey (1992), op. cit., pp. 158, 160.
16. Baker and Selvey (1992), op. cit., p. 159.
17. Baker and Selvey (1992), op. cit., p. 159.
18. Gary E. Elkins, L. A. Gamino, and R. R. Rynearson, "Mass Psychogenic Illness, Trance States and Suggestion," *American Journal of Clinical Hypnosis* 30 (1988): 447.
19. Elkins et al. (1988), op. cit., p. 448.
20. B. Nemery, B. Fischler, M. Boogaerts, D. Lison, and J. Willems, "The Coca-Cola Incident in Belgium, June 1999," *Food and Chemical Toxicology* 40 (2002): 1657–58; A. Gallay and S. Demarest, *Case Control Study Among Schoolchildren on the Incident Related to Complaints Following the Consumption of Coca-Cola Company Products, Belgium, 1999* (Scientific Institute of Public Health, Epidemiology Unit, November 1999), http://www.iph.fgov.be/epidemio/epien/cocacola.htm, accessed April 10, 2002.

21. Nemery et al. (2002), op. cit., pp. 1658–59.
22. A. Bernard and S. Fierens, "The Belgian PCB/Dioxin Incident: A Critical Review of Health Risks Evaluations," *International Journal of Toxicology* 21.5 (2002): 333–40; P. J. Schepens, A. Covaci, P. G. Jorens, L. Hens, S. Scharpe, and N. van Larebeke, "Surprising Findings Following a Belgian Food Contamination with Polychlorobiphenyls and Dioxins," *Environmental Health Perspectives* 109.2 (2001): 101–03; N. van Larebeke, L. Hens, P. Schepens, A. Covaci, J. Baeyens, K. Everaert, J. L. Bernheim, R. Vlietinck, and G. De Poorter, "The Belgian PCB and Dioxin Incident of January–June 1999: Exposure Data and Potential Impact on Health," *Environmental Health Perspectives* 109.3 (2001): 265–73; K. Bester, P. de Vos, L. Le Guern, S. Harbeck, F. Hendrickx, G. N. Kramer, T. Linsinger, I. Mertens, H. Schimmel, B. Sejerøe-Olsen, J. Pauwels, G. De Poorter, G. G. Rimkus, and M. Schlabach, "Preparation and Certification of a Reference Material on PCBs in Pig Fat and Its Application in Quality Control in Monitoring Laboratories During the Belgian 'PCB-Crisis,'" *Chemosphere* 44.4 (2001): 529–37; Nemery et al. (2002), op. cit., p. 1659.
23. Nemery et al. (2002), op. cit., pp. 1659–60.
24. B. Nemery, B. Fischler, M. Boogaerts, and D. Lison, "Dioxins, Coca-Cola, and Mass Sociogenic Illness in Belgium," *The Lancet* 354.9172 (July 3, 1999): 77; "Het Coca-Cola incident juni 1999 in België. Evaluatie van de gebeurtenissen, discussie, besluit en aanbevelingen," Ad Hoc Werkgroep van de Hoge Gezondheidsraad. Ministerie van Volksgezondheid, Brussels, March, 2000, http://www.health.fgov.be/CSHHGR/Nederlands/Advies/Coca-colaNl.htm, accessed April 10, 2003.
25. "Coke Adds Life, but Cannot Always Explain It" (editorial), *Lancet* 354.9174 (July 17, 1999): 173; Scott Leith, "3 Years After Recall, Coke Sales in Belgium at Their Best," *The Atlanta Journal-Constitution*, August 26, 2002; "Het Coca-Cola incident juni 1999 in België," op. cit.; Nemery et al. (2002), op. cit., p. 1662.
26. K. Durbin, T. Vogt, "Fumes…," *Columbian*, September 29, 2001.
27. R. L. Villanueva, M. C. Payumo, and K. Lema, "Flu Scare Sweeps Schools," *Business World* (Philippines), October 3, 2001, p. 12.

28. CNN, "Special Report Live with Aaron Brown," Atlanta, Georgia, October 16, 2001, 10–11 P.M.
29. "Update: Rashes Among Schoolchildren — 27 States, October 4, 2001–June 3, 2002," *Morbidity and Mortality Weekly Report* (Center for Disease Control, Atlanta) 51.24 (June 21, 2002): 524–52, http://www.cdc.gov/mmwr/preview/mmwrhtml/mm510 8a1.htm; "Rashes Among Schoolchildren — 14 States, October 4, 2001–February 27, 2002," *Morbidity and Mortality Weekly Report* (Center for Disease Control, Atlanta) 51.8 (March 1, 2002): 161–64, http://www.cdc.gov/mmwr/preview/mm wrhtml/mm 5108a1.htm; Robert E. Bartholomew and Benjamin Radford, "Rash of Mysterious Rashes May be Linked to Mass Hysteria," *The Skeptical Inquirer* 26.3 (2002): 8.
30. R. M. Rockney and T. Lemke, "Casualties from a Junior High School During the Persian Gulf War: Toxic Poisoning or Mass Hysteria?" *Journal of Developmental and Behavioral Pediatrics* 13 (1992): 339–42; R. M. Rockney and T. Lemke, "Response," letter, *Journal of Developmental and Behavioral Pediatrics* 15 (1) (1994): 64–65.
31. M. F. Goldsmith, "Physicians with Georgia on their Minds," *Journal of the American Medical Association* 262 (1989): 603–04.
32. Baruch Modan, Moshe Tirosh, Emil Weissenberg, Cilla Acker, T. A. Swartz, Corina Coston, Alexander Donagi, Moshe Revach, and Gaston Vettorazzi, "The Arjenyattah Epidemic," *The Lancet* 2 (1983): 1472–74.
33. A. Hafez, "The Role of the Press and the Medical Community in an Epidemic of Mysterious Gas Poisoning in the Jordan West Bank," *American Journal of Psychiatry* 142 (1985): 834–35.
34. Modan et al. (1983), op. cit., p. 1472.
35. Hafez (1985), op. cit., p. 834.
36. Modan et al. (1983), op. cit., p. 1472.
37. Hafez (1985), op. cit., p. 834.
38. Modan et al. (1983), op. cit., pp. 1472–73.
39. Modan et al. (1983), op. cit.
40. Report issued by the United Nations Educational Scientific and Cultural Organization (UNESCO) Executive Board, June 13, 1983 (116th Session) 116 EX/16 Add., Paris, June 9, 1983, Item 5.1.5 of the agenda: "Implementation of 21 C/Resolution 14.1 Concerning Educational and Cultural Insti-

tutions in the Occupied Arab Territories: Report of the Director-General," http://domino.un.org/UNISPAL.NSF/0/1198eaeac7114c0585256970005642d8?OpenDocument, accessed February 1, 2005.

41. Report issued by the United Nations Educational Scientific and Cultural Organization (UNESCO) Executive Board, June 13, 1983, op. cit.

42. Philip Landrigan and Bess Miller, "The Arjenyattah Epidemic: Home Interview Data and Toxicological Aspects," *The Lancet* 2 (1983): 1474–75.

43. Raphael Israeli, "Poison: The Use of Blood Libel in the War Against Israel," *Jerusalem Letter* 476 (April 15, 2002): 2, http://www.jcpa.org/jlv p476.htm.

44. Associated Press; "Spring Fever," *Fortean Times* 69 (June–July 1993), p.16.

45. Douglas Jehl, "Of College Girls Betrayed and Vile Chewing Gum," *New York Times*, July 10, 1996; discussion in *Fortean Times* 91 (Oct. 1996), p.14.

46. Raphael Israeli (2002), op. cit., p. 4.

47. Reuters New Agency, May 28, 1997; *Jerusalem Post* June 7 and 14, 1997; *New York Post*, June 29, 1997.

48. Hafez (1985), op. cit., pp. 836–37.

49. Paul Sieveking, "Behind the Battles in the Balkans," *Fortean Times* 124 (July 1999), p. 9.

50. *Independent*, March 24 and 27, 1990; *Observer* March 25, 1990; *Daily Telegraph* April 4, July 16, 1990; *Fortean Times* 55 (Autumn 1990): 24; Z. Radovanovic, "On the origin of mass casualty incidents in Kosovo, Yugoslavia, in 1990," *European Journal of Epidemiology* 11, (1995): 1–13. A separate investigation conducted by Dr. Bernard Cohen of the organization Physicians for Human Rights, after examining the video records of 3,000 patients, also concluded that mass hysteria was the most likely explanation. See Pal Kolsta, ed., *Media Discourse and Yugoslav Politics: Representations of Self and Other* (Burlington, VT: Ashgate, 2009), p. 93.

51. Debora MacKenzie, "Ethnic Strife Triggers Psychosomatic Illness," *New Scientist*, January 25, 1997, p. 5.

52. Associated Press, December 1, 2002; *Fortean Times* 169 (April 2003): 20.

53. Paul Sieveking, "Crazed Laughter in Chechnya," *Fortean Times* 210 (June 2006): 22–23.

54. Sieveking, op. cit.

55. Sieveking, op. cit.

56. R. M. Philen, E. M. Kilbourn, and T. W. McKinley, "Mass Sociogenic Illness by Proxy: Parentally Reported in an Elementary School," *The Lancet* 2 (1989): 1372–76.

57. Philen et al., pp. 1373, 1375.

58. M. T. Yasamy, A. Bahramnezhad, and H. Ziaaddini, "Postvaccination Mass Psychogenic Illness on an Iranian Rural School," *East Mediterranean Health Journal* 5.4 (1999): 710–15.

59. S. Kharabsheh, H. Al-Otoum, J. Clements, A. Abbas, N. Khuri-Bulos, A. Belbesi, T. Gaafar, and N. Dellepiane, "Mass Psychogenic Illness Following Tetanus-Diphtheria Toxoid Vaccination in Jordan," *Bulletin of the World Health Organization* 79.8 (2001): 765.

60. Kharabsheh, op. cit., pp. 765, 767.

61. Kharabsheh, op. cit., p. 769.

62. "National Affairs," *Newsweek*, April 4, 1983, p. 35.

63. "National Affairs," *Newsweek*, April 4, 1983, p. 35.

64. John Nova Lomax blog, blogs.houstonpress.com/hairballs/2008/07/the_year_the_smurfs_attacked.php July 14, 2008.

65. Stephanie McGrath, "Our Wayward Children," *The Houston Chronicle*, March 3, 1985, p. 1.

66. "On a Spot of Bother," *Sydney Morning Herald*, October 10, 1944, p. 1; "Hypnotist Lectures Pupils, Gets Unexpected Reaction," *Wisconsin Rapids Daily Tribune*, January 17, 1953, p. 8.

67. Stephen C. Smith, "Students Go Berserk at Miami School," *Austin Herald* (Minnesota), October 27, 1979, p. 3.

68. "Colombian Magician Arrested for Hypnotizing 41 Kids," *Hispanically Speaking News*, September 2, 2011, http://www.hispanicallyspeakingnews.com/notitas-de-noticias/2011/09/02/, accessed October 9, 2012. The title is misleading, as he was placed in police protection for his own safety.

69. "Colombian Magician Arrested for Hypnotizing 41 Kids," *Hispanically Speaking News*, op. cit.; "Hypnosis at Colombian School Ends in Mass Hysteria," Indo Asian News Service, September 3, 2011; Laura Hibbard, "Miller Zambrano Posada, Magician, Arrested," Huffington Post, 2012, http://in.news.yahoo.com/hypnosis-colombian-school-ends-mass-hysteria-054044654.html, accessed October 8, 2012.

70. CBC News Canada, "Hypnotized Students in Mass Trance Needed Emergency Help," June 15, 2012, http://news.ca.msn.

com/top-stories/hypnotized-students-in-mass-trance-needed-emergency-help, accessed October 12, 2012.

Chapter 4

1. Miles Richardson, cited in Robert E. Bartholomew, *Exotic Deviance* (Boulder, CO: University of Colorado Press, 2000), ii.
2. This is a composite account based on a collection of over 500 Malaysian press reports detailing separate outbreaks since the late 1950s.
3. The author (R.B.) and his Malay wife have multiple firsthand experiences in negotiating Malaysian traffic fines.
4. Susan Ellen Ackerman, *Cultural Process in Malaysian Industrialization: A Study of Malay Women Factory Workers*, Ph.D. thesis, University of California at San Diego (Ann Arbor, MI: University Microfilms, 1980).
5. Jin-Inn Teoh and Eng-Seng Tan, "An Outbreak of Epidemic Hysteria in West Malaysia," in *Culture-Bound Syndromes, Ethnopsychiatry, and Alternate Therapies*, vol. 4 of *Mental Health Research in Asia and the Pacific*, ed. William P. Lebra, pp. 32–43 (Honolulu: University Press of Hawaii, 1976); Sivagnanachelvi Selvadurai, *Problems of Residential Students in a Secondary Technical School*, Master's thesis, University of Malaya, Kuala Lumpur, 1985; George Orwell, *1984: A Novel* (London: Secker and Warburg, 1949). "George Orwell" was a pen name for British writer Eric Arthur Blair (1903–1950).
6. Jin-Inn Teoh, Saesmalijah Soewondo, and Myra Sidharta, "Epidemic Hysteria in Malaysia: An Illustrative Episode," *Psychiatry* 8.3 (1975): 260.
7. The name of the affected community and school are pseudonyms, as are the names of the girls involved.
8. Teoh et al. (1975), op. cit., 260.
9. Teoh and Teoh (1975), op. cit., p. 261.
10. Teoh and Teoh (1975), op. cit., p. 265.
11. Teoh et al. (1975), op. cit., p. 260.
12. Teoh et al. (1975), op. cit., p. 260.
13. Soewondo Teoh and Sidharta (1975), op. cit., pp. 263–64.
14. Soewondo Teoh and Sidharta (1975), op. cit., p. 264.
15. Soewondo Teoh and Sidharta (1975), op. cit., p. 264.
16. Soewondo Teoh and Sidharta (1975), op. cit., p. 264.
17. Walter William Skeat, *Malay Magic* (London: Macmillan, 1900); John Desmond Gimlette, *Malay Poisons and Charm Cures* (London: Oxford University Press, 1915); P. C. Y. Chen, "Indigenous Malay Psychotherapy," *Tropical and Geographical Medicine* 22 (1970): 409; Kirk Endicott, *An Analysis of Malay Magic* (Oxford: Clarendon, 1970).
18. Justus Friedrich C. Hecker, *The Dancing Mania of the Middle Ages*, translated by B. Babington (New York: B. Franklin, 1837 [1970]); Louis Florentin Calmeil, *De la Folie, Considérée Sous le Point de vue Pathologique, Philosophique, Historique et Judiciaire* [*On the Crowd, Considerations on the Point of Pathology, Philosophy, History and Justice*] (Paris: Baillere, 1845); Richard Robert Madden, *Phantasmata or Illusions and Fanaticisms of Protean Forms Productive of Great Evils* (London: T. C. Newby, 1857); R. B. Davy, "St. Vitus' Dance and Kindred Affection; The Recent Epidemic at the Ursulin Convent in Brown County, Ohio; A Sketch of the Historic Disease," *Cincinnati Lancet and Clinic* 4 (1880): 440–45, 467–73; Samuel Garnier, *Barbe Buvée, en Religion, Sœur Sainte-Colombe et la Prétendue Possession des Ursulines d'Auxonne* [*Barbara Buvée, and Religion, Sister Columbe and the Feigned Possession of the Ursulines at Auxonne*] (Paris: Felix Alcan, 1895); Jean Loredan, *Un Grand Proces de Sorcellerie au XVIIe siècle, L'Abbé Gaufridy et Madéleine de Demandolx (1600–1670)* [*The Grand Process of Witchcraft in the Seventeenth Century, L'Abbe Gaufridy and Madeleine de Demandolx (1600–1670)*] (Paris: Perrin et Cie, 1912); Aldous Huxley, *The Devils of Loudun* (New York: Harper, 1952); George Rosen, *Madness in Society* (London: Routledge and Kegan Paul, 1968); Keith Thomas, *Religion and the Decline of Magic* (London: Weidenfeld and Nicolson, 1971); Robert E. Bartholomew, "Tarantism, Dancing Mania and Demonopathy: The Anthro-Political Aspects of 'Mass Psychogenic Illness,'" *Psychological Medicine* 24 (1994): 281–306.
19. Refer to the following Malaysian newspaper articles: T. Abdul Rahman, "As I See It ... Will the Hysteria Return?" *The New Straits Times* (Malaysia), July 6, 1987; "Hysterical Pupils Take Schoolmates Hostage," *The New Straits Times*, May 19, 1987, p. 1; "Hysteria: Schoolgirls 'Confess,'" *The New*

Straits Times, May 21, 1987, p. 3; "Hysteria Blamed on 'Evil Spirits': School Head Wants the Ghosts to Go," *The New Straits Times,* May 23, 1987, p. 7; "Council to Meet Over Hysteria Stricken Girls," *The New Straits Times,* May 24, 1987, p. 4; "Seven Girls Scream for Blood: Hysterical Outbursts Continue," *The New Straits Times,* May 25, 1987, p. 4; "Interview: Fatimah, 'I Only Fulfilled My Parents' Wishes,'" *The New Straits Times,* May 31, 1987, p. 7; "I Can't Believe It, Says Pupil," *The New Straits Times,* May 31, 1987, p. 7; "100 Pupils and Two Teachers Yet to Return," *The New Straits Times,* July 10, 1987; "Transfer Plan for Girls Hit by Hysteria," *The New Straits Times,* July 21, 1987; "First Group of Hysteria Girls Sees Psychiatrist," *The New Straits Times,* August 11, 1987; "Hysteria: Second Batch Visits 'Shrink,'" *The New Straits Times,* August 13, 1987.

20. Eng-Seng Tan, "Epidemic Hysteria," paper read at the Scientific Session of the Annual General Meeting of the Malaysian Medical Association held at the General Hospital, Johor Baru, on April 12, 1963, and published in Eng-Seng Tan, "Epidemic Hysteria," *The Medical Journal of Malaya* 18.2 (December 1963): 72.

21. Tan (1963), op. cit., p. 72.

22. This is also true of people around the world, who commonly blend the scientific and supernatural.

23. Tan (1963), op. cit., p. 73.

24. Tan (1963), op. cit., p. 75.

25. The name of the college and those of the participants have been changed by Tan to protect the privacy of participants.

26. Raymond Lai Ming Lee and Susan Ellen Ackerman, "The Sociocultural Dynamics of Mass Hysteria: A Case Study of Social Conflict in West Malaysia," *Psychiatry* 43 (1980): 82.

27. Lee and Ackerman (1980), op. cit., p. 83.

28. Lee and Ackerman (1980), op. cit., p. 83.

29. Lee and Ackerman (1980), op. cit., pp. 83, 85. Lee and Ackerman further state: "By attributing undesirable actions to the spirit world, one is able to negotiate a problematic situation without causing embarrassment to oneself or the parties involved. It is immaterial whether other people suspect that claims of spirit involvement are contrived as long as one admits guilt but mitigates it by apportioning blame to malevolent spirits" (p. 85).

30. Umaporn Trangkasombat, Umpon Su-umpan, Veera Churujikul, Kamthorn Prinksulka, Orawan Nukhew, and Vilailuk Haruhanpong, "Epidemic Dissociation Among School Children in Southern Thailand," *Dissociation* 8.3 (1995): 134.

31. Trangkasombat et al. (1995), op. cit., p. 134.

32. Trangkasombat et al. (1995), op. cit., p. 133.

33. Trangkasombat et al. (1995), op. cit., p. 140.

34. Aphaluck Bhatiasevi, "Belief in Ghosts Sparks Hysteria: Students Freak Out at School Camp," *Bangkok Post,* February 4, 2001.

35. *The Bangkok Post* (dated August 8, 2003), http://www.ucg.org/worldnews/asiapacific/AP03.htm, accessed January 2, 2004. The feeling of suffocation, or of a weight pressing down on one's chest while sleeping, also occurs in other narrative genres of paranormal experience, most notably in the "Night Hag" tales of "sleep paralysis" from New England, studied by David Hufford in his *The Terror that Comes in the Night* (University of Pennsylvania Press, 1982).

36. Bournemouth *Daily Echo,* July 3, 1993.

37. "Five Women Treated by Exorcist After Visit to Fossil Site," July 2, 2002, http://www.ananova.com/news/story/sm_620143.html?menu=, accessed January 2, 2003, citing *The Bangkok Post.*

38. "Five Women Treated by Exorcist...," op. cit.

39. Http://www.ananova.com/news/story/sm_621181.html?menu=, accessed January 2, 2003, citing "Fear may have caused students' fossil site collapse," *The Bangkok Post,* July 3, 2002.

40. Http://www.ananova.com/news/story/sm_787527.html?menu=, accessed on January 2, 2003, citing: "Exorcist leads hunt for 'entrail-eating ghosts,'" *The Bangkok Post,* June 4, 2003.

41. "Devil Worship Terror Grips Lebanon's Kids," *The Business Times Singapore* online edition, March 17, 2003, http://www.spi.com.sg/haunted/katong_cult/devil_worship.htm, accessed January 2, 2004.

42. "Science Students Exorcise Ghosts," Tribune News Service, 2002, http://www.tribuneindia.com/2002/20021116/cth2.htm, accessed July 30, 2004.

43. "'Football ghost' keeps Indian schoolchildren off school," Ananova News Agency,

2004, http://www.ananova.com/news/story/sm_822542.html?menu =news.latestheadlines, accessed April 2, 2004.

44. "Exorcism Planned for School Toilet 'Ghost,'" Ananova News Agency, circa June 1, 2003.

45. "Mass Hysteria Hits Girls in Nepal School," http://www.tribuneindia.com/2003/20030909/world.htm#5, accessed July 30, 2004, citing the PTI news agency.

46. "'Possessed' Schoolgirls Treated," September 2003, http://iafrica.com/news/quirky/ 267749.htm, accessed July 6, 2004.

47. "Indian city spooked by 'ghost' photo," September 2003, http://www.ananova.com/news/ story/sm_820471.html, accessed July 31, 2004. This appears to have been part of the worldwide media scare that followed the release of the Japanese horror movie *The Ring* in 1998 directed by Hideo Nakata and adapted from the novel of the same name by Koji Suzuki, itself a re-telling of the Japanese folk tale "Bancho Sarayashiki." On East Asian Internet chat forums, particularly, there was an extensive wave of people mocking up images of friends with the iconic and eerie form of Sadako's ghost behind them, or somewhere else in the picture. Nearly all of these "ghosts" were said to have spontaneously appeared in a photograph taken of an uneventful scene.

48. "Feline Spirits Force Orissa School to Close," August 5, 2004, report from India's IANI news service, http://www.webindia123.com/news/show details.asp?id =44859&cat=India, accessed August 21, 2004; "School Shut Amid Fears that Some Girls Possessed," IANS News Service, http://news.newkerala.com/indianews/ index. php?action=fullnews &id=6702, accessed September 12, 2004.

49. "School Shut Amid Fears That Some Girls Possessed," op. cit.

Chapter 5

1. Walter Lippman, *Public Opinion* (New York: Harcourt, Brace, 1922), cited in F. MacDonnell, *Insidious Foes* (New York: Oxford University Press, 1995), p. 2.

2. Robert Conley, "Laughing Malady a Puzzle in Africa. 1000 Along Lake Victoria Afflicted in 18 Months—Most Are Youngsters. Schools Close Down," *New York Times*, August 8, 1963, p. 29.

3. A. M. Rankin and P. J. Philip, "An Epidemic of Laughing in the Buboka District of Tanganyika," *Central African Journal of Medicine* 9 (1963): 167–70.

4. Rankin and Philip (1963), op. cit., p. 167.

5. Rankin and Philip (1963), op. cit.

6. Conley (1963), op. cit.; *New York Times*, August 9, 1963, p. 4.

7. Rankin and Philip (1963), op. cit.; G. J. Ebrahim, "Mass Hysteria in School Children, Notes on Three Outbreaks in East Africa," *Clinical Pediatrics* 7 (1968): 437.

8. Kagwa (1964), op. cit., pp. 560–61.

9. Kagwa (1964), op. cit., pp. 561–62.

10. "Two Schools Close in Tanzania Till Siege of Hysteria Ends," *New York Times*, May 25, 1966, p. 36.

11. C. C. Adomakoh, "The Pattern of Epidemic Hysteria in a Girls' School in Ghana," *Ghana Medical Journal* 12 (1973): 408–09.

12. Adomakoh (1973), op. cit., p. 409.

13. Adomakoh (1973), op. cit., p. 411.

14. Robert K. Utley, *The Last Days of the Sioux Nation* (New Haven and London: Yale University Press, 1963), pp. 31–334.

15. David L. Miller, *Introduction to Collective Behavior and Collective Action*, 2nd ed. (Prospect Heights, IL: Waveland, 2000), p. 423

16. See also Emily A. Schultz and Robert H. Lavenda, *Anthropology: A Perspective on Human Culture* (Mountain View, CA: Mayfield, 1995), p. 545; James Davidson, Pedro Castillo, and Michael Stoff, *The American Nation* (Upper Saddle River, NJ: Prentice-Hall, 2000), pp. 519–20.

17. Many people would not consider this to be mainstream Christianity; it has been described more as "voodoo Christianity" due to its absorption of African elements.

18. Winkie Pratney, *Revival* (Lafayette, LA: Huntington House, 1984), p. 267.

19. http://www.thewaycm.com/pages/section5/perspectives_pages/africa.html.

20. Dr. Jack Partain, telephone interview by Robert Bartholomew, January 17, 2004; Dr. Partain is professor emeritus of religion at Gardner-Webb College in Boiling Springs, North Carolina, and taught at the Baptist Seminary of East Africa, Arusha, Tanzania, for 13 years.

21. Jack Partain, "Christians and Their Ancestors: A Dilemma of Theology," *Christian Century*, November 26, 1986, p. 1066.

22. Ibid.

23. R. Murray Thomas, ed., *International

Comparative Education: Practices, Issues, and Prospects (New York: Pergamon, 1991), p. 204.

24. Jack Partain (1986) op. cit.

25. G. M. Setiloane, "How the Traditional World-View Persists in the Christianity of the Sotho-Tswana," in *Christianity in Independent Africa,* ed. Edward Fashole-Luke, Richard Gray, Adrian Hastings, and Godwin Tasie (Bloomington, IN: Indiana University Press, 1978), p. 407.

26. Partain (2004), op. cit.

27. Greg Makeham, "12 Months of the Toronto Blessing," 1995, http://members.iinet.net.au/~gregga/ toronto/testimonies/12tb-1.html, accessed December 31, 2003.

28. Dr. Richard Needham, "The Toronto Blessing — Part One," http://www.geocities.com/bob_hunter/needham1.htm, accessed April 5, 2004. Dr. Needham is on the faculty of the Highland Theological College, Dingwall, Scotland IV15 9HA, United Kingdom.

29. Gino Geraci, "Look Before You Laugh," 1995, http://www.banner.org.uk/tb/look.html, accessed April 5, 2004; Dirk Anderson, "Great Signs and Wonders II," http://www.intowww.org/articles/art9708.htm, accessed December 31, 2003.

30. Anderson, op. cit.

31. Edward Tarkowski, "Laughing Phenomena: Its History and Possible Effects on the Church, Part III: The Abrahamic Covenant And Joyous Feast Of Tabernacles," http://users.stargate.net/~ejt/apos3.htm, accessed December 21, 2003.

32. Needham, op. cit.

33. J. R. Muhangi, "Mass Hysteria in an Ankole School," *East African Medical Journal* 50 (1973): 304–09.

34. Muhangi (1973), op. cit., p. 308.

35. Muhangi (1973), op. cit., p. 309.

36. Not her real name.

37. Manohar Dhadphale and S. P. Shaikh, "Epidemic Hysteria in a Zambian School: 'The Mysterious Madness of Mwinilunga,'" *British Journal of Psychiatry* 142 (1983): 85–88.

38. Dhadphale and Shaikh, op. cit., p. 87.

39. *Daily Times* (Malawi), June 14, 1993.

40. Malcolm MacLachlan, Dixie Maluwa Banda, and Eilish McAuliffe, "Epidemic Psychological Disturbance in a Malawian Secondary School: A Case Study in Social Change," *Psychology and Developing Societies* 7(1) (1995): 85.

41. MacLachlan et al. (1995), op. cit., p. 85.

42. MacLachlan et al. (1995), op. cit., p. 85.

43. Gideon Nkala, "Mass Hysteria Forces School Closure," *Middle East Intelligence Wire,* March 13, 2000.

44. Wene Owino, "Mass Hysteria Causes School's Temporary Closure," *Pan African News Agency,* March 8, 2000.

45. "Medics Call for School's Closure as Students Go Crazy," *Pan African News Agency,* March 3, 2000.

46. "Medics Call for School's Closure as Students Go Crazy," op. cit.

47. Lawson R. Wulsin and Athanase Hagengimana, "PTSD in Survivors of Rwanda's 1994 War," *Psychiatric Times* 15.4 (April 1998), http://www.psychiatrictimes.com/p980412.html, accessed December 31, 2003.

48. Wulsin and Hagengimana (1998), op. cit.

49. Conerly Casey, "'Dancing Like They Do in Indian Film': Media Images, Possession, and Evangelical Islamic Medicine in Northern Nigeria," Paper presented at the American Anthropological Association Meetings, 1999. I am grateful to Casey Conerly for granting me permission to quote from this draft paper.

50. Conerly Casey (1999), op. cit.

51. Conerly Casey (1999), op. cit. Teleportation (a word coined by Charles Fort in 1931) refers to the hypothetical ability of beings or objects to disappear from one place and reappear instantly in another without physically traversing the distance between them. It has been suggested as an explanation for mysterious appearances and disappearances, and is supposed to be a paranormal ability that can be done at will.

52. Conerly Casey (1999), op. cit.

53. Conerly Casey (1999), op. cit.

54. Dan Lamla Mkize and Reginald T. Ndabeni, "Mass Hysteria with Pseudoseizures at a South African High School," *South African Medical Journal* 92.9 (2002): 698.

55. Adrienne Carlisle, "Stress May Have Caused 'Mass Hysteria,'" *South African Dispatch,* May 29, 1999, http://www.dispatch.co.za/1999/05/29/easterncape/CAUSED.HTM.

56. Ajith Bridgraj, "A Mysterious 'Madness,'" 1999, *The Teacher,* http://www.teacher.co.za/9908/demon.html.

57. *Sunday Herald Sun* (Melbourne, Australia), June 13, 1999.

58. Bridgraj (1999), op. cit.

59. *Sunday Herald Sun* (Melbourne, Australia), June 13, 1999.

60. Mkize and Ndabeni (2002), op. cit., p. 698.

61. Other incidents occurred in the Kirinyaga district, at the Wang'uru Girls' Secondary School, at the Gathigi Primary School about thirty miles north of Nairobi, and at the Kambaa Girls' High School near Nairobi.
62. Tervil Okoko, "Ghosts Invade Kenyan Schools," *Pan Africa News Agency*, July 19, 2000; "Ghosts Beat Up Pupils at Kenyan School," AFP news agency, July 20, 2000, citing local newspapers; "I Hired Ghosts to Torment Schoolgirls," *The Star* (South Africa), June 5, 2000 (Reuters report).
63. Lucas Barasa (2001), op. cit.
64. Lucas Barasa (2001), op. cit.
65. "Headmaster Flees as Hysteria Grips School," *The Daily News* (Zimbabwe), July 30, 2002.
66. "Headmaster Flees as Hysteria Grips School," op. cit.
67. "Headmaster Flees as Hysteria Grips School," op. cit.
68. Although the word *tokoloshe* is believed to be Xhosa in origin, variants (e.g., *tokolosh, tikolosi, thokolosi, teikolosha*) are widely used throughout Southern Africa. A *tokoloshe* is a pot-bellied, dwarf-like spirit familiar that combines aspects of a zombie, a poltergeist, and a shape-changer, and is usually sent by a witch or wizard to cause mischief or sexual harassment.
69. "Headmaster Flees as Hysteria Grips School," op. cit.
70. "Headmaster Flees as Hysteria Grips School," op. cit.
71. Sifelani Tsiko, "Mysterious Hysteria Hits Moleli High School," *The Zimbabwe Herald On-line* (Zimbabwe), Friday, September 13, 2002.
72. Sifelani Tsiko (2002), op. cit.
73. Sifelani Tsiko (2002), op. cit.
74. Damian Zane, "Mass Fainting Hits Ethiopian Students," British Broadcasting Corporation, Friday, February 14, 2003, http://news.bbc.co.uk/2/hi/ africa/2763141.stm, accessed June 27, 2003.
75. Charles Wendo, "Uganda: A Village Possessed by Mass Hysteria," *All Africa Global Media*, July 6, 2002.
76. Wendo, op. cit.
77. Moses Nsubuga and Chris Kiwawulo, "Demons Attack Kiboga Pupils," *New Vision*, July 6, 2004, http://www.newvision.co.ug/D/8/26/370664, accessed November 21, 2012.
78. "Demons Hit School," *New Vision*, February 4, 2008.
79. "Demons in Hoima District," *New Vision*, February 9, 2008.
80. Francis Kagolo, "Kitebi Primary School Remains Closed over Mass Hysteria," *New Vision*, March 30, 2011.
81. Kagolo, op. cit.
82. "Kitebi Closed, Christian and Traditionalists Wage War," *Uganda News Picks*, April 18, 2011.
83. Elizabeth Ritchie, "The Ritchies in Uganda. Demons, Ghosts and Evil Spirits," 2011, http://ritchiesinuganda.blogspot.co.nz/2011/04/220411-demons-ghosts-and-evil-spirits.html, accessed November 22, 2012.
84. Paul Boyer and Steven Nissenbaum, *Salem Possessed: The Social Origins of Witchcraft* (Cambridge: Harvard University Press, 1974.
85. James Onen, "'Demonic Attacks' in Ugandan Primary Schools," *Free Thought Kampala*, April 4, 2011, http://freethoughtkampala.wordpress.com/2011/04/04/woo-takedown-03-demonic-attacks-in-ugandan-primary-schools/, accessed November 22, 2012.
86. Elizabeth Namazzi and Carol Kasujja, "Uganda: "What's Happening at Kitebi Primary School," *New Vision*, April 9, 2011.
87. John Kibego, "School Closed After 'Demon Attacks,'" *The Observer*, October 16, 2011; Frederick Kivabulaya, "Hoima School Closed over Alleged Demon Attacks," Ugandan Radio Network transcript, October 13, 2011.
88. Kibego (2011), op. cit.; Frederick Kivabulaya, "Hoima School Closed over Alleged Demon Attacks," Ugandan Radio Network transcript, October 13, 2011.
89. I thank Julie Parle for allowing me to quote from her unpublished study on *umhayizo*, and for reading over this section of the manuscript and offering her views. While Julie takes exception to my use of the word witchdoctor, I explain my rationale for this in the acknowledgments.
90. Michael Gamache, personal communication to Robert Bartholomew, February 5, 2004; Gamache is a science teacher at Mill River Union High School in North Clarendon, Vermont.

Chapter 6

1. "The Quotations Page," http://www.quotationspage.com/quotes/Oliver_Wen

dell_Holmes_Jr./, accessed on August 12, 2004.

2. "Ara" and the names of the other people afflicted by the hysteria are pseudonyms.

3. Stephen Frankel, "Mass Hysteria in the New Guinea Highlands: A Telefomin Outbreak and Its Relationship to Other New Guinea Hysterical Reactions," *Oceania* 47 (1976): 107–08, 117.

4. Frankel (1976), op. cit., pp. 113, 114.

5. Frankel (1976), op. cit., pp. 111–13.

6. Frankel (1976), op. cit., p. 115.

7. Frankel (1976), op. cit., p. 120.

8. Frankel (1976), op. cit., p. 121.

9. Frankel (1976), op. cit.

10. Reay (1960), op. cit., p. 138.

11. Reay (1960), op. cit., p. 139; Marie Reay, "'Mushroom Madness' in the New Guinea Highlands," *Oceania* 31.2 (1960): 137–39.

12. Roger Heim and R. Gordon Wasson, "The 'Mushroom Madness' of the Kuma," *Botanical Museum Leaflets* (Harvard University) 21.1 (1965): 20.

13. Marie Reay, "Mushrooms and Collective Hysteria," *Australian Territories* 5 (1965): 22–24.

14. "Boletus Manicus," http://www.entheogen.com/boletusm.html, accessed June 5, 2003.

15. Benjamin Thomas, "'Mushroom Madness' in the Papua New Guinea Highlands: A Case of Nicotine Poisoning?" *Journal of Psychoactive Drugs* 34.3 (2002): 321–23.

16. Marie Reay, "Ritual Madness Observed: A Discarded Pattern of Fate in Papua New Guinea," *The Journal of Pacific History* 12 (1977): 55–79.

17. Reay (1977), op. cit., pp. 59–60, cited in Benjamin Thomas, http://www.shamanaustralis.com/~benjaminthomas/Komugl_Tai_and_Acute_Nicotine_Intoxication.htm, accessed June 5, 2003.

18. Aubrey L. Parke, "The Qawa Incident in 1968 and Other Cases of 'Spirit Possession,'" *The Journal of Pacific History* 30 (1995): 210–26, citing the *Fiji School of Medicine Journal* 4.12 (December 1969): 4.

19. Parke, op. cit., p. 217.

20. Parke, op. cit., p. 218.

21. Parke, op. cit., p. 218.

22. Parke, op. cit., pp. 218–19.

23. Parke, op. cit., p. 220; "Yaqona (Kava)," *Islands Travel*, Lot 7, Qanville Estate, Box 10146, Nadi Airport, Fiji, South Pacific, http://www.fiji-island.com.

24. Parke, op. cit., p. 220.

25. Parke, op. cit., p. 221.

26. Parke, op. cit., p. 222–23.

27. Parke, op. cit., p. 226.

28. "Fiji: Kidnap Hysteria Leads to Assaults," November 10, 2003, http://www.pacificislands.cc/pina/pinadefault.php?urlpinaid =9726, accessed January 2, 2004, citing the *Fiji Times*.

29. "Schoolchildren Possessed by 'Devil' in Manila," Reuters News Service report, January 28, 1994.

30. Sol Jose Vanzi, "Nueva Vizcaya Students 'possessed' by Evil Spirits," Philippine Headline News Online, 2003, http://www.newsflash.org/2003/05/ht/ht003563.htm.

31. Francis Allan Angelo, *The Guardian* (Iloilo, The Phillipines), February 16–17, 2004.

32. The following report is based on a firsthand visit to the Rizal Elementary School by the reporter. Jaime Licauco, "Dwarves in Iloilo School," "Inner Awareness" column, Inquirer News Service, February 16, 2004, http://www.inq7.net/lif/2004/feb/17/lif_22-1.htm, accessed August 24, 2004.

33. Licauco (2004), op. cit. Western fairy traditions also stress the necessity of being polite to fairies lest they take offense. This includes referring to them indirectly as the "Good Folk." When Bob Rickard was researching the associations between fairies, crop circles and whirlwinds, he came across an old Irish belief that one must take off their hat to a whirling eddy because of the belief that these were used by (or caused by the passage of) fairies through the air: "A few days after making this discovery, I was astonished by the coincidence of meeting a man from Kerry who, unbidden, told me how he was about to cross a bridge when he stopped his car because there was a small whirlwind of dust in the way. He said his passengers had laughed when he got out and asked its permission to pass."

34. "Panic After 'Devil Attack' at School," *The Trinidad Guardian*, November 12, 2010, http://www.guardian.co.tt/archives/news/general/2010/11/11/panic-after-devil-attack-school, accessed January 14, 2012.

35. "Panic After 'Devil Attack' at School," op. cit.

36. Marion O'Callaghan, "The Devil Arrives in Moruga," *Trinidad and Tobago Newsday*, November 22, 2012, http://www.newsday.co.tt/commentary/0,131243.html, accessed January 14, 2012.

37. Marion O'Callaghan (2012), op. cit.

Chapter 7

1. Clifford Geertz, *The Interpretation of Cultures* (New York: Basic, 1973), p. 5.
2. Nashyiela Loa Zavala, "The Expulsion of Evil and Its Return: An Unconscious Fantasy Associated with a Case of Mass Hysteria in Adolescents," *The International Journal of Psychoanalysis* 91.5 (2010): 1157–78.
3. Not her real name.
4. According to British psychologist Chris French, Ouija boards can be explained using conventional psychology. He says that when someone asks a question, the participants rest their finger or fingers lightly against the glass and it will seemingly answer the question by sliding into either a series of letters that spell out answers, or onto the section that says "yes," "no" or "maybe." French says that this can be explained by the Idiomotor effect, in which people are unaware that they are actually pushing the glass. French says that an easy way to prove that it is a psychological effect is to blindfold the participants and have them try answering the questions without being able to see where they are pushing the glass. Inevitably, they end up with garbled, incomprehensive messages. See Chris French, "Debunking the Paranormal," *Health and Wellbeing*, http://www.videojug.com/expertanswer/debunking-the-paranormal-2/how-does-a-ouija-board-work.
5. Loa Zavala (2010), op. cit., p. 1162.
6. Loa Zavala (2010), op. cit., p. 1163.
7. Loa Zavala (2010), op. cit., p. 1163.
8. Loa Zavala (2010), op. cit., p. 1164.
9. Loa Zavala (2010), op. cit., p. 1164.
10. Loa Zavala (2010), op. cit., p. 1164.
11. Loa Zavala (2010), op. cit., p. 1168.
12. Loa Zavala (2010), op. cit., pp. 1169–70.
13. Richard Leonardi, "Nicaraguan Leprechauns," *Essays on Nicaragua*, http://www.nicaraguaphoto.com/essays/update_nicaraguaSept2003.shtml, accessed November 13, 2010.
14. Leonardi (2010), op. cit.
15. Paul Hoffman, *Sex with the Devil*, August 10, 2009, http://bigthink.com/ideas/15839, accessed October 30, 2010.
16. Nicola Fell, "She Ran Around Like a Maniac,' *BBC News*, April 20, 2009, http://news.bbc.co.uk/1/hi/health/8007895.stm, accessed October 30, 2010.
17. Fell (2010), op. cit.
18. Phil Dennis, "Grisi Siknis Among the Miskito," *Medical Anthropology* 5.4 (1981): 445–505; Phil Dennis, "Grisi Siknis in Miskito Culture," in *The Culture-Bound Syndromes*, Ronald C. Simons and Charles C. Hughes, eds. (Holland: D. Reidel, 1985), pp. 289–306.
19. Charles Napier Bell, *In Tangweera: Life and Adventures Among Gentle Savages* (London: Arnold, 1899), p. 97.
20. Nicola Ross, "Nicaragua's Crazy Sickness: An Indigenous Community Grapples with a Mysterious Ailment," *The Walrus*, June 2006, http://www.walrusmagazine.com/articles/2006.06-anthropology-nicaragua-grisi-siknis/, accessed October 30, 2010.
21. Robert Widdicombe, "Nicaragua Village in Grip of Madness," *Guardian*, December 17, 2003.
22. Nicola Fell, "She Ran Around Like a Maniac," *BBC News*, April 20, 2009, http://news.bbc.co.uk/1/hi/health/8007895.stm, accessed October 30, 2010.
23. For a discussion of the widespread fear of contamination of wells and reservoirs, and why it seems unlikely, see Andy Roberts' "Reservoir Drugs," *Fortean Times* 262 (May 2010): 38–42.
24. Video clips of victims in their throes can be found on YouTube that do, indeed, show some young male victims, e.g., http://www.youtube.com/watch?v=5kWbhdm6-6E, accessed October 30, 2010.
25. Charles Napier Bell (1899), op. cit., p. 97.
26. Dennis (1981), op. cit.
27. Robert Widdicombe, "Nicaragua Village in Grip of Madness," *Guardian*, December 17, 2003.
28. Bell (1899), op. cit., p. 97.
29. Tim Rogers, "Grisi Siknis Illness Grips Indigenous Nicaraguan Communities," TicoTimes.net, also as a YouTube report, posted August 5, 2009, http://www.youtube.com/watch?v=7i-vbei4D4Q&feature=related, transcription by B.R. Rogers, compares the incident to the spectacle at Salem. This may not be a frivolous comparison; at least one other commentator (to an online blog) reminded readers that the Salem children were influenced by a maid, Tituba, who came from the Caribbean, to which Nicaragua is adjacent.
30. Mondale Smith and Jenelle Carter, "Mass School Hysteria Spread Across Guyana," Kaieteur News Online, 2009, http://www.kaieteurnewsonline.com/2009/11

/07/mass-school-hysteria-spreads-across-guyana/, accessed October 19, 2012.

31. Leroy Smith, "Spiritual Manifestation Creates Panic at City," *Guyana Chronicle*, March 15, 2012, http://www.guyanachronicle online.com/site/index.php?option= com_content&id=40707:spiritual-manifes-tation-creates-panic-at-city-school&Itemid= 8, accessed January 14, 2012.

32. Kristen Macklingam, "Another 'Demon Attack' at St. Winefride's," Kaieteur News, March 27, 2012, http://www.kaieteur newsonline.com/2012/03/27/another-%E2%80%9Cdemon-attack%E2%80%9D-at-st-winefride%E2%80%99s/, accessed January 14, 2013.

Chapter 8

1. Cited in Rhoda T. Tripp, compiler, *The International Thesaurus of Quotations* (New York: Harper & Row, 1970), p. 303.

2. The main sequence of events was reconstructed from the following reportage and Robert Rickard's notes taken as the incident unfolded; all dates are in 1980: *Daily Mail*, July 14, 15, 16, 17, and 26; *Daily Mirror*, July 14, 16, 17, and 23; *Daily Star*, July 14, 15, and 16; *Daily Express*, July 14, 15, and 16; *Daily Telegraph*, July 14 and 16; *The Times*, July 14, 15, 24, and 26; *Western Mail*, July 14 and 16; *Guardian* July 14, 15, and 17; *London Evening Standard*, July 14; *Mansfield and North Nottinghamshire Chronicle and Advertiser*, July 17, 31, and August 14; *The Sunday Times*, July 20; *Observer*, July 20; *Shropshire Star*, July 14; *New Scientist*, July 31, August 28. This is a revision and expansion of material that appeared in *Fortean Times* 33 (Autumn 1980): 22–27.

3. Terry Bingham was frequently wrongly referred to as an organizer of the event; he was secretary to the Zingaris Band from Clay Cross, Derbyshire (*Daily Express*, July 15, 1980).

4. Denise Winn, "Hysteria Tests on Festival Victims," *Daily Express*, July 20, 1980. According to Ms. Winn's research, "The panic spread when alarming messages, such as 'Don't eat the ice cream. It's been poisoned.' and 'Don't stand on the grass. It's been sprayed,' were relayed across the Tannoy."

5. The *Sun* seems to have got the verdict right early on — "'KO'd by 'Hysteria,'" *Sun*, July 16, 1980 — although they favored the 'anti-hysteria' lobby in some of their reporting.

6. A hospital spokesman later said their initial diagnosis "has since been ruled out by chemical tests." *Guardian*, July 17, 1980.

7. Oliver Gillie and Toni Turner, "Mystery Epidemic may have been Sparked off by The Blebs," *Sunday Times*, July 20, 1980.

8. "More Band Children Ill," *Daily Express*, July 21, 1980.

9. "Band Bug Hits Kids," *Sun*, 28 July 1980.

10. "Children Collapse on Parade," Wolverhampton *Express & Star*, July 28, 1980.

11. *Daily Mail* and *Daily Telegraph*, July 21, 1980.

12. Denise Winn, op cit.

13. *Western Mail*, August 8, 1980.

14. "New theory on 'mass hysteria.'" BBC News, 23 September, 2003, online at: http://news.bbc.co.uk/1/ hi/england/nottingham shire/ 3128402.stm. Accessed 17/05/2010.

15. The BBC TV regional magazine *Inside Out: East Midlands* produced a documentary called "The Hollinwell Incident," first broadcast on Monday, September 22, 2003. The BBC's info page on the program — carries three viewers' responses which demonstrate the level of skepticism about the 'official explanations.' Harold Ashby said that "that blaming mass hysteria is a way of covering up the truth," by which he meant "this incident was caused by the crop spraying." He probably represents a sizeable mindset that has no interest in facts which contradict deeply held beliefs. "No one will ever convince me that just one child fainting could cause over two hundred to come down with those symptoms." David Haslam, an author who also appeared in the program, asked: "If pesticides were the cause why didn't medical tests on victims show this?" Kerry Randall had a question of her own: "If as they say it was mass hysteria, why did it affect babies and adults as well as the children?" See: http://www.bbc.co.uk/insideout/eastmidlands/series4/holinwell_incident. shtml.

16. Don Concannon and Frank Haynes, *Guardian*, July 15, 1980. Dennis Skinner, *Daily Mirror*, July 16, 1980.

17. Oliver Gillie and Toni Turner, op cit.

18. Denise Winn, op cit.

19. Oliver Gillie and Toni Turner, op cit.

20. H. C. T. Smith and E. J. Eastham, "Outbreak of Abdominal Pain,' *The Lancet* 2 (1973): 956–58.

21. Smith and Eastham (1973), op cit., p. 957.

22. Smith and Eastham (1973), op cit., p. 957.
23. Smith and Eastham (1973), op cit., p. 958.
24. Smith and Eastham (1973), op cit., p. 958.
25. Smith and Eastham (1973). op cit., p. 958; David Hambling, "Contagious Fear: Mass Sociogenic Smell Weapon," *Wired*, January 28, 2008, http://www.wired.com/dangerroom/2008/01/contagious-fe. Accessed 17 May 2010. Hambling compares the Hazlerigg event to the panic cause by a meteorite that fell in Caracas on 15 September 2007. "According to witnesses, the crater filled with boiling liquid and noxious gas poured out. Up to six hundred people were said to be affected, including seven police officers who had to be taken to hospital. An official said that fumes from the crater caused 'nausea, vomiting, diarrhea, headaches and stomach pain.'" Other, more 'conventional' cases of mass hysteria are mentioned also. Hambling's point is that "the combination of smell and fear is frequently the trigger for outbreaks of mass illness." He cites a US meteor hunter, who proposes that the meteoric impact on the swampy water and the mineral rocks beneath it resulted in a cloud of noxious sulphur-dioxide which *could* be compared to the "stench from a pigsty" frequently blamed for the Hazlerigg collapse. Ever since, in most mentions of the Hazlerigg incident, the 'pigsty stench' is usually given, without qualification, as the cause of the panic. It may well have been the 'trigger' but it could not, of itself, account for the widespread symptoms.
26. *Daily Mirror*, July 10, 1973; *BBC News*, September 23, 2003, op cit.; *Daily Telegraph*, July 14, 1980.
27. R. Levine, "Epidemic Faintness and Syncope in a School Marching Band." *Journal of the American Medical Association* 238.22 (1977): 2373–74.
28. Levine (1977), op cit., p. 2376.
29. Levine (1977), op cit., p. 2373; P. H. Pfeiffer, "Mass Hysteria Masquerading as Food Poisoning," *Journal of the Maine Medical Association* 55 (1964): 27.
30. "165 Girls Faint at Football Game; Mass Hysteria Grips 'Pep Squad,'" *New York Times*, September 14, 1952, p. 1; "'Tigerettes' Faint Like Flies; Gridiron Looks Like Race Track." *Waukesha Daily Freeman* [Waukesha, Wisconsin], September 13, 1952, p. 1; "165 Girls 'Faint Like Flies,' All Rushed Off By Ambulances." *Great Bend Daily Tribune* [Great Bend, Kansas], September 13, 1952, p. 1.
31. "Mass Hysteria Sends 165 Girls to Hospital," *Daily Redlands Facts* [Redlands, California], September 13, 1953, p. 1; "160 H.S. Must Take Football Less Seriously," *The Mt. Pleasant News* [Iowa], September 13, 1952, p. 1; "165 Girls 'Faint Like Flies,' All Rushed Off By Ambulances," op cit., p. 1.
32. "Mass Hysteria Mars the Music," *Science News* (September 21, 1991) 140(12): 187.
33. "Exhaust Fumes and Hysteria KO Some 500 Students at Festival," *Stevens Point Daily Journal* [Wisconsin], November 24, 1959, p. 2.
34. "Choir Hit by Fainting Spells," *The Times Recorder* [Zanesville, Ohio]. December 13, 1953, p. 1.
35. "Mass Fainting Hits Chorus," *Mansfield News-Journal* [Ohio], December 22, 1952.
36. Peter D. Moss and Colin P. McEvedy, "An Epidemic of Overbreathing Among Schoolgirls," *British Medical Journal* 2 (1966): 1295–1300. Just about any startling event can trigger a fainting episode. At a school in Minnesota in 1927, it was the igniting of flash powder from a camera. On November 10, three girls fainted during the assembly after someone took a "flashlight" picture. This highly public event may have made others anxious as it set off a series of fainting spells over several weeks. See, Willard C. Olson, "Account of a Fainting Epidemic in a High School," *Psychology Clinic* (Philadelphia) 18(1928): 34–38.
37. M. E. Moffat, "Epidemic Hysteria in a Montreal Train Station," *Pediatrics* 70 (1982): 308-10.
38. Moffatt (1982), op cit., pp. 309–10.
39. Moffatt (1982), op cit., p. 310.
40. Thanks to Bruce Francis for these observations.
41. "Makhlok2 Daripada Dunia Lain Mendarat di-Johor?" [Beings From Another Planet Landed in Johor?], *Berita Harian*, July 4, 1969. "Makhlok2<in> is the proper spelling.
42. *The Straits Times*, August 22, 1970.
43. *The Straits Times*, August 21, 1970.
44. *The Straits Times*, August 22, 1970; "Malaysian Sightings," *The Echo*, 1980 (exact date unknown).
45. *The Straits Times*, August 21, 1970.
46. "Orang Orang Kenit Angkasa Lepas Mendarat Pula di Rawang?" [Beings From

Space Landed in Rawang?], *Utusan Malaysia*, August 28, 1970; "'Spaceship' in Rawang. School Staff, Pupils Saw 'Object,'" *Malay Mail*, August 31, 1970.

47. "I was Shot by 3-inch Aliens, Says Kid," *The Star*, May 20, 1979; *The Star*, May 23, 1979; "Police to Probe 'Alien Landing,'" *The Star*, May 21, 1979. In addition to Khor, the other primary students who witnessed the event were Cheah Seow Boon, Tan Teik Hwa, Goh Kah Pin, Tan Goon Heng, and Teh See Phui.

48. "We Saw Midgets, Say Pupils," *The New Straits Times*, August 26, 1982; "Ball of Fire Causes Excitement in Town," *The Star*, August 18, 1982; "Sarikei 'Fireball' Could be a Distress Signal," *The Star*, August 22, 1982; "Api Dari Langit Gemparkan Penduduk Sarikei" [Fire from the Sky Shocks Residents of Sarikei], *Utusan Malaysia*, August 18, 1982; "Jabatan Kajicuaca Beri Penjelasan Mengenai Bola Api Dari Langit" [The Meteorology Office Explained about the Fireball from the Sky], *Utusan Malaysia*, August 19, 1982.

49. *The New Straits Times*, October 11, 1974; "Kisah 'Orang Kenit' Gemparkan Sekolah Pangkalan Tentera Kuantan" [Story About Tiny Beings Shocked Pangkalan Tentera School in Kuantan], *Berita Harian*, October 11, 1974. Information on the second incident was compiled by Ahmad Jamaludin from individuals who are aware of the incidents in their area but did not participate in the actual sighting.

50. *Berita Harian*, October 12, 1974.

51. "Children Say They Saw 'Aliens,'" *New Straits Times*, October 18, 1985; "Murid Dakwa Jumpa Makhluk Asing," *Berita Harian*, October 18, 1985; "Detik-Detik Pertemuan Dengan Makhluk Asing" [Moments of Meeting with Aliens], *Bacaria*, October 27, 1985; "Guru Sahkan Murid Jumpa UFO" [Teacher Admits Students Saw UFO], *Bacaria*, October 27, 1985.

52. Sajaratul Noor Kamal Hijaz, "Awang Kenit Muncul di Sekolah" [Gnomes Appear in School], *Watan*, April 4 1989; "Gigi Awang Kenit Taajam — Faizul" [Gnomes Have Sharp Teeth], *Watan*, April 4, 1989; "Guru Besar: Cuma Khayalan Murid" [Head Master: Just Student Imagination], *Watan*, April 4, 1989.

53. "Murid Dakwa Terserempak 'Orang Kenit'" [Pupils Claim Encounter with Tiny Entities], *Berita Harian*, May 15, 1991.

54. *Nanyang Siang Pau*, July 24, 1991.

55. Mustafa Kamil Jamaluddin (1992). "Sekumpulan Pelajar Dakwa Terserempak..." [A Group of Students Claimed to have Met....], *Bacaria*, October 3.

56. J. Abdullah, *A Report of the Interview with the Female Teacher and Students at the Hishamuddin Secondary Islamic School, Klang*, confidential report, n.d.; R. E. Bartholomew, *Miracle or Mass Delusion: What Happened in Klang, Malaysia?* A study compiled for Pusat Islam, The Prime Minister's Department, Kuala Lumpur, Malaysia, 1993.

57. *The Daily Telegraph*, June 16, 1990.

58. Adam Sisman, ed., *The Best of the Fortean Times* (New York, Avon, 1992), p. 63.

59. Tim Ryan and Jurek Kirakowski, *Ballinspittle, Moving Statues and Faith* (Cork, Ireland: Mercier, 1985), p. 53.

60. Ryan and Kirakowski, 1985, op cit., p. 53; *The Scotsman*, October 24, 1985.

61. Bob Rickard, "A Moving Experience," *Fortean Times* 45: 6–7; "The Moving Statues of Ireland," *Fortean Times* 45: 30–34; Lionel Beer, *The Moving Statue of Ballinspittle and Related Phenomena* (Middlesex, UK, Spacelink Books, 1986).

Chapter 9

1. Quoted in Rhonda T. Tripp, compiler, *The International Thesaurus of Quotations* (New York: Thomas Y. Crowell, 1970), p. 158.

2. David Maybury-Lewis, *Millennium: Tribal Wisdom and the Modern World* (New York: Viking, 1992), p. 8.

3. David L. Miller, *Introduction to Collective Behavior and Collective Action* (Prospect Heights, IL: Waveland, 2000), p. 95.

4. R. H. Barnes, "Construction Sacrifice, Kidnapping and Headhunting Rumours on Flores and Elsewhere in Indonesia," *Oceania* 64 (1993): 146–58; G. Forth, "Construction Sacrifice and Head-Hunting Rumours in Central Flores (Eastern Indonesia): A Comparative Note," *Oceania* 61 (1991): 257–66; Richard Allen Drake, "Construction Sacrifice and Kidnapping: Rumor Panics in Borneo," *Oceania* 59 (1989): 269–78; R. A. Drake, letter to Robert Bartholomew, August 19, 1989.

5. The Agence France-Press (AFP) report was picked up by the *South China Morning Post*, March 22, 1993.

6. Gordon W. Allport and Leo Postman, *The Psychology of Rumor* (New York: Henry Holt, 1947).

7. "Mystery Infection Closes Rostraver's Lebanon School," *The Valley Independent* (Monessen, Pennsylvania), December 12, 1961, pp. 1, 5; "Mystery Infection Called Not Serious," *The Valley Independent*, December 13, 1961, p. 1; "Mystery Infection — Lebanon School Open; Reports Are Awaited," *The Valley Independent*, December 18, 1961, p. 1; "Mystery Infection at Lebanon Is Discounted," *The Valley Independent*, December 19, 1961, p. 1; Judith S. Mausner and Horace M. Gezon, "Report on a Phantom Epidemic of Gonorrhea," *American Journal of Epidemiology* 85 (1967): 324.

8. "School Approved — Pitt Report Clears Up Lebanon Infection," *The Valley Independent*, January 11, 1962, p. 1; Mausner and Gezon (1967), op. cit., p. 327.

9. J. Teoh, S. Soewondo, and M. Sidharta, "Epidemic Hysteria in Malaysia: An Illustrative Episode," *Psychiatry* 8.3 (1975): 258–68; Adrienne Carlisle, "Stress May Have Caused 'Mass Hysteria,'" South African *Dispatch*, May 29, 1999, http://www.dispatch.co.za/1999 /05/29/easterncape /CAUSED.HTM; Ajith Bridgraj, "A Mysterious 'Madness,'" *The Teacher*, 1999, http://www.teacher. co.za/9908/demon.html.

10. A. Hafez, "The Role of the Press and the Medical Community in an Epidemic of Mysterious Gas Poisoning in the Jordan West Bank," *American Journal of Psychiatry* 142 (1985): 833–37; James R. Stewart, "The West Bank Collective Hysteria Episode: The Politics of Illness," *The Skeptical Inquirer* 15 (1991): 153–60.

11. Edgar A. Schuler, Vincent J. Parenton, "A Recent Epidemic of Hysteria in a Louisiana High School," *Journal of Social Psychology* 17 (1943): 221–35.

12. F. Aemmer, *Eine Schulepidemie von Tremor Hystericus [A School Epidemic of Hysterical Tremor]*. Inaugural dissertation, Basel, 1893; J. Truper, "Zur Frage der Schulerselbstmorde," *Zeitschrift für Kinderforschung* 143 (1908): 75–86.

13. Neil J. Smelser, *Social Change in the Industrial Revolution* (London: Routledge and Kegan Paul, 1962); Neil J. Smelser, "Theoretical Issues of Scope and Problems," in *Readings in Collective Behavior*, ed. Robert R. Evans, 89–94 (Chicago: Rand McNally, 1971), p. 92; S. W. Wong, B. Kwong, Y. K. Tam, and M. M. Tsoi, "Psychological Epidemic in Hong Kong," *Acta Psychiatrica Scandinavica* 65 (1982): 430.

14. E. L. Goldberg, "Crowd Hysteria in a Junior High School," *Journal of School Health* 43 (1973): 362–66; C. P. McEvedy, A. Griffith, and T. Hall, "Two School Epidemics," *British Medical Journal* 2 (1966): 1300–02; Moss and McEvedy (1966), op. cit.; J. A. Knight, T. I. Friedman, and J. Sulianti, "Epidemic Hysteria: A Field Study," *American Journal of Public Health* 55 (1965): 858–65; W. C. Olson, "Account of a Fainting Epidemic in a High School," *Psychology Clinic* (Philadelphia) 18 (1928): 34–38; P. Olczak, E. Donnerstein, T. Hershberger, and I. Kahn, "Group Hysteria and the MMPI," *Psychological Reports* 28 (1971): 413–14; J. Teoh and K. Yeoh, "Cultural Conflict in Transition: Epidemic Hysteria and Social Sanction," *Australian and New Zealand Journal of Psychiatry* 7 (1973): 283–95; Y. K. Tam, M. M. Tsoi, G. B. Kwong, and S. W. Wong, "Psychological Epidemic in Hong Kong, Part 2, Psychological and Physiological Characteristics of Children Who Were Affected," *Acta Psychiatrica Scandinavica* 65 (1982): 437–49; Wong et al. (1982), op. cit.; G. W. Small, M. W. Propper, E. T. Randolph, and S. Eth, "Mass Hysteria Among Student Performers: Social Relationship as a Symptom Predictor," *American Journal of Psychiatry* 148 (1991): 1200–05. K. T. Goh, "Epidemiological Enquiries into a School Outbreak of an Unusual Illness," *International Journal of Epidemiology* 16.2 (1987): 265–70; L. Michaux, T. Lemperiere, and C. Juredieu, "Considérations Psychopathologiques sur une Épidémie d'hystérie Convulsive dans un Internat Professionnel [Considerations of an Epidemic of Convulsive Hysteria in a Boarding School]," *Archives Francaises Pédiatrie* (Paris) 9 (1952): 987–90; Schuler and Parenton (1943), op. cit.; W. Theopold, "Induzierter Amplexus neuralis bei Mädchen einer Schulklasse [Induced Neural Amplexus in Girls in a School Class]," *Monatsschrift für Kinderheilkunde* 103 (1955): 79–80.

15. A. C. Kerckhoff, "A Social Psychological View of Mass Psychogenic Illness," in *Mass Psychogenic Illness: A Social Psychological Analysis*, ed. M. Colligan, J. Pennebaker, and L. Murphy, pp. 199–215 (Hillsdale, NJ: Lawrence Erlbaum, 1982); R. L. Lee, *The Social Meaning of Mass Hysteria in West Malaysia and Singapore*, Ph.D. thesis, University of Massachusetts, 1979.

16. D. C. Taylor, "Hysteria, Belief, and

Magic," *British Journal of Psychiatry* 155 (1989): 391–398, cited in Robert E. Bartholomew, "Tarantism, Dancing Mania and Demonopathy: The Anthro-Political Aspects of 'Mass Psychogenic Illness,'" *Psychological Medicine* 24 (1994): 300.

17. Taylor (1989), op. cit.

18. Solomon Moore (reporter for the *Los Angeles Times*), telephone interview with Robert Bartholomew, March 14, 2000; Solomon Moore and M. Ramirez, "3 Sickened Pacoima Students Ingested LSD; 11 Other Hospitalized 4th Graders Had No Drugs in System…," *Los Angeles Times*, September 25, 1998.

19. Parsons Talcott, "Family Structures and the Socialization of the Child," in *Family, Socialization, and the Interaction Process*, ed. Talcott Parsons and R. Bales, pp. 35–131 (New York: The Free Press, 1955); Colligan and Murphy (1979), op. cit.

20. D. F. Klein, "False Suffocation Alarms, Spontaneous Panics, and Related Conditions: An Integrative Hypothesis," *Archives of General Psychiatry* 50 (1993): 306–17; H. Aro and V. Taipale, "The Impact of Timing of Puberty on Psychosomatic Symptoms Among Fourteen to Sixteen-Year-Old Finnish Girls," *Child Development* 58 (1987): 261–68; American Psychiatric Association (1994), op. cit., p. 455.

21. Ackerman (1980), op. cit.; R. L. Lee and S. E. Ackerman, "The Sociocultural Dynamics of Mass Hysteria: A Case Study of Social Conflict in West Malaysia," *Psychiatry* 43 (1980): 85.

22. Margaret McCartney, "Don't Panic! Could 'Mass Hysteria' Explain Why 55 Pupils and Staff from Collenswood School in Hertfordshire Fell Mysteriously Ill Last Week?" *The Guardian* (London), September 14, 2004.

23. C. G. Schmidt, "The Group-Fantasy Origin of AIDS," *Journal of Psychohistory* 12.1 (1984): 37–78; G. R. Elkins, L. A. Gamino, and R. R. Rynearson, "Mass Psychogenic Illness, Trance States, and Suggestion," *American Journal of Clinical Hypnosis* 30 (1988): 267–75; L. A. Gamino, G. R. Elkins, and K. U. Hackney, "Emergency Management of Mass Psychogenic Illness," *Psychosomatics* 30 (1989): 448; H. S. Faust and L. B. Brilliant, "Is the Diagnosis of 'Mass Hysteria' an Excuse for Incomplete Investigation of Low-Level Environmental Contamination?" *Journal of Occupational Medicine* 23 (1981): 22–26.

24. Bernadette Wittstock, Lydia Rozental, and Charlene Henn, "Mass Phenomena at a Black South African Primary School," *Hospital and Community Psychiatry* 42 (1991): 852; Rozental Wittstock and Henn Wittstock (1991), op. cit., p. 852.

25. Clyde Kluckhohn, *Mirror for Man* (New York: McGraw-Hill, 1949), p. 11.

Bibliography

Abdul Rahman, T. "As I See It ... Will the Hysteria Return?" *The New Straits Times* (Malaysia), July 6, 1987.

Abdullah, J. *A Report of the Interview with the Female Teacher and Students at the Hishamuddin Secondary Islamic School, Klang.* Unpublished, undated, circa 1992.

Ackerman, Susan Ellen. *Cultural Process in Malaysian Industrialization: A Study of Malay Women Factory Workers.* Doctoral thesis, University of California at San Diego. Ann Arbor, MI: University Microfilms, 1980.

Adomakoh, C. C. "The Pattern of Epidemic Hysteria in a Girls' School in Ghana." *Ghana Medical Journal* 12 (1973): 407–11.

Aemmer, Fritz. *Eine Schulepidemie von Tremor Hystericus [A School Epidemic of Hysterical Tremor].* Inaugural dissertation, Basel, 1893.

Allport, Gordon W., and Leo Postman. *The Psychology of Rumor.* New York: Henry Holt, 1947.

Anderson, Dirk. "Great Signs and Wonders II." http://www.intowww.org/articles/art 9708.htm. Accessed December 31, 2003.

Armainguad, M. "Recherches Cliniques sur L'hystérie; Relation d'une Petite Épidémie d'hystérie Observée à Bordeaux. [Clinical Research on Hysteria and Its Relation to a Small Epidemic of Hysteria Observed in Bordeaux]." *Mémoire et Bulletin de la Société de Médecine et Chirurgie de Bordeaux*, 1879, 551–79.

Aro, H., and V. Taipale. "The Impact of Timing of Puberty on Psychosomatic Symptoms Among Fourteen to Sixteen-Year-Old Finnish Girls." *Child Development* 58 (1987): 261–68.

Baker, P., and D. Selvey. "Malathion-induced Epidemic Hysteria in an Elementary School." *Veterinary and Human Toxicology* 34 (1992): 156–60.

Baring-Gould, Sabine. *The Book of Werewolves: Being an Account of a Terrible Superstition.* London: Smith, Elder, 1865.

Barnes, R. H. "Construction Sacrifice, Kidnapping and Headhunting Rumours on Flores and Elsewhere in Indonesia." *Oceania* 64 (1993): 146–58.

Bartholomew, R. E. *Miracle or Mass Delusion: What Happened in Klang, Malaysia?* A study compiled for Pusat Islam, the prime minister's department, Kuala Lumpur, Malaysia, 1993.

Bartholomew, Robert E. "Tarantism, Dancing Mania and Demonopathy: The Anthro-Political Aspects of 'Mass Psychogenic Illness.'" *Psychological Medicine* 24 (1994): 281–306.

Bartholomew, Robert E., and Benjamin Radford. "Rash of Mysterious Rashes May be Linked to Mass Hysteria." *The Skeptical Inquirer* 26.3 (2002): 8.

Bekhterev, Vladimir Mikhailovich. *Suggestion and Its Role in Social Life.* 3rd ed. Translated from the Russian by Tzvetanka Dobreva-Martinova. New Brunswick, NJ: Transaction, 1998 (1908).

Bekker, Balthasar. *Le Monde Enchanté.* Volume 4. Amsterdam: Pierre Rotterdam, 1694.

Benaim, Silvio, John Horder, and Jennifer Anderson. "Hysterical Epidemic in a Classroom." *Psychological Medicine* 3 (1973): 366–73.

Bernard, A., and S. Fierens. "The Belgian PCB/Dioxin Incident: A Critical Review of Health Risks Evaluations." *International Journal of Toxicology* 21.5 (2002): 333–40.

Bester, K., P. de Vos, L. Le Guern, S. Harbeck, F. Hendrickx, G. N. Kramer, T. Linsinger, I. Mertens, H. Schimmel, B. Sejerøe-Olsen,

J. Pauwels, G. De Poorter, G. G. Rimkus, and M. Schlabach. "Preparation and Certification of a Reference Material on PCBs in Pig Fat and Its Application in Quality Control in Monitoring Laboratories During the Belgian 'PCB-Crisis.'" *Chemosphere* 44.4 (2001): 529–37.

Bhatiasevi, Aphaluck. "Belief in Ghosts Sparks Hysteria: Students Freak Out at School Camp." *Bangkok Post*, February 4, 2001.

Boyer, Paul, and Steven Nissenbaum. *Salem Possessed: The Social Origins of Witchcraft*. Cambridge: Harvard University Press, 1974.

Bridgraj, Ajith. "A Mysterious 'Madness.'" *The Teacher*. 1999. http://www.teacher.co.za/9908/demon.html.

Burnham, W. H. "Suggestion in School Hygiene." *Pedagogical Seminary* 19 (1912): 228–49.

Burnham, William H. *The Normal Mind*. New York: D. Appleton, 1924.

Butler, Edgar W., Hiroshi Fukurai, Jo-Ellen Dimitrius, and Richard Krooth. *Anatomy of the McMartin Child Molestation Case*. Lanham, MD: University Press of America, 2001.

Calmeil, L. F. *De la Folie, Considérée Sous le Point de vue Pathologique, Philosophique, Historique et Judiciaire* [*On the Crowd, Considerations on the Point of Pathology, Philosophy, History and Justice*]. Vol. 1. Paris: Baillere, 1845.

Carlisle, Adrienne. "Stress May Have Caused 'Mass Hysteria.'" *South African Dispatch*, May 29, 1999. http://www.dispatch.co.za/1999/05/29/easterncape/CAUSED.HTM.

Casey, Conerly. "'Dancing Like They Do in Indian Film': Media Images, Possession, and Evangelical Islamic Medicine in Northern Nigeria." Paper presented at the American Anthropological Association Meetings, 1999.

Ceci, Stephen J., and Maggie Bruck. "Child Witnesses: Translating Research into Policy." *Social Policy Report* 7.3 (1993): 2–32.

Chen, P. C. Y. "Indigenous Malay Psychotherapy." *Tropical and Geographical Medicine* 22 (1970): 409.

"Children Collapse on Parade." *Wolverhampton Express and Star*, July 28, 1980.

"Choir Hit by Fainting Spells." *The Times Recorder* (Zanesville, Ohio). December 13, 1953, p. 1.

CNN. "Special Report Live with Aaron Brown." Atlanta, Georgia. October 16, 2001, 10–11P.M.

"Colombian Magician Arrested for Hypnotizing 41 Kids." *Hispanically Speaking News*, September 2, 2011. http://www.hispanicallyspeakingnews.com/notitas-de-noticias/2011/09/02/. Accessed October 9, 2012.

Conley, Robert. "Laughing Malady a Puzzle in Africa. 1000 Along Lake Victoria Afflicted in 18 Months—Most Are Youngsters. Schools Close Down." *New York Times*, August 8, 1963, p. 29.

"Council to Meet over Hysteria Stricken Girls." *The New Straits Times*, May 24, 1987, p. 4.

Darnton, Robert. *The Great Cat Massacre and Other Episodes in French Cultural History*. New York: Basic, 1984.

Davidson, James, Pedro Castillo, and Michael Stoff. *The American Nation*. Upper Saddle River, NJ: Prentice-Hall, 2000.

De Lancre, Pierre. *Tableau de l'inconstance des Mauvais anges et Démons*. Paris: Buon, 1613.

"Demons in Hoima District." *New Vision*, February 9, 2008.

"Denver Deluged. Storm of Rain, Hail and Wind Causes Excitement." *The Democratic Standard* (Coshocton, Ohio), June 4, 1897.

"Detik-Detik Pertemuan Dengan Makhluk Asing [Moments of Meeting with Aliens]." *Bacaria*, October 27, 1985.

"Devil Worship Terror Grips Lebanon's Kids." *The Business Times Singapore* online edition, March 17, 2003. http://www.spi.com.sg/haunted/katong_cult/devil_worship.htm. Accessed January 2, 2004.

Dhadphale, Manohar, and S. P. Shaikh. "Epidemic Hysteria in a Zambian School: 'The Mysterious Madness of Mwinilunga.'" *British Journal of Psychiatry* 142 (1983): 85–88.

Drake, Richard Allen. "Construction Sacrifice and Kidnapping: Rumor Panics in Borneo." *Oceania* 59 (1989): 269–78.

Dumville, B. "Should the French System of Moral Instruction Be Introduced into England." In *Moral Instruction and Training in Schools: Report of an International Inquiry*, vol. 2. Edited by M. E. Sadler. London: Longmans, Green, 1908, pp. 116–117.

Durbin, K., and T. Vogt. "Fumes..." *Columbian*, September 29, 2001.

Eberle, Paul, and Shirley Eberle. *The Abuse of Innocence: The McMartin Preschool Trial*. Buffalo, NY: Prometheus, 1993.

Ebrahim, G. J. "Mass Hysteria in School

Children: Notes on Three Outbreaks in East Africa." *Clinical Pediatrics* 7 (1968): 437–38.

Elkins, G. R., L. A. Gamino, and R. R. Rynearson. "Mass Psychogenic Illness, Trance States, and Suggestion." *American Journal of Clinical Hypnosis* 30 (1988): 267–75.

Endicott, Kirk. *An Analysis of Malay Magic*. Oxford: Clarendon, 1970.

"Exhaust Fumes and Hysteria KO Some 500 Students at Festival." *Stevens Point Daily Journal* (Wisconsin), November 24, 1959, p. 2.

"Exorcism Planned for School Toilet 'Ghost.'" Ananova News Agency, circa June 1, 2003.

"Exorcist Leads Hunt for 'Entrail-Eating Ghosts.'" *The Bangkok Post*, June 4, 2003.

"Explanation Sought for Teen-Age fainting Spells." *Stevens Point Daily Journal* (Wisconsin), April 10, 1976, p. 11.

"Feline Spirits Force Orissa School to Close." India's IANI news service. August 5, 2004. http://www.webindia123.com/news/show details.asp?id =44859&cat=India. Accessed August 21, 2004.

"Fainting Spells Making School Nervous." *Oshkosh Daily Northwestern*, April 10, 1976, p. 1.

Faust, H. S., and L. B. Brilliant. "Is the Diagnosis of 'Mass Hysteria' an Excuse for Incomplete Investigation of Low-Level Environmental Contamination?" *Journal of Occupational Medicine* 23 (1981): 22–26.

"Fear May Have Caused Students' Fossil Site Collapse." *The Bangkok Post,* July 3, 2002.

"Fiji: Kidnap Hysteria Leads to Assaults." November 10, 2003. http://www.pacificislands.cc/pina/pinadefault.php?urlpinaid =9726, citing *The Fiji Times*. Accessed January 2, 2004.

"First Group of Hysteria Girls Sees Psychiatrist." *The New Straits Times*, August 11, 1987.

"Five Women Treated by Exorcist After Visit to Fossil Site." Tuesday, July 2, 2002. http://www.ananova.com/news/story/sm_620143.html?menu=, citing *The Bangkok Post.* Accessed January 2, 2003.

"'Football Ghost' Keeps Indian Schoolchildren Off School." Ananova News Agency. 2004. http://www.ananova. com/news/story/sm_822542.html?menu=news.latestheadlines. Accessed April 2, 2004.

Fort, Charles. *The Complete Books of Charles Fort*. New York: Dover, 1974.

Forth, G. "Construction Sacrifice and Head-Hunting Rumours in Central Flores (Eastern Indonesia): A Comparative Note." *Oceania* 61 (1991): 257–66.

"Four Girls Fainted." *Brooklyn Daily Eagle*, June 16, 1897, p. 16.

Frankel, Stephen. "Mass Hysteria in the New Guinea Highlands: A Telefomin Outbreak and Its Relationship to Other New Guinea Hysterical Reactions." *Oceania* 47 (1976): 105–33.

Gallay, A., and S. Demarest. *Case Control Study Among Schoolchildren on the Incident Related to Complaints Following the Consumption of Coca-Cola Company Products, Belgium, 1999*. Scientific Institute of Public Health, Epidemiology Unit. November 1999. http://www.iph.fgov.be/epidemio/epien/cocacola.htm. Accessed April 10, 2002.

Gamino, L. A., G. R. Elkins, and K. U. Hackney. "Emergency Management of Mass Psychogenic Illness." *Psychosomatics* 30 (1989): 446–49.

Garnier, Samuel. *Barbe Buvée, en Religion, Sœur Sainte-Colombe et la Prétendue Possession des Ursulines d'Auxonne [Barbara Buvée, and Religion, Sister Columbe and the Feigned Possession of the Ursulines at Auxonne]*. Paris: Felix Alcan, 1895.

Geraci, Gino. "Look Before You Laugh." 1995. http://www.banner.org.uk/tb/look. html. Accessed April 5, 2004.

"Ghosts Beat Up Pupils at Kenyan School." AFP news agency, July 20, 2000.

Gillie, Oliver, and Toni Turner. "Mystery Epidemic May Have Been Sparked Off by the Blebs." *Sunday Times*, July 20, 1980.

Gimlette, John Desmond. *Malay Poisons and Charm Cures*. London: Oxford University Press, 1915.

Goh, K. T. "Epidemiological Enquiries into a School Outbreak of an Unusual Illness." *International Journal of Epidemiology* 16.2 (1987): 265–70.

Goldberg, E. L. "Crowd Hysteria in a Junior High School." *Journal of School Health* 43 (1973): 362–66.

Goldsmith, M. F. "Physicians with Georgia on Their Minds." *Journal of the American Medical Association* 262 (1989): 603–04.

Goode, Erich. *Deviant Behavior*. 6th ed. Upper Saddle River, NJ: Prentice-Hall, 2001.

Görres, Johann Joseph von. *La Mystique Divine, Naturelle et Diabolique*. Translated from the 1845 German *Christliche Mystik*. Vol. 5. Paris: Poussielgue-Rusand, 1855.

Gove, Philip B., ed. *Webster's Seventh New Collegiate Dictionary*. Springfield, MA: G. and C. Merriam, 1972.

"Guru Besar: Cuma Khayalan Murid [Head Master: Just Student Imagination]." *Watan*, April 4, 1989.

"Guru Sahkan Murid Jumpa UFO" [Teacher Admits Students Saw UFO], *Bacaria*, October 27, 1985.

Hafez, A. "The Role of the Press and the Medical Community in an Epidemic of Mysterious Gas Poisoning in the Jordan West Bank." *American Journal of Psychiatry* 142 (1985): 833–37.

Hagenbach E. "Chorea-epidemie [Epidemic Chorea]." *Kor-Blatt f Schweit Arzte* (Basel) 23 (1893): 631–32.

Hambling, David. "Contagious Fear: Mass Sociogenic Smell Weapon." *Wired*, January 28, 2008. http://www.wired.com/dangerroom/2008/01/contagious-fe. Accessed May 17, 2010.

Harrison, Cal. "Mysterious Ailment Strikes Students at Welsh." *Lake Charles American Press*, March 28, 1962, p. 1.

"Headmaster Flees as Hysteria Grips School." *The Daily News* (Zimbabwe), July 30, 2002.

Hecker, Justus Friedrich. *Epidemics of the Middle Ages*. Translated from the German by B. Babington. London: Sydenham Society, 1844.

Hecker, Justus Friedrich C. *The Dancing Mania of the Middle Ages*. Translated by B. Babington. New York: B. Franklin, 1837 (1970).

Heim, Roger, and R. Gordon Wasson. "The 'Mushroom Madness' of the Kuma." *Botanical Museum Leaflets, Harvard University* 21.1 (1965): 1–36.

Hibbard, Laura. "Miller Zambrano Posada, Magician, Arrested." *Huffington Post*. 2012. http://in.news.yahoo.com/hypnosis-colombian-school-ends-mass-hysteria-054044654.html. Accessed 8 October 2012.

Hirt, L. "Eine Epidemie von Hysterischen Krämpfen in einer Schleisischen Dorfschule [An Epidemic of Hysterical Cramp in a Village School in Schleisischen]." *Zeitschrift für Schulgesundheitspflege* 6 (1893): 225–29. Summary of an article by L. Hirt in the *Berliner Klinische Wochenschrift*.

Hoekema, Anthony A. *What About Tongue-Speaking?* Grand Rapids, MI: William B. Eerdmans, 1966.

Howells, John, ed. *World History of Psychiatry*. New York: Brunner/Mazel, 1975.

Huefer, Oliver Madox. *The Book of Witches*. East Ardsley, UK: EP, 1973 (1908).

Hufford, David. *The Terror That Comes in the Night*. Philadelphia: University of Pennsylvania Press, 1982.

Huxley, Aldous. *The Devils of Loudun*. New York: Harper, 1952.

"Hypnosis at Colombian School Ends in Mass Hysteria." Indo Asian News Service, September 3, 2011.

"Hypnotist Lectures Pupils, Gets Unexpected Reaction." *Wisconsin Rapids Daily Tribune*, January 17, 1953, p. 8.

"Hypnotized Students in Mass Trance Needed Emergency Help," CBC News Canada. June 15, 2012. http://news.ca.msn.com/top-stories/hypnotized-students-in-mass-trance-needed-emergency-help. Accessed October 12, 2012.

"Hysteria Blamed on 'Evil Spirits': School Head Wants the Ghosts to Go." *The New Straits Times*, May 23, 1987, p. 7.

"Hysteria: Schoolgirls 'Confess.'" *The New Straits Times*, May 21, 1987, p. 3.

"Hysteria: Second Batch Visits 'Shrink.'" *The New Straits Times*, August 13, 1987.

"Hysterical Pupils Take Schoolmates Hostage." *The New Straits Times*, May 19, 1987, p. 1.

"I Can't Believe It, Says Pupil." *The New Straits Times*, May 31, 1987, p. 7.

"I Hired Ghosts to Torment Schoolgirls." *The Star* (South Africa), June 5, 2000. Reuters report.

"Indian City Spooked by 'Ghost' Photo." September 2003. http://www.ananova.com/news/story/sm_820471.html. Accessed July 31, 2004.

"Interview: Fatimah, 'I Only Fulfilled My Parents' Wishes.'" *The New Straits Times*, May 31, 1987, p. 7.

Israeli, Raphael. "Poison: The Use of Blood Libel in the War Against Israel." *Jerusalem Letter* 476 (April 15, 2002): 2. http://www.jcpa.org/jlv p476.htm.

"Jabatan Kajicuaca Beri Penjelasan Mengenai Bola Api Dari Langit [The Meteorology Office Explained About the Fireball from the Sky]," *Utusan* (Malaysia), August 19, 1982.

Jamaluddin, Mustafa Kamil. "Sekumpulan Pelajar Dakwa Terserempak... [A Group of Students Claimed to Have Met....]." *Bacaria*, October 3, 1992.

Jehl, Douglas. "Of College Girls Betrayed and Vile Chewing Gum." *New York Times*, July 10, 1996.

Johnson, H. "Moral Instruction and Training in France." In *Moral Instruction and Training in Schools: Report of an International Inquiry, Volume 2*. Edited by Sir Michael Sadler. London: Longmans, Green, 1908, pp. 1–50.

"Just a Curtain Fire." *The North Adams Evening Transcript*, February 2, 1899, citing *The New York Sun*.

Kagolo, Francis. "Kitebi Primary School Remains Closed over Mass Hysteria." *New Vision* (Uganda), March 30, 2011.

Kerckhoff, A. C. "A Social Psychological View of Mass Psychogenic Illness." In *Mass Psychogenic Illness: A Social Psychological Analysis*. Edited by M. Colligan, J. Pennebaker, and L. Murphy. Hillsdale, NJ: Lawrence Erlbaum, 1982, pp. 199–215.

Kharabsheh, S., H. Al-Otoum, J. Clements, A. Abbas, N. Khuri-Bulos, A. Belbesi, T. Gaafar, and N. Dellepiane. "Mass Psychogenic Illness Following Tetanus-Diphtheria Toxoid Vaccination in Jordan." *Bulletin of the World Health Organization* 79.8 (2001): 764–70.

Kibego, John. "School Closed After 'Demon Attacks.'" *The Observer*, October 16, 2011.

"Kisah 'Orang Kenit' Gemparkan Sekolah Pangkalan Tentera Kuantan [Story About Tiny Beings Shocked Pangkalan Tentera School in Kuantan]." *Berita Harian*, October 11, 1974.

"Kitebi Closed, Christian and Traditionalists Wage War." *Uganda News Picks*, April 18, 2011.

"Kitebi Primary School Remains Closed Over Mass Hysteria." *New Vision* (Uganda), March 30, 2011.

Kivabulaya, Frederick. "Hoima School Closed Over Alleged Demon Attacks." Ugandan Radio Network transcript, October 13, 2011.

Klein, D. F. "False Suffocation Alarms, Spontaneous Panics, and Related Conditions: An Integrative Hypothesis." *Archives of General Psychiatry* 50 (1993): 306–17.

Kluckhohn, Clyde. *Mirror for Man*. New York: McGraw-Hill, 1949.

Knight, James A., Theodore I. Friedman, and Julie Sulianti. "Epidemic Hysteria: A Field Study." *American Journal of Public Health* 55 (1965): 858–65.

Knox, Ronald A. *Enthusiasm*. Oxford: Clarendon, 1950.

Kolsta, Pal, ed. *Media Discourse and Yugoslav Politics: Representations of Self and Other*. Burlington, VT: Ashgate, 2009.

Landrigan, Philip, and Bess Miller. "The Arjenyattah Epidemic: Home Interview Data and Toxicological Aspects." *The Lancet* 2 (1983): 1474–76.

Laquer, L. "Über eine Chorea-Epidemie [An Epidemic of Chorea]." *Deutsche Medizinische Wochenschrift* (Leipzig) 14 (1888): 1045–46.

Lee, Raymond Lai Ming. *The Social Meaning of Mass Hysteria in West Malaysia and Singapore*. Ph.D. thesis, University of Massachusetts, 1979.

Lee, Raymond Lai Ming, and Susan Ellen Ackerman. "The Sociocultural Dynamics of Mass Hysteria: A Case Study of Social Conflict in West Malaysia." *Psychiatry* 43 (1980): 78–88.

Leith, Scott. "3 Years After Recall, Coke Sales in Belgium at Their Best." *The Atlanta Journal-Constitution*, August 26, 2002.

Levine, R. "Epidemic Faintness and Syncope in a School Marching Band." *Journal of the American Medical Association* 238.22 (1977): 2373–76.

Licauco, Jaime. "Dwarves in Iloilo School" Inner Awareness Column. Inquirer News Service, February 16, 2004. http://www.inq7.net/lif/2004/feb/17/lif_22–1.htm. Accessed August 24, 2004.

Lippman, Walter. *Public Opinion*. New York: Harcourt, Brace, 1922.

Loredan, Jean. *Un Grand Proces de Sorcellerie au XVIIe siècle, L'Abbé Gaufridy et Madéleine de Demandolx (1600–1670) [The Grand Process of Witchcraft in the Seventeenth Century, L'Abbe Gaufridy and Madeleine de Demandolx (1600–1670)]*. Paris: Perrin et Cie, 1912.

Lukas, Joseph. *Der Schulmeister von Sadowa*. Maniz: Kirchheim, 1878.

MacDonnell, F. *Insidious Foes*. New York: Oxford University Press, 1995.

Mackay, Charles. *Memoirs of Extraordinary Popular Delusions and the Madness of Crowds, Volume 2*. London: Office of the National Illustrated Library, 1852.

MacKenzie, Debora. "Ethnic Strife Triggers Psychosomatic Illness." *New Scientist*, January 25, 1997, p. 5.

Macklingam, Kristen. "Another 'Demon Attack' at St. Winefride's." *Kaieteur News*, March 27, 2012. http://www.kaieteur

newsonline.com/2012/03/27/another-%E2%80%9Cdemon-attack%E2%80%9D-at-st-winefride%E2%80%99s/. Accessed January 14, 2013.

MacLachlan, Malcolm, Dixie Maluwa Banda, and Eilish McAuliffe. "Epidemic Psychological Disturbance in a Malawian Secondary School: A Case Study in Social Change." *Psychology and Developing Societies* 7.1 (1995): 79–90.

Madden, Richard Robert. *Phantasmata or Illusions and Fanaticisms of Protean Forms Productive of Great Evils*. T. C. Newby: London, 1857.

Makeham, Greg. "12 Months of the Toronto Blessing." 1995. http://gregga/toronto/testimonies/12tb-1.html. Accessed December 31, 2003.

"Makhlok2 Daripada Dunia Lain Mendarat di-Johor? [Beings from Another Planet Landed in Johor?]" *Berita Harian*, July 4, 1969. "Makhlok2" is the proper spelling.

Maple, Eric. *Witchcraft: The Story of Man's Search for Supernatural Power*. London: Octopus, 1973.

"Mass Fainting Hits Chorus." *Mansfield News-Journal* (Ohio), December 22, 1952.

"Mass Hysteria Hits Girls in Nepal School." http://www.tribuneindia.com/2003/20030909/world.htm#5, citing the PTI news agency. Accessed July 30, 2004.

"Mass Hysteria Mars the Music." *Science News* 140.12 (September 21, 1991): 187.

"Mass Hysteria Sends 165 Girls to Hospital." *Daily Redlands Facts* (Redlands, California), September 13, 1953, p. 1.

Mausner, Judith S., and Horace M. Gezon. "Report on a Phantom Epidemic of Gonorrhea." *American Journal of Epidemiology* 85 (1967): 320–31.

Maybury-Lewis, David. *Millennium: Tribal Wisdom and the Modern World*. New York: Viking, 1992.

McCartney, Margaret. "Don't Panic! Could 'Mass Hysteria' Explain Why 55 Pupils and Staff from Collenswood School in Hertfordshire Fell Mysteriously Ill Last Week?" *The Guardian* (London), September 14, 2004.

McEvedy, C. P., A. Griffith, and T. Hall. "Two School Epidemics." *British Medical Journal* 2 (1966): 1300–02.

"Medics Call for School's Closure as Students Go Crazy." Pan African News Agency, March 3, 2000.

Michaux, L., T. Lemperiere, and C. Juredieu. "Considérations Psychopathologiques sur une Épidémie d'hystérie Convulsive dans un Internat Professionnel [Considerations of an Epidemic of Convulsive Hysteria in a Boarding School]." *Archives Francaises Pédiatrie* (Paris) 9 (1952): 987–90.

Miller, David L. *Introduction to Collective Behavior and Collective Action*. 2nd ed. Prospect Heights, Illinois: Waveland, 2000.

Mkize, Dan Lamla, and Reginald T. Ndabeni. "Mass Hysteria with Pseudoseizures at a South African High School." *South African Medical Journal* 92.9 (2002): 697–99.

Modan, Baruch, Moshe Tirosh, Emil Weissenberg, Cilla Acker, T. A. Swartz, Corina Coston, Alexander Donagi, Moshe Revach, and Gaston Vettorazzi. "The Arjenyattah Epidemic." *The Lancet* 2 (1983): 1472–74.

Moffat, M. E. "Epidemic Hysteria in a Montreal Train Station." *Pediatrics* 70 (1982): 308–10.

Montgomery, J. D. "The Education of Girls in Germany: Its Methods of Moral Instruction and Training." In *Moral Instruction and Training in Schools: Report of an International Inquiry, Volume 2*. Edited by M. E. Sadler. London: Longmans, Green, 1908, pp. 231–41.

Moore, Simon. Telephone interview by Robert Bartholomew. March 14, 2000. Moore is a reporter for the *Los Angeles Times*.

Moore, Solomon, and M. Ramirez. "3 Sickened Pacoima Students Ingested LSD; 11 Other Hospitalized 4th Graders Had No Drugs in System..." *Los Angeles Times*, September 25, 1998.

Moss, Peter D., and Colin P. McEvedy. "An Epidemic of Overbreathing Among Schoolgirls." *British Medical Journal* 2 (1966): 1295–1300.

Muhangi, J. R. "Mass Hysteria in an Ankole School." *East African Medical Journal* 50 (1973): 304–09.

"Murid Dakwa Jumpa Makhluk Asing." *Berita Harian*, October 18, 1985.

"Murid Dakwa Terserempak 'Orang Kenit' [Pupils Claim Encounter with Tiny Entities]." *Berita Harian*, May 15, 1991.

"Mystery Infection at Lebanon Is Discounted." *The Valley Independent* (Monessen, Pennsylvania), December 19, 1961, p. 1.

"Mystery Infection Called Not Serious." *The Valley Independent* (Monessen, Pennsylvania), December 13, 1961, p. 1.

"Mystery Infection Closes Rostraver's Lebanon School." *The Valley Independent* (Monessen, Pennsylvania), December 12, 1961, pp. 1, 5.

"Mystery Infection — Lebanon School Open; Reports Are Awaited." *The Valley Independent* (Monessen, Pennsylvania), December 18, 1961, p. 1.

Namazzi, Elizabeth, and Carol Kasujja. "Uganda: 'What's Happening at Kitebi Primary School." *New Vision*, April 9, 2011.

Needham, Richard. "The Toronto Blessing — Part One." http://www.geocities.com/bob_hunter/needham1.htm. Accessed April 5, 2004.

Nemery, B., B. Fischler, M. Boogaerts, and D. Lison. "Dioxins, Coca-Cola, and Mass Sociogenic Illness in Belgium." *The Lancet* 354.9172 (July 3, 1999): 77.

Nemery, B., B. Fischler, M. Boogaerts, D. Lison, and J. Willems. "The Coca-Cola Incident in Belgium, June 1999." *Food and Chemical Toxicology* 40 (2002): 1657–67.

Nitzkin, Joel L. "Epidemic Transient Situational Disturbance in an Elementary School." *Journal of the Florida Medical Association* 63 (1976): 357–59.

Nkala, Gideon. "Mass Hysteria Forces School Closure." Middle East Intelligence Wire, March 13, 2000.

Okoko, Tervil. "Ghosts Invade Kenyan Schools." Pan Africa News Agency, July 19, 2000.

Olczak, P., E. Donnerstein, T. Hershberger, and I. Kahn. "Group Hysteria and the MMPI." *Psychological Reports* 28 (1971): 413–14.

Olson, W. C. "Account of a Fainting Epidemic in a High School." *Psychology Clinic* (Philadelphia) 18 (1928): 34–38.

Onen, James. "'Demonic Attacks' in Ugandan Primary Schools." *Free Thought Kampala*, April 4, 2011. http://freethoughtkampala.wordpress.com/2011/04/04/woo-takedown-03-demonic-attacks-in-ugandan-primary-schools/. Accessed November 22, 2012.

"Orang Orang Kenit Angkasa Lepas Mendarat Pula di Rawang? [Beings from Space Landed in Rawang?]" *Utusan Malaysia*, August 28, 1970.

Orwell, George. *1984: A Novel*. London: Secker and Warburg, 1949.

Owino, Wene. "Mass Hysteria Causes School's Temporary Closure." Pan African News Agency, March 8, 2000.

Palmer, Dr. "Psychische seuche in der Sbersten Slasse einer Sadchenschule [A Psychic Epidemic in the First Class of a Girls School]." *Zentralblatt für Nervenheilkunde und Psychiatrie* 3 (1892): 301–08.

Parke, Aubrey L. "The Qawa Incident in 1968 and Other Cases of 'Spirit Possession.'" *The Journal of Pacific History* 30 (1995): 210–26.

Parsons, Talcott. "Family Structures and the Socialization of the Child." In *Family, Socialization, and the Interaction Process*. Edited by Talcott Parsons and R. Bales. New York: Free Press, 1955, pp. 35–131.

Partain, Jack. Telephone interview by Robert Bartholomew, January 17, 2004. Partain is professor emeritus of religion at Gardner-Webb College in Boiling Springs, North Carolina, and taught at the Baptist Seminary of East Africa, Arusha, Tanzania, for 13 years.

_____. "Christians and Their Ancestors: A Dilemma of Theology." *Christian Century*, November 26, 1986, p. 1066.

Pfeiffer, P. H. "Mass Hysteria Masquerading as Food Poisoning." *Journal of the Maine Medical Association* 55 (1964): 27.

Philen, R. M., E. M. Kilbourn, and T. W. McKinley. "Mass Sociogenic Illness by Proxy: Parentally Reported in an Elementary School." *The Lancet* 2 (1989): 1372–76.

Pinsent, Arthur. *The Principles of Teaching-Method with Special Reference to Secondary Education*. 3rd ed. rev. London: George G. Harrap, 1969.

Pratney, Winkie. *Revival*. Lafayette, LA: Huntington House, 1984.

Rabinowitz, Dorothy. "From the Mouths of Babes to a Jail Cell: Child Abuse and the Abuse of Justice: A Case Study." *Harper's Magazine*, May 1990, pp. 52–63, quoted in http://www.law.umkc.edu/faculty/projects/ftrials/evil/evilP18.html.

Radovanovic, Z. "On the Origin of Mass Casualty Incidents in Kosovo, Yugoslavia, in 1990." *European Journal of Epidemiology* 11 (1995): 1–13.

Rankin, A. M., and P. J. Philip. "An Epidemic of Laughing in the Buboka District of Tanganyika." *Central African Journal of Medicine* 9 (1963): 167–70.

Reay, Marie. "Mushrooms and Collective Hysteria." *Australian Territories* 5 (1965): 22–24.

_____. "'Mushroom Madness' in the New Guinea Highlands." *Oceania* 31.2 (1960): 137–39.

_____. "Ritual Madness Observed: A Discarded Pattern of Fate in Papua New Guinea." *The Journal of Pacific History* 12 (1977): 55–79.

Regnard, M., and J. Simon. "Sur une Épidémie de Contracture des Éxtrêmités Observée à Gentilly [On an Epidemic of Limb Contracture Observed in Gentilly]." *Comptes Rendus des Séances de la Société de Biologie* (Paris) 3 (1887): 344–47, 350–53.

Rembold, S. "Acute Psychiche Contagion in Einer Mädchenschule [Acute Psychic Contagion in a Girls' School]." *Berliner Klinische Wochenschrift* 30 (1893): 662–63.

Rickard, Robert, and John Michell. *Unexplained Phenomena: A Rough Guide Special*. London: Rough Guides, 2001.

Ritchie, Elizabeth. "The Ritchies in Uganda: Demons, Ghosts and Evil Spirits." 2011. http://ritchiesinuganda.blogspot.co.nz/2011/04/220411-demons-ghosts-and-evil-spirits.html. Accessed November 22, 2012.

Roach, E. Steven, and Ricky L. Langley. "Episodic Neurological Dysfunction Due to Mass Hysteria." *Archives of Neurology* 61.8 (August 2004): 1269–72.

Robbins, Rossell Hope. *The Encyclopedia of Witchcraft and Demonology*. New York: Crown, 1966.

Rockney, R. M., and T. Lemke. "Casualties from a Junior High School During the Persian Gulf War: Toxic Poisoning or Mass Hysteria?" *Journal of Developmental and Behavioral Pediatrics* 13 (1992): 339–42.

_____. "Response." Letter. *Journal of Developmental and Behavioral Pediatrics* 15.1 (1994): 64–65.

Rosen, George. *Madness in Society*. London: Routledge and Kegan Paul, 1968.

Rosen, George S. "Psychopathology in the Social Process: Dance Frenzies, Demonic Possession, Revival Movements and Similar So-Called Psychic Epidemics. An Interpretation." *Bulletin of the History of Medicine* 36 (1962): 13–44.

Roueche, Berton. "Annals of Medicine: Sandy." Interview with Dr. Joel Nitzkin. *The New Yorker* 21 (1978): 63–70.

"St. Vitus' Dance and Kindred Affection; The Recent Epidemic at the Ursulin Convent in Brown County, Ohio; A Sketch of the Historic Disease." *Cincinnati Lancet and Clinic* 4: 440–45, 467–73.

Sajaratul Noor Kamal Hijaz. "Awang Kenit Muncul di Sekolah [Gnomes Appear in School]." *Watan*, April 4, 1989.

Satiloane, G. M. "How the Traditional World-View Persists in the Christianity of the Sotho-Tswana." *Christianity in Independent Africa*. Edited by E. Fashole-Luke, et al. London: Rex Collings, 1978, pp. 402–412.

Schepens, P. J., A. Covaci, P. G. Jorens, L. Hens, S. Scharpe, and N. van Larebeke. "Surprising Findings Following a Belgian Food Contamination with Polychlorobiphenyls and Dioxins." *Environmental Health Perspectives* 109.2 (2001): 101–03.

Schmidt, C. G. "The Group-Fantasy Origin of AIDS." *Journal of Psychohistory* 12.1 (1984): 37–78.

Schoedel, Johannes. "Über Induzierte Krankheiten [On Induced Illness]." *Jahrbuch für Kinderheilkunde* 14 (1906): 521–28.

"School Approved — Pitt Report Clears Up Lebanon Infection." *The Valley Independent*, January 11, 1962, p. 1.

"School Shut Amid Fears That Some Girls Possessed." IANS News Service. http://news.newkerala.com/indianews/index.php?action=fullnews &id=6702. Accessed September 12, 2004.

"Schoolchildren Possessed by 'Devil' in Manila." Reuters News Service, January 28, 1994.

Schuler, E. A., and V. J. Parenton. "A Recent Epidemic of Hysteria in a Louisiana High School." *Journal of Social Psychology* 17 (1943): 221–35.

Schultz, Emily A., and Robert H. Lavenda. *Anthropology: A Perspective on Human Culture*. Mountain View, CA: Mayfield, 1995.

Schutte, P. "Eine neue form Hysterischer Zustande bei Schulkindern [A New Form of Hysterical Conditions in School Children]." *Münchener Medizinsche Wochenschrift* 53 (1906): 1763–64.

"Science Students Exorcise Ghosts." Tribune News Service. 2002. http://www.tribuneindia.com/2002/20021116/cth2.htm. Accessed July 30, 2004.

Selvadurai, Sivagnanachelvi. "Problems of Residential Students in a Secondary Technical School." Master's thesis, University of Malaya, Kuala Lumpur, 1985.

"Seven Girls Scream for Blood: Hysterical Outbursts Continue." *The New Straits Times*, May 25, 1987, p. 4.

"...Seven Hundred School Children Panic-Stricken by Fire." *The Daily Gazette* (Colorado Springs, Colorado), February 21, 1883, p. 1.

Sidky, H. *Witchcraft, Lycanthropy, Drugs, and Disease: An Anthropological Study of the European Witch-Hunts*. New York: Peter Lang, 1997.

Sieveking, Paul. "Behind the Battles in the Balkans." *Fortean Times* 124 (July 1999): 9.

———. "Crazed Laughter in Chechnya," *Fortean Times* 210 (June 2006): 22–23.

Sisman, Adam, ed. *The Best of the Fortean Times*. New York: Avon, 1992.

Sjoberg, Richard L. "The Catechism Effect: Child Testimonies During a 17th-Century Witch Panic as Related to Educational Achievement." *Memory* 8.2 (2000): 65–69.

———. "False Allegations of Satanic Abuse: Case Studies from the Witch Panic in Rattvik 1670–71." *European Child and Adolescent Psychiatry* 6 (1997): 219–26.

Skeat, Walter William. *Malay Magic*. London: Macmillan, 1900.

Small, G. W., M. W. Propper, E. T. Randolph, and S. Eth. "Mass Hysteria Among Student Performers: Social Relationship as a Symptom Predictor." *American Journal of Psychiatry* 148 (1991): 1200–05.

Smelser, Neil J. *Social Change in the Industrial Revolution*. London: Routledge and Kegan Paul, 1962.

———. "Theoretical Issues of Scope and Problems." *Readings in Collective Behavior*. Edited by Robert R. Evans. Chicago: Rand McNally, 1971, pp. 89–94.

Smith, H. C. T., and E. J. Eastham. "Outbreak of Abdominal Pain." *The Lancet* 2 (1973): 956–58.

Smith, Leroy. "Spiritual Manifestation Creates Panic at City." *Guyana Chronicle*, March 15, 2012. http://www.guyanachronicleonline.com/site/index.php?option=com_content&id=40707:spiritual-manifestation-creates-panic-at-city-school&Itemid=8. Accessed January 14, 2012.

Smith, Mondale, and Jenelle Carter. "Mass School Hysteria Spread Across Guyana," Kaieteur News Online. 2009. http://www.kaieteurnewsonline.com/2009/11/07/mass-school-hysteria-spreads-across-guyana/. Accessed October 19, 2012.

"'Spaceship' in Rawang. School Staff, Pupils Saw 'Object.'" *Malay Mail*, August 31, 1970.

Spanos, Nicholas P., Wendy Cross, Mark Lepage, and Marjorie Coristine. "Glossolalia as Learned Behavior: An Experimental Demonstration" *Journal of Abnormal Psychology* 95.1 (1987): 21–23.

Spiller, G. "An Educational Democracy: Moral Instruction and Training in the Schools of Switzerland." In *Moral Instruction and Training in Schools: Report of an International Inquiry, Volume 2*. Edited by M. E. Sadler. London: Longmans, Green, 1908, pp. 196–206.

———. "Moral Education in the Boys' Schools of Germany." In *Moral Instruction and Training in Schools: Report of an International Inquiry, Volume 2*. Edited by M. E. Sadler. London: Longmans, Green, 1908, pp. 213–230.

Stewart, James R. "The West Bank Collective Hysteria Episode: The Politics of Illness." *The Skeptical Inquirer* 15 (1991): 153–60.

Talbot, Margaret. "The Devil in the Nursery." *New York Times Magazine*, January 7, 2001.

Tam, Y.K., M. M. Tsoi, G. B. Kwong, and S. W. Wong. "Psychological Epidemic in Hong Kong, Part 2: Psychological and Physiological Characteristics of Children Who Were Affected." *Acta Psychiatrica Scandinavica* 65 (1982): 437–49.

Tan, Eng-Seng. "Epidemic Hysteria." *The Medical Journal of Malaya* 18.2 (December 1963): 72–76.

Tarkowski, Edward. "Laughing Phenomena: Its History and Possible Effects on the Church, Part III: The Abrahamic Covenant and Joyous Feast of Tabernacles." http://users.stargate.net/~ejt/apos3.htm. Accessed December 21, 2003.

Taylor, D. C. "Hysteria, Belief, and Magic." *British Journal of Psychiatry* 155 (1989): 391–398.

Teoh, J., and K. Yeoh. "Cultural Conflict in Transition: Epidemic Hysteria and Social Sanction." *Australian and New Zealand Journal of Psychiatry* 7 (1973): 283–95.

Teoh, Jin-Inn, and Eng-Seng Tan. "An Outbreak of Epidemic Hysteria in West Malaysia." In *Culture-Bound Syndromes, Ethnopsychiatry, and Alternate Therapies, Volume IV of Mental Health Research in Asia and the Pacific*. Edited by William P. Lebra. Honolulu: University Press of Hawaii, 1976, pp. 32–43.

Teoh, Jin-Inn, Saesmalijah Soewondo, and Myra Sidharta. "Epidemic Hysteria in Malaysia: An Illustrative Episode." *Psychiatry* 8.3 (1975): 258–68.

Theopold, W. "Induzierter Amplexus neuralis bei Mädchen einer Schulklasse

[Induced Neural Amplexus in Girls in a School Class]." *Monatsschrift für Kinderheilkunde* 103 (1955): 79–80.

Thomas, Benjamin. "'Mushroom Madness' in the Papua New Guinea Highlands: A Case of Nicotine Poisoning?" *Journal of Psychoactive Drugs* 34.3 (2002): 321–23.

Thomas, Keith. *Religion and the Decline of Magic.* London: Weidenfeld and Nicolson, 1971.

Thomas, R. Murray, ed. *International Comparative Education: Practices, Issues, and Prospects.* New York: Pergamon, 1991.

Thorndike, E. and R. S. Woodworth. "The Influence of Improvement on One Mental Function upon the Efficiency of Other Functions." *Psychological Review* 8 (1901): 247–61.

"'Tigerettes' Faint Like Flies; Gridiron Looks Like Race Track." *Waukesha Daily Freeman* (Waukesha, Wisconsin), September 13, 1952, p. 1.

"To Reward Heroine. Costly Present for Girl Scholar Who Stopped Fire Panic." *The Daily Northwestern* (Oshkosh, Wisconsin), October 20, 1900.

Trangkasombat, Umaporn, Umpon Suumpan, Veera Churujikul, Kamthorn Prinksulka, Orawan Nukhew, and Vilailuk Haruhanpong. "Epidemic Dissociation Among School Children in Southern Thailand." *Dissociation* 8.3 (1995): 130–41.

"Transfer of Training." *Encyclopedia Britannica.* 2004. http://www.britannica.com/eb/article?eu=114763. Accessed July 25, 2004.

"Transfer Plan for Girls Hit by Hysteria." *The New Straits Times*, July 21, 1987.

Tripp, R. T., compiler. *The International Thesaurus of Quotations.* New York: Thomas Y. Crowell, 1970.

Truper, J. "Zur Frage der Schulerselbstmorde." *Zeitschrift für Kinderforschung* 143 (1908): 75–86.

Tsiko, Sifelani. "Mysterious Hysteria Hits Moleli High School." *The Zimbabwe Herald* online, Friday, September 13, 2002.

"Two Schools Close in Tanzania Till Siege of Hysteria Ends." *New York Times*, May 25, 1966, p. 36.

Utley, Robert K. *The Last Days of the Sioux Nation.* New Haven and London: Yale University Press, 1963.

Van Larebeke, N., L. Hens, P. Schepens, A. Covaci, J. Baeyens, K. Everaert, J. L. Bernheim, R. Vlietinck, G. De Poorter. "The Belgian PCB and Dioxin Incident of January–June 1999: Exposure Data and Potential Impact on Health." *Environmental Health Perspectives* 109.3 (2001): 265–73.

Vanzi, Sol Jose. "Nueva Vizcaya Students 'Possessed' by Evil Spirits." *Philippine Headline News.* 2003. http://www.newsflash.org/2003/05/ht/ht003563.htm.

Victor, Jeffrey S. "The Search for Scapegoat Deviants." *The Humanist*, September/October 1992, 10–13.

Villanueva, R. L., M. C. Payumo, and K. Lema. "Flu Scare Sweeps Schools." *Business World* (Philippines), October 3, 2001, p. 12.

"We Saw Midgets, Say Pupils." *The New Straits Times*, August 26, 1982.

Welch, Steven R. *Subjects or Citizens? Elementary School Policy and Practice in Bavaria 1800–1918.* Melbourne, Australia: University of Melbourne, Department of History Monograph 26, 1998.

Wellert, Robb, and Gary H. Grossman, producers. *History's Mysteries: Legends of the Werewolves.* Weller/Grossman Productions for the History Channel, 1998.

Wendo, Charles. "Uganda: A Village Possessed by Mass Hysteria." All Africa Global Media, July 6, 2002.

Wessely Simon. "Mass Hysteria: Two Syndromes?" *Psychological Medicine* 17 (1987): 109–20.

Wichmann, R. "Eine Sogenannte Veitstanzepidemie in Wildbad [A So-called Epidemic of St. Vitus Dance in Wildbad]." *Deutsche Medizinische Wochenschrift* (Leipzig) 16 (1890): 632–36, 659–63.

Wier, Jean (Weyer, Johann). *Histoires, Disputes et Discours Des Illusions et Impostures des Diables, des Magiciens Infames, Sorcières et Empoisonneurs.* Vol. 1. Translated from the 1563 Latin original. Paris: Bureaux du Progrès Médical, 1885.

Wildavsky, Aaron. *But Is It True? A Citizen's Guide to Environmental Health and Safety Issues.* Boston, MA: Harvard University Press, 1997.

Wilson, David S., and Angus Gillespie. *Rooted in America: Foodlore of Popular Fruits and Vegetables.* Knoxville: University of Tennessee Press, 2000.

Winn, Denise. "Hysteria Tests on Festival Victims." *Daily Express*, July 20, 1980.

Wittstock, Bernadette, Lydia Rozental, and Charlene Henn. "Mass Phenomena at a Black South African Primary School." *Hospital and Community Psychiatry* 42 (1991): 851–53.

Wolf, M. "Witchcraft and Mass Hysteria in Terms of Current Psychological Theories." *Journal of Practical Nursing and Mental Health Services* (March 1976): 23–28.

Wong, S. W., B. Kwong, Y. K. Tam, and M. M. Tsoi. "Psychological Epidemic in Hong Kong." *Acta Psychiatrica Scandinavica* 65 (1982): 421–36.

Wulsin, Lawson R., and Athanase Hagengimana. "PTSD in Survivors of Rwanda's 1994 War." *Psychiatric Times* 15.4 (April 1998). http://www.psychiatrictimes.com/p980412.html. Accessed December 31, 2003.

Yasamy, M. T., A. Bahramnezhad, and H. Ziaaddini. "Postvaccination Mass Psychogenic Illness on an Iranian Rural School." *East Mediterranean Health Journal* 5.4 (1999): 710–15.

Zane, Damian. "Mass Fainting Hits Ethiopian Students." British Broadcasting Corporation, Friday, 14 February, 2003. http://news.bbc.co.uk/2/hi/ africa/2763141. Accessed June 27, 2003.

Zollinger, E. "Über die Pädagogische Behandlung des Nervösen Zitterns der Schulkinder [On the Educational Treatment of Nervous Trembling in School Children]." *Jahrbuch der Schweiz Gesellschaft für Schulgesundheitspflege* 7 (1906): 20–47.

Index

Abdul Rahman, Tunku 79
Abdullah, Dr. Jariah 169
Abu, Haji Abdul Aziz 167
Addis Ababa University (Ethiopia) 114
Afendi, Faizul 167
Agence France-Press 178
Ahmad, Maimunah 166
Alabama 155–56
Alar 44
Albania 61–62
albularyo 131
Aldine School District (Texas) 67
Alexandra, Egypt 59
Algeria 169
al-Haya al-Jadida 60
Ali, Mohamed 164
Allport, Gordon 178
Alor Star, Malaysia 79
Altamirano, Bismarck 139
Altamirano, Darwin 139
Älvdalen, Sweden 15–16
amafufunyana. 110
American Community School (Beirut) 89
American National Institute for Occupational Safety and Health 150
aminotriazole 44
Amok 125, 140
Amsterdam, Holland 12–14, 17, 25
Ann, Neo Lee 166
Anthrax Scare of 2001 6, 11, 53, 175
Antonio Alvarado, José 142
Antwerp, Belgium 51
anxiety hysteria 8, 87, 176
Ariffin bin Mokhtar, Mohamed 163
Arizona Agriculture Department 49
Arrabah (Israeli-occupied West Bank) 55–58
Arrabah Girls' School (Israeli-occupied West Bank) 56
asbestos scare 40
Asdee, County Kerry (Ireland) 170
Ashfield Imperials Band 149
assembly line hysteria 150
aurat 169

Baan Thab Sawai School (Thailand) 87
Bacillus anthracis 175
Bacon, Francis 12
Bagabag 131
Balkans 61–62
Ballinspittal, Ireland 170, 172
Bametie 14
Banda, Hastings Kamuza 105
Bandar Baru Sentul, Kuala Lumpur 168
Banusawan, Liam 88
barking children of Hoorn, Holland 17
barking nuns 14
Barnes, Dr. James 156
Barricada Internacional 138
Bartholomew, Robert E. 1
Basel, Switzerland 30
Battle in Space 162
Bavaria, Germany 28
Bay Harbor Elementary School 45
BBC (British Broadcasting Corporation) 151
Beirut, Lebanon 89
Bekker, Balthasar 17
Beletus manicus 126
Belgian Coca-Cola Scare 51–53
Belgian Congo 99
Belgian Poison Control Centre 52
Bellevue, Louisiana 34
Berger, Peter 1
Bertrand, Emilie 69
Besharov, Douglas 18
Bethume Negro School (Welch, Louisiana) 36, 176
Bhabut 129
Bhanja, Chittaranjan 90
Biberach, Germany 28
Bilwi, Nicaragua 140, 143
"Bin Laden Itch" 6, 53
bin Omar, Baharuddin 166
Bingham, Terry 147, 151
Bissem, Julius 112
Bla 143
Black Angels of Lille, France 14–15
Blackburn, England 159–160
Blåkulla 16

224   Index

blebs" 149, 152
"bloody Mary" 68
Bolante, Joy 131
bomoh 73–74, 76, 80–81
Bornem, Belgium 51–52
Borneo 165, 177
Bosnia 61
Bourignon, Antoinette 14–15
Boyle, Robert 12
Brilliant, Lawrence 184
Brugge, Belgium 51
Buckey, Peggy McMartin 19
Buckey, Ray 19–21, 24
Bulileka, Fiji 128
Bulo, Bongeka 110
Burabika Hospital, Kampala, Uganda 96
Burundi 100

Cairo, Egypt 59–60
Canada 53, 69, 102, 160–61
Canyon Creek Middle School (Washington State) 53
Carns, Ireland 170
Carson, Rachel 44
Casey, Conerly 108–109
"cat children" 13
cat girls: Fiji 128; India 91–92
Catholic University de Louvain (Brussels) 52
cats 5, 12, 13, 91, 92
Centers for Disease Control 6, 54, 64
Chakraphand, Dr. Somchai 87
Chao, Jose 143
Chao, Rafaela 143
Chechnya 62
Chemnitz, Germany 31
Cheong, Margie 135
Chew, Khor Boon 164
Chinese Zombie Robot Scare 177–78
Chongqing (Sichuan Province, China) 177–78
Chulalongkorn University (Thailand) 85
Collège du Sacré-Coeur (Sherbooke, Canada) 69
The Coming Revival 102
Commission on Arab Women 58
Congo (now the Democratic Republic of Congo) 99, 100
conversion disorder 1, 4, 6, 25, 31, 40, 41, 65, 107, 180, 183
Cork City, Ireland 170–171
Coussin, Dr. Brian 60
Coxsackie virus 149
Croatia 61
Cropper, Paul 41
culture bound syndromes 140
curandera 140–41

Dade County Health Office (Florida) 45
Dagestan, Chechnya 63

Daily Mirror 148, 151
Daily Telegraph 150
Dalsayev, Musa 63
Damanhour, Egypt 59
Darnton, Robert 13
Darwin, Charles 93, 39
datura stramonium 95
Davis, Daniel 21
Dawes, Glenn 1
Dennis, Phil 140–42–43
Derby, England 29
Destination Moon 162
dibenzofurans 52
dioxin 52
Djenin (Israeli-occupied West Bank) 56–57, 60
Djenin Hospital 57, 60
Dnevnik 62
dogs 17, 68, 159
Dolagobind, India 91
Donne, John 121
Drake, Richard 177
Dublin, Ireland 170
Los duendes (Nicaraguan elves) 139
Dupont, James 41
durians 165
Dzimrevski, Jordan 62

East Denver High School, Colorado 33
East Templeton, Massachusetts 157–58
Eastham, E. 154
Eben-Al Abas School (Jordan) 65
ecstasy 42
Edwards, Felicity 111
Ehselayev, Vaha Dardeyevich 63
Elkins, Dr. Gary 50, 184
Elliott, Kerry 147
Elliott, Linda 147
Ellzey, Dr. James 67
Emberto, Lola 140–41
endwara ya kucheka ("the laughing trouble") 95
Epperly, G. 159
Ericsen, Eric 15
Ernst, E. 67
Essay Concerning Human Understanding 12
European Witch Scare 5, 12, 17–18
The Exorcist 13, 73

Facebook (and mass hysteria) 42
false memories 21
Fansidar (malaria drug) 105
Fariñas, Joel 131
Ferryville, Louisiana 35
Fijian kidnapping scare 130–131
Finland (witch scare) 16
Flynn, Elizabeth 170
Frankel, Stephen 123–25
Freud, Sigmund 4
Friedland, Prussia 15

Ganesh (elephant god) 129, 170
Gardasil 40
Gaza Strip 60
Geddes, Linda 142
Geertz, Clifford 134
Georgia Department of Public Health 64
Ghana 97–98, 173
ghost attacks 8, 87, 90, 111, 114, 120
Ghost Dance religion 99
"ghost nests" in Malaysia 79
Gishu, Uasin 112
Gitogo secondary school (Kenya) 111
globus hystericus 183
Goalsara Primary School (India) 90
golden staph 40
Graham, Mrs. Eileen 171–72
great East African religious revival 100
great preschool scare 18–19
great *Puja* ceremony 129
great Smurf scare 66
great Swedish witch panic (1664–76) 16
Grisi Siknis 139–43
Gross-tinz, Germany 30
Guan, Ooi Keat 164
The Guardian 84, 132, 148, 151
Gulliver's Travels 126
Gumare, Botswana 106
Gymkhana 149

Ha'Aretz 57
Hafez, Albert 57, 60
Hagengimana, Athanase 107
Halilovna Aliyeva, Jamilya 63
Hantus 78
Hanza, Iran 65
Harelbeke, Belgium 51
Harfoush, Julie 89
Hausa people 108–09
Hazlerigg, Northumberland 152–54
headhunter scares 177
health scares 44
Hebrew University 60
Heger, Dr. Astrid 23
Heim, Roger 126
"Helang" Malaysia 73
Herzegovina 61, 169
Hishamuddin Secondary Islamic School (Klang, Malaysia) 168
Hjarne, Urban 16
Holland 1, 12, 17–18, 25, 179
Hollinwell incident 146–152
Holmes, Enid 149
Holmes, Oliver Wendell, Jr. 121
Holy Bible 98, 101–102, 133, 137, 144, 179
Holy Koran 74, 77, 83, 169, 179, 181
Holy Laugh 102, 176
Holy Laugh Movement 102
Honduras 142
Houston, Texas 66–67, 178
Howard-Browne, Rodney 102

Huffington Post 42
Hughes, Andrew 130
Human Papillomavirus (HPV) 40
hydrogen sulphide 52, 58
hypnosis 28, 67–69, 184

Indian masala films 108
Invaders from Mars 162
Ipswich High School (Massachusetts) 67
Islamic Sabbath 77
Islamic Salvation Front Party 169
Ismailia, Egypt 59
Israeli, Raphael 60
Israeli Mossad 60
Israeli-occupied West Bank 55
Itokela Girls' Secondary School (Kenya) 111

Jakab, Zsuzsanna 62
James Cook University, Australia 1
Japanese Americans (internment of) 25
Jasmin, Gloria 131
Jenin (Israeli-occupied West Bank) 55–57, 60
jinn spirits 74, 179
Jit Sin Primary School (Penang) 164
Johnson, Judy 19
Johor Baru General Hospital 80
Juju (evil spells) 98

Kagwa, Benjamin 96
Kambaa school (Kenya) 111
Kamla, Nicaragua 140, 143
Kampung Buluhan 168
Kampung Melayu (Gambang, Malaysia) 166
Kano, Nigeria 108–09
Kapurawala, India 90
Karam, Dr. Elie 142
Kashasha School (Tanganyika) 96
Kashasha village, Tanganyika (now Tanzania) 94
Kassam, Farida 169
Kathuma Primary School (Kenya) 111
Kayayimba, Uganda 115
Kayiira, Julius 115
"killer apples" 44
Kilton Concordes Band 150
Kim Guan, Yew 166
King Charles XI 15
Kirakwski, Jurek 171
Kizito, Dr. M. 115
Klang, Malaysia 168, 170
Kluckhohn, Clyde 186
Knight, Dr. James 37
Komugi Taï 125–26
komugl people 126–27
Kortrijk, Belgium 51
Kramer, Heinrich 12
Krin Krin, Nicaragua 141, 143

Kuantan, Malaysia 166
Kuhlmeyer, Harry, Jr. 19–20
Kuma people 62, 125–26
Kumanovo, Macedonia 62
Kutama Mission Hospital (Zimbabwe) 113
Kuwait 169

Labasa Hospital, Fiji 127
lallang (tall weeds) 166
LaMay, Dan 68
Landrigan, Philip 58
Langley, Rick 39
laughing 6, 27, 67, 82, 94–104, 106–7, 115, 120, 135, 139, 175–76
laughing mania 6, 96, 99–102, 104, 106–07, 115, 175–76
"Laughing Revival" 102
Law Wai Chow 168
Lazario, Paul 165
Lebanon Elementary School (Fellsburg, Pennsylvania) 178
Leicester, England 150, 169
Leicestershire (United Kingdom) 150
Leonardi, Richard 139
Leroy Central School (vocal tics) 40
Lertkrai, Panya 88
Levine, Dr. Richard 155
Levy, Florence 142
Lewis, Ioan 183
Lewis, Dr. Malcolm 151
Liang, Raymond 164
Lichter, Dr. David 42
Lippman, Walter 94
Lison, Dominique 52
Lochristi, Belgium 51
Locke, John 12
Lomax, John Nova 67
London School "drop attacks" 33–34
Loreto Day Secondary School (Kenya) 112
Loreto-Matunda Secondary School (Kenya) 112
Los Angeles, California 19
Louisiana Health Department 37–38
"Love Madness" (South Africa) 118
Lower Koti, Nepal 91
LSD 182
Lucas, Joseph 28
Luckmann, Thomas 1
lycanthropy 13
lyme disease 42

Ma'Ariv 56–57
magnesium deficiency 42
Mahmud, Nor Akmar 166
Maimi, Florida 28
Majozi, Makhosi 111
Makerere University College 95
malathion 48–51
Malaysia 3, 6, 71–84, 92, 136, 140, 161–170, 173, 176, 179, 182, 184

Malleus Maleficarum (Hammer of Witches) 11–12
Managua, Nicaragua 139
Manhattan Beach, California 18–20
Manhattan Beach Police 19–21
Mansfield and North Nottinghamshire Chronicle and Advertiser 150
Mansour, Fathy 59
Mansura, Egypt 59
Manton (United Kingdom) 150
Marina, Evaristo 68
mass hysteria by proxy 64
Maxwell High School (Kuala Lumpur, Malaysia) 168
Mayberry-Louis, David 173
Mbale, Uganda 96
McDavis, Pablo 142
McEvoy, James 67
McMartin, Virginia 18–21
McMartin Preschool scare 18–25
Mecca 169
Mechtler, Laszlo 40–41
Meissen, Germany 31
meningitis 109
"mental discipline" 5, 26–27, 32, 174
meowing nuns 14
Merriman, Petula 147
Metz, France 13
Mexico City, Mexico 7, 134–35
Miami Aerospace Academy 68
Middle East 3, 6, 55, 58, 64, 66
Miller, Bess 58
Miller, David 99
Miller, Henry 173
Minkailova, Taisa 62–63
Miskito people 139–43
Mitchell, Steven 154
Mitchelstown, Ireland 170–171
Mocoa City, Columbia 68
Modan, Baruch 57–58
Moffatt, Dr. M.E. 161
Mohamad, Norzidi 167
Mohapatra, Sasmita 92
Moleli High School (Zimbabwe) 113–114
Montenegra, Alejandra 139
Montenegro 61
Montreal, Canada 160–161
Montreal Central Train Station 160
Montreal Children's Hospital 161
Mooncoin, Ireland 171
mor phi (Thai exorcist) 88
Mora, Daniel 68
Mora, Sweden 16
Moscow, Russia 62–63, 109
motor hysteria 8, 27, 40, 42, 130, 176–77
Mount Melfry, Ireland 171
Mount Pleasant, Mississippi 38–39
Mountcollins, Ireland 170
moving statue "epidemic" 170–172
Mualang peoples, Borneo 177

Index

Mubobobo 113
Muhairwe, Annette 115
Muhangi, Joseph 103–04
Mukerere University (Uganda) 103
"Murai Secondary School" Malaysia 73
"mushroom madness" 125–26
Muslim-American profiling 25
Musoma, Tanzania 97
Mwinilunga, Zambia 104
My Favorite Martian 163
Myron T. Herrick Junior High (Cleveland, Ohio) 159
The Mysterians 162
"mysterious madness" (Zambia) 104
mystery rashes 53–54
Mywali, Charles 97

n-butylbenzene sulfonamide 158
Nadeau, Maxime 69
"Naked Movie Star Game" 23
Nakhon Ratchasima province (Thailand) 87
Napier Bell, Charles 141
Natchez, Mississippi 156
National Center on Child Abuse and Neglect 18
National Institute of Technology (Nicaragua) 140
Neal, Paul 156
Nepal Rashtriya Secondary School 91
Neville High School (Monroe, Louisiana) 156
New Delhi, India 109
New Guinea Nursing "Madness" 122–125
New Indian Express 90
New Scientist 62
New York City 32
New York State Health Department 40
Newark (United Kingdom) 150
Newcastle University Hospitals 154
Nigamananda Saraswat hermitage 92
Nitzkin, Dr. Joel 45–47
Nonda 125–25
North Carolina (pseudo-seizures) 39, 42
Nottingham (United Kingdom) 148, 150–51
Nottingham Public Health Laboratory 151
Nottinghamshire (United Kingdom) 146, 148–50
Nshamba, Tanganyika 96
Ntali, Reverend Ebenezer 110
Nueva Ecija, Philippines 131
El Nuevo Diario 139
nunneries 14, 78–79, 136, 176
Nyanungo, Ms. Kwadzanai 14
Nyanza Secondary School (Rwanda) 107

The Observer 150
O'Connor, Dennis 172
Ogden, Eric 149
Okavango Community Jr. Secondary School (Botswana) 106
Oklahoma State University 158
O'Leary, Dr. Eugene 178
organophosphate poisoning 50
Orieno, Ms. Hermie 132
Orwell, George 72
Ottoman Empire 61
ouija board 7, 134–35, 38
Owino, Wene 106

Pahang, Malaysia 165
Paka Primary School (Terengganu, Malaysia) 166
Palestinian Ministry of Supplies 60
Palethorpe, Margaret 137, 152
PANDAS 40
Pande, Manjubala 92
Panjab University (India) 90
pantang 77
Panyakorn, Phra Khru Udom 89
Papua New Guinea 3, 7, 122, 125–26, 179
pari-pari 162–63
Partain, Jack 101
pawang 77
PCBs 52
Peacock, Arthur 151
Pearl Harbor (bombing) 25
Pedan Cave, Thailand 88
pee-paub 89
penusggus spirits 84
People magazine 18
People's Elementary School (Germany) 31
People's School 29
Persian Gulf War 54
pesticides 42, 54
Phantom Gonorrhea Outbreak 78
phenobarbital 114
Philadelphia, Pennsylvania 67
Philip, P. 95
Philippines 7, 53, 131–32
pibloktoq ("Arctic hysteria") 140
Pinsent, Arthur 32
Podujevo, Albania 62
Posada, Miller Zambrano 68–69
Postman, Leo 178
post–September 11th terror scares 53
post-traumatic stress disorder 4, 107
pregnancy scare 34, 36, 38, 176
Pretoria, South Africa 185
Progesterone 60
Prophet Mohammed 73
pseudocyesis (false pregnancy) 34
pseudoparalysis 161
psychogenic pain disorder 183
Puasakul, Inthira 88
Puerto Cabezas, Nicaragua 140, 142
Pujari (Fijian "man of prayer") 129

Qawa Primary School (Fiji) 127
Quebec City, Canada 160
Quebec province, Canada 69
Queens Medical Centre, Nottingham 148

Rabinowitz, Dorothy 25
Raiti, Nicaragua 141
Rajabaht Institute, Thailand 88
Ramashenye Girls' Middle School (Tanganyika) 96
rambutans 80
Rana, Purshotam 91
Randall, R. 127
Rankin, Dr. A. 95
Rättvik, Sweden 15–16
Rawang, Selangor, Malaysia 164
Ray, David 184
Rayess, Samir 89
Reay, Marie 125–26
Reid, Thomas 26
Rembold, Dr. S. 28–29
Rhode Island elementary school (terror scare) 54
Rhodes University (Cape Town) 111
Richardson, Miles 71
Rickard, Bob 1
Riewleung, Sunthorn 87
Ritalin 42
Rizal Elementary School (Iloilo, Philippines) 132
Roach, Steven 39
Rogers, Tim 143
Rorschach ink blot test 170
Ross, Nicola 142–43
Royal Malaysian Air Force Primary School (Padang Geroda) 165
Rubin, Lael 21–22
rumor 1, 4–7, 15, 30, 35, 37–38, 45, 50, 53, 55, 57–59, 61–62, 65–67, 82, 86, 8–90, 93, 109, 111–112, 114–15, 131, 135–36, 146, 149, 152, 158, 161, 176–79, 181–82, 185–86
Russell, Bertrand 44
Rwanda 11, 107
Ryan, Tim 171

Sabri Zubit, Mohmed 166
St. John's College (Umtata, South Africa) 109
St. Mark's Secondary School (Mhondoro, Zimbabwe) 112
Salem Village 24
Sallam, Ismail 59
Salomon Taylor, Carlos 141
Sanders, Bill 67
Sandino, Porcela 140–41
Santa Monica, California 157
Santa Muerte (Saint Death) 135
Sarikei, Borneo 165
satanism scare 5, 13, 18–19, 24, 89, 111
Schmidt, Casper 184

Schoedel, Dr. Johannes 3, 31
Scorgie, Fiona 119
Scully, Michael 170
Selayang Baru Primary School (Selangor, Malaysia) 167
September 11, 2001 5–6, 25, 53–54
Serbia 61–62
Setiloane, Gabriel 101
Severn-Trent Water Authority (United Kingdom) 148
Shaheen, Abdel Aziz 60
Shaitan (Fijian spirit) 128
Shakespeare, William 70
Shona language 113
Showalter, Elaine 53
Sibanda, Dr. Peter 114
Siegel, Dr. Marc 40
Sieveking, Paul 63
Silent Spring 44
Simón Bolívar School (Nicaragua) 138
Singh, Hakim 90
Sirdar, Mara 129
Sjöberg, Richard 16
Skinner, Denis 151
Small, Dr. Gary 157, 181
Smelser, Neil J. 181
Smith, Anadina 140, 143
Smith, H. 154
Smith, Leroy 144
Smith, Stephen 68
Smith, Thornton 156
Smurf scare 66–67, 178
Snell, D. 128
Songkok 166
sookia 141
South Normanton (United Kingdom) 150
Soviet Georgia (phantom gas attack) 3, 54
Sprenger, Jakob 12
Springfield High School (Pennsylvania) 67
Starogladovsk, Chechnya 63
Staroshchedrinskaya, Chechnya 63
Stella Maris Secondary School (Blantyre, Malawi) 105
Stillwater High School (Oklahoma) 159
Stockholm (witch scare) 16
Stowell English Primary School (Penang, Malaysia) 163
Stuttgart, Germany 29
Sultan Sulaiman Primary School (Kuala Terengganu, Malaysia) 167
Sumbuka 108–9
Sunday Times 151–52
Sunday World 171
Svensen, Gertrude 15
Swedo, Dr. Susan 40
Swift, Jonathan 126

Tampoi Mental Hospital 79
Tan, Eng-Seng 79
Tanganyika 94, 96, 99–100

Tangweera 141
Tapah Secondary School (Perak, Malaysia) 167
Taveuni, Fiji 128
Taylor, David 141, 182
Telefomin, Papua New Guinea 122, 124–26
Teleportation 109
Tel-Hashomer Hospital 60
Teller, Henry 99
Temenggong Abdul Rahman Primary School (Johor Baru, Malaysia) 162
Teoh, Jin-Inn 72
tetanus-diphtheria vaccine (Td) 65
Tetovo, Macedonia 62
Texas Tech University 140
Thai Fossil Scare 88
Thanthi newspaper 91
Thasala Elementary School (Thailand) 84
theories of mass hysteria 179–85
Thorndike, Edward Lee 27
thyroid cancer 44
The Times 151
"Timor College" (Malaysia) 81
Tipton, West Midlands (United Kingdom) 150
Tiruchi, India 91
Tito, Marshal 61
Tokoloshe 113
Toronto Blessing 102–3, 176
Tourette's Syndrome 40
toyl 78, 162–3
trance states 5, 8, 13, 25–7, 43, 100, 110, 176
Trangkasombat, Umaporn 85–6
"trembling disease" 3, 31, 180
Tridemorph 151
Trifiletti, Rosario 40
Tulane University 37
Turner, Franklin 67
Twain, Mark 146
twitching epidemics 1, 5, 8, 25–27, 29, 34–36, 39, 40, 43, 101, 104, 110, 127–29, 153, 174, 176, 180, 183, 186
Twitter (and mass hysteria) 42

Uganda 96, 100, 103, 115, 117
Ugandan Running Sickness 115
Umhayizo ("Love Madness") 119
Umpat, Marilyn 131
Umtata, Grahamstown, South Africa 109
University of Ghana Medical School 98
University of Kebangsaan Malaysia 169
University of Pittsburgh 179
Uraccan University (Nicaragua) 142
ustaz 83

vaccine panics 64
Valium 106
Valle, Austria 29, 125
Veerasamy, Mr. R. 164
vertigo 161
Victor, Jeff 24
Virgil's *Georgics* 32
Voltaire 26
von Wolff, Christian 26, 174
voodoo 38–39, 136

Warren High School (Ohio) 159
Wasson, R. Gordon 126
Wells, Edna 142, 148
Wessely, Simon 27
West Bank 55, 60
Western Mail 151
Weyer, Johann 13–14
Whitbread, Richard 69
Wickramasena, Suriakumar 168
Wigneswaran, K. 163
Wigwam 166
William Byrd High School (twitching outbreak) 39
Winn, Denise 160
witchcraft 5, 9, 11–15, 18, 25–26, 43, 69, 79, 94, 106, 108–9, 115–19, 133, 186
witches' sabbat 15–16
Wittstock, Bernadette 186
Wood, Dr, John 149
Woodland Gladers band 152
World Health Organization 55, 62
Wounded Knee Creek, South Dakota 99
writing tremor 4, 29
Wulsin, Lawson 107

yagya 90
yaqona (Fijian drink) 128–29
Yasamy, Dr. M.T. 65
Yattah (Israeli-occupied West Bank) 55, 57
Yedi'Ot Ahronot 56
Youtube (and mass hysteria) 42
Yyuri, Yasmin Hadyah 168

Zaidi, Mohamed Izainurie Nor 167
Zakaria, Hafiza 167
Zavala, Nashyiela Loa 134, 136–38
Zimbabwe National Traditional Healers' Association 114
Zulkifli, Mohamed 164
Zulu language 113
Zululand 119
Zvikwambo 113

www.ingramcontent.com/pod-product-compliance
Ingram Content Group UK Ltd.
Pitfield, Milton Keynes, MK11 3LW, UK
UKHW041948140426
5217IPUK00014B/707